MW00720131

AUXILIO

THE CANADIAN COAST GUARD 1962-2002

SEMPER

Canadian Hydrographic Services Crest

Coast Guard Crest

Fisheries Protection Crest

FLAGS

Governor General's Honorary Flag

Minister's Flag

Deputy Minister's Flag

Canadian Coast Guard Commissioner's Flag

Canadian Coast Guard Deputy
Commisionner's Flag

Canadian Coast Guard Fleet Director General's Pennant

Canadian Coast Guard Senior Officer's Pennant

Canadian Coast Guard Vessel Jack

Canadian Coat Guard Auxiliary Services Pennant

Fisheries Patrol Vessel Pennant

Canadian Hydrographic Services Flag

THE CANADIAN COAST GUARD
1962-2002

CHARLES D. MAGINLEY

Vanwell Publishing Limited
St. Catharines, Ontario

Vanwell Publishing acknowledges the financial support of the Government of Canada through the Book Publishing Industry Development Program for our publishing activities.

Vanwell Publishing acknowledges the Government of Ontario through the Ontario Media Development Corporation's Book Initiative.

Design: Linda Moroz-Irvine
Cover: Painting of *Louis S. St Laurent*, *Polar Sea* and *Yamal* at the North Pole, by Yves Bérubé

Vanwell Publishing Limited
1 Northrup Crescent
P.O. Box 2131
St. Catharines, Ontario L2R 7S2
sales@vanwell.com
1-800-661-6136
fax 905-937-1760

In the United States:
P.O. Box 1207
Lewiston, NY 14092
USA

Printed in Canada

National Library of Canada Cataloguing in Publication

Maginley, Charles D. (Charles Douglas), 1929-
    The Canadian Coast Guard, 1962-2002 : auxilio semper / Charles D. Maginley.

Includes bibliographical references and index.
ISBN 1-55125-075-6

1. Canadian Coast Guard–History. I. Title.

VG55.C3M32 2003   363.28'6'0971   C2003-904204-9

The Coast Guard's motto, *Saluti Primum, Auxilio Semper* is usually translated as "Safety First, Service Always," but "Safety First" is what the Coast Guard hopes its clients will practise, not how it conducts its own operations, because risks must be taken when necessary. The second part of the motto, "Service Always," is not actually a literal translation from the Latin. *Auxilio* means assistance or help, so perhaps the phrase could be taken to mean "we are always here to help." But however it is translated, *Auxilio Semper* is the essence of the way in which the Coast Guard contributes to the safety and well-being of Canadian and visiting mariners.

For me, Charles Maginley's book is a very engaging technical history of the modern Coast Guard, written to help celebrate the fortieth anniversary of one of Canada's great national institutions. The history of the Coast Guard, so admirably captured in this text, corroborates my current vision of the Canadian Coast Guard as a national service institution with a strong commitment to operational readiness, maritime safety and navigable waters.

Key factors were identified as leading to the formation of the Coast Guard in 1962: public demand for improved Search and Rescue facilities, considerations of Arctic sovereignty and development, and the need to respond to the continuing growth in shipborne traffic and technological advances in mobile platforms, navigation and marine communications. Today, these same factors continue to drive the need for a strong and innovative Coast Guard, and many of the essential services that we now provide have been in demand since well before Confederation. The need for service persists and grows even as we alter the means to achieve the results in ways that we can afford.

While tracing the evolving Coast Guard institution with meticulous attention to technical detail on the development of its fleet of ships, hovercraft and aircraft, and of its navigation and communication systems, Charles Maginley has been careful to also tell us about the all-important human dimension. Through the inclusion of selected profiles of individuals who have personally made a significant difference in the development of Canada's Coast Guard, the essential human element has been brought to the fore.

You will read about Coast Guard leaders such as Captain Joseh Elzéar Bernier of L'Islet, Quebec who, as commander of the third northern voyage of the vessel *Arctic* and Canada's premier Arctic sailor, proclaimed the sovereignty of Canada on Dominion Day, July 1, 1909, over the entire Arctic archipelago. Also highlighted are the considerable accomplishments of Dr Gordon Stead, DSC and Bar, who as Director General, Marine Services, and Assistant Deputy Minister, Marine, at the Department of Transport from 1958 through 1970, welded a collection of locally-oriented regional agencies into one national institution. He also played a vital part in the formation of the Coast Guard in 1962 and in the founding of the Coast Guard College in 1965. Today, we are equally committed to training the next generation of operational and technical personnel who will constitute and make possible the Coast Guard of the future.

The author clearly presents the historic and continuing significance of the Canadian Coast Guard's many contributions to exploration, scientific research, social, economic and sovereign development activity in the Canadian Arctic. Many Coast Guard vessels have transited the Arctic Passage in both directions while performing a variety of rescue, Arctic supply, commercial vessel icebreaking support, hydrological and science support missions. On all such missions the Coast Guard makes a unique visual contribution to the Canadian national consciousness and sense of identity through the display of red and white markings on its vessels.

The Arctic voyage, more than any other operational mission, exemplifies the Canadian Coast Guard experience and its service to Canada. For example, on her annual voyages the Eastern Arctic patrol ship *C.D. Howe* stopped at every coastal settlement and station in Labrador, the south coast of Hudson Strait, the south and east coasts of Baffin Island and at points on Ellesmere Island. The ship had well-equipped hospital, staff and dental facilities and accommodations for personnel from various federal departments and agencies and was a welcome sight for northern residents.

Another important theme that emerges from my reading of this book is the interplay between the unfortunate occurrence of marine tragedies and subsequent administrative actions designed to prevent repetition of such occurrences. The theme of marine tragedy and response makes it clear that it is the responsibility of everyone involved to anticipate and manage the wide range of risks associated with real-time events and state conditions in the Canadian maritime domain. The Coast Guard must always be a learning institution that consciously applies its expertise, knowledge and leadership, in the light of changing circumstances, to create public value through service to Canadians.

An overview is provided of various studies that have examined the operations of, and institutional arrangements for, federal maritime fleets with a view to improving their efficiency and effectiveness. Practical insights are provided into the types of issues that I, as Commissioner, currently face in the management of the Coast Guard. One very basic issue concerns how best to fund the provision of marine services to commercial shipping, to those in need of icebreaking services, and to increase safety in pleasure craft use. This resourcing challenge arises in the context of a vast marine geography, a legislated mandate of substantive breadth, and a continuance of fiscal discipline in a dynamic business and technological environment. Based on its past record of performance the Canadian Coast Guard will successfully rise to the occasion.

It gives me pleasure, in my position as Coast Guard Commissioner, to sincerely thank Charles Maginley for his dedication of the past five years in so carefully researching and assembling the definitive chronology of the Canadian Coast Guard over its forty-year history. I also wish to extend my appreciation to the many Coast Guard and departmental personnel, both active and retired, who have so generously assisted the author in making this book a most welcome and timely addition to the documentation of Canada's maritime history.

John Adams
Commissioner, Canadian Coast Guard

In the nineteen-sixties the Coast Guard was fortunate to have an official historian, John Appleton, who was given the task of producing a history of the organization (and its predecessors) to commemorate Canada's centennial in 1967. His book, *Usque ad Mare,* was published by the Queen's Printer, Ottawa, in 1969 and some 3000 copies were issued in English and French.

By the nineteen-eighties it was apparent that an updated history was needed. *Usque ad Mare* had become a collector's item, occasionally available in nautical bookstores. My first idea was to create a second edition, keeping much of the original but adding material to bring the story up to date. As time went by, during which several unsuccessful proposals to the Coast Guard management were made, (all of which seemed to coincide with periods of financial retrenchment), the proposal changed to one for a new volume, *Usque ad Mare II*, together with a re-issue of the original. This concept was accepted and in April 1998 I re-located to Ottawa and started work. I was to discover that one year is really not enough to properly complete a project of this nature but, nevertheless, in March 1999, a text was ready. However, a new period of cost-cutting had commenced and I was thanked and told that further expenditure on such a project was impossible in the then current financial climate.

While working on *Usque ad Mare II*, I had recruited Bernard Collin to help with the illustrations. We then utilized his expertise in jointly creating *The Ships of Canada's Marine Services*, a pictorial book with considerable historic content in the text, which was published by Vanwell Publishing. The book received Coast Guard approval and the launching ceremony was held in the lobby of DFO Headquarters in Ottawa in November 2001. This had the added benefit of reviving interest in the Coast Guard history in a new form: a book to commemorate the fortieth anniversary of the founding of the Coast Guard in 1962. It would be quite unrelated to *Usque ad Mare* but in an echo of Appleton's choice of a title from part of the motto of Canada, *Auxilio Semper: The Canadian Coast Guard 1962-2002* contains a reference to a part of the motto of the Coast Guard: *Saluti Primum, Auxilio Semper.*

The usually unsung work of the men and women of the Coast Guard deserves to be commemorated and I hope that this volume will be read by Canadians who, perhaps, have not realized that the nation has been served for forty years by a thoroughly professional organization whose members are engaged in skilled and often dangerous tasks on the seas, rivers and lakes of our great nation.

ACKNOWLEDGEMENTS

This book could not have been completed without the input and assistance of many present and former members of the Canadian Coast Guard. Much of the credit should be given to two of my former colleagues at the Coast Guard College: Jim Kelly and Jim Calvesbert. During their appointments in Ottawa, they were instrumental in persuading Coast Guard senior management of the need for an updated history. Once the project was underway, Deputy Commissioner Michael Turner and (later) Newfoundland Director-General John Butler provided material support as well as encouragement.

During the research phase I visited all the Regions and was able to see, at first hand, Coast Guard personnel at work: in an icebreaker (the *Sir John Franklin*), a Mackenzie River navigation aids tender, (the *Dumit*) and a hovercraft (the *Waban-aki*). I was privileged to meet and interview Captain Paul Fournier O.C. and Captain Gordon Warren C.M., both of whom had prominent roles in some of the incidents recounted in the book, as well as other distinguished Coast Guard captains and senior managers. Many people in Headquarters, the Regions and the Fleet willingly answered my questions and provided information. In particular, Wayne Ellwood assisted greatly in helping me to understand recent organizational changes while Dick Theedom in Ottawa and Christina Penney in Newfoundland contributed to the biographical notes. The staff of the National Archives and the libraries of Transport Canada, Fisheries and Oceans and the Coast Guard College all facilitated my research.

Finally, Ron Barrie of Coast Guard Maritimes Region meticulously reviewed the text and Bernard Collin provided the illustrations and processed them for publication. I must also thank my wife June for her patience during the many hours I spent at the computer and for her unfailing support.

Charles Douglas Maginley
Mahone Bay, Nova Scotia
December 2002

Dedicated to the men and women of the
Canadian Coast Guard, ashore and afloat

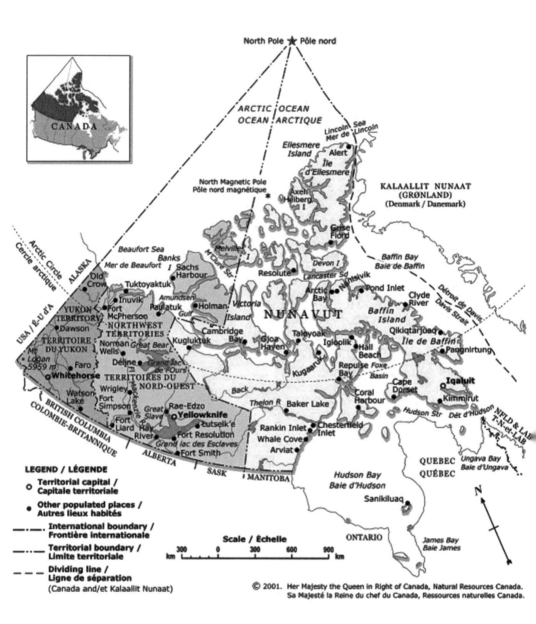

North Pole ★ Pôle nord

ARCTIC OCEAN
OCEAN ARCTIQUE

Lincoln Sea
Mer de Lincoln

Ellesmere
Island
Alert
Île
d'Ellesmere

KALAALLIT NUNAAT
(GRØNLAND)
(Denmark / Danemark)

North Magnetic Pole
Pôle nord magnétique

Axell
Heiberg
I

Grise
Fiord

Arctic Circle
Cercle arctique

Beaufort Sea
Mer de Beaufort

Banks
I

Melville
I

Devon I

Baffin Bay
Baie de Baffin

Sachs
Harbour

Resolute

Lancaster Sd

ALASKA

Old
Crow

Tuktoyaktuk

Amundsen

Arctic
Bay

Nanisivik

Pond Inlet

Clyde
River

Détroit de Davis

USA / É-U d'A

Inuvik
Fort
McPherson

Paulatuk

Holman

Gulf

Victoria
Island

NUNAVUT

Baffin
Island

Qikiqtarjuaq

Davis Strait

YUKON
TERRITORY

Cambridge
Bay

Kugluktuk

Gjoa
Haven

Taloyoak

Igloolik

Île de Baffin

Pangnirtung

Dawson

NORTHWEST
TERRITORIES

Norman
Wells

Great Bear

Hall
Beach

TERRITOIRE
DU YUKON

Mt
Logan
5959 m

Déline

Grand lac
de l'Ours

Kugaaruk

Repulse Foxe
Bay Basin

Faro

Whitehorse

TERRITOIRES DU
NORD-OUEST

Back

Cape
Dorset

Iqaluit

Kimmirut

Watson
Lake

Wrigley
Fort
Simpson

Great
Slave

Rae-Edzo
Yellowknife

Thelon R

Baker Lake

Coral
Harbour

Hudson Str Dét d'Hudson

NFLD & LAB
T-N-et-LAB

BRITISH COLUMBIA
COLOMBIE-BRITANNIQUE

Fort
Liard

Hay
River

Lutselk'e
Fort Resolution
Fort Smith

Rankin Inlet

Chesterfield
Inlet

Mackenzie

Grand lac des Esclaves

Whale Cove

Arviat

QUEBEC
QUÉBEC

Ungava Bay
Baie d'Ungava

ALBERTA

SASK

MANITOBA

Hudson Bay
Baie d'Hudson

N

LEGEND / LÉGENDE

○ Territorial capital /
  Capitale territoriale

● Other populated places /
  Autres lieux habités

–·–·– International boundary /
       Frontière internationale

—·—·— Territorial boundary /
        Limite territoriale

– – – Dividing line /
       Ligne de séparation

(Canada and/et Kalaallit Nunaat)

Sanikiluaq

ONTARIO

James Bay
Baie James

Scale / Échelle

300   0   300   600   900
km   km

© 2001. Her Majesty the Queen in Right of Canada, Natural Resources Canada.
Sa Majesté la Reine du chef du Canada, Ressources naturelles Canada.

CANADA

The Creation of the Coast Guard

The Canadian Coast Guard officially came into existence on 26 January 1962, when the Honourable Leon Balcer, Minister of Transport in the government of Mr John Diefenbaker, rose in the House of Commons and announced that the government had decided that the Department of Transport fleet of ships would, in the future, be known as the Canadian coastguard [sic]. Mr Balcer went on to say that: "the decision to adopt the new name was taken in recognition of the tremendous expansion the fleet had undergone in the scope of its activities, in the number of vessels and in the standards of operation that had been achieved. It had also been decided to adopt a new colour scheme of a red hull and white superstructure with a stylised red maple leaf on the funnel, instead of the former black, white and yellow combination. The use of red was of significant practical utility, especially for icebreakers and vessels engaged in Search and Rescue. New types of uniforms were to be issued, and the essential civilian character of the service was to be unchanged."

Lionel Chevrier, a former Liberal Minister of Transport, responded that all honourable members would agree with the statement. Another member, D.M. Fisher, representing Port Arthur, also welcomed the announcement and anticipated an expansion of Search and Rescue operations, particularly in the Great Lakes. In fact, the establishment of a marine Search and Rescue branch or specialty was one of the main reasons for the creation of a Coast Guard and it is significant that "Search and Rescue" is the subject heading for the announcement in the published House of Commons Debates (Hansard).

Search and Rescue was not, however, the only reason for this important change. Another was the question of Arctic sovereignty and the need for a visible Canadian presence to support the joint U.S.-Canadian defence installations in the far north and to foster economic development. A third influence was the growth of world shipborne trade, requiring not only national regulations and safety rules, but also the need to work with international bodies and United Nations—notably the International Maritime Organization (IMO), originally the International Maritime Consultative

CHAPTER 1

The Coast Guard and its Predecessors

Organization (IMCO). By 1962 it had become apparent that a national maritime body, staffed with trained professionals, was needed to support and promote our national interests in the nautical field, while leaving our sea defences and contributions to the North Atlantic Treaty Organization (NATO) in the hands of the Royal Canadian Navy (which, with its limited resources, could not be distracted by non-military tasks—no matter how important). A Coast Guard was the indicated solution.

The Department of Marine and Fisheries

To find the origins of the Canadian government marine services, we must go back to the creation of Canada in 1867. The new dominion inherited from the previous colonial regimes, and particularly from the Province of Canada, marine services that were commensurate with their resources and the practices of the time. One of the first measures taken by the new Parliament was to pass an Act for the Organization of the Department of Marine and Fisheries of Canada, which received vice-regal assent on 22 May 1868. The Department would be responsible for the administration of any laws made or to be made relating to:

- Sea, coastal and inland fisheries;
- Pilots and pilotage;
- Lighthouses, beacons and buoys and their maintenance;
- Government harbours, ports and wharves and government vessels (except gunboats and other vessels of war);
- Harbour commissioners and harbour masters;
- Classification of vessels and examination and granting of certificates of masters, mates (later) engineers;
- Shipping masters and shipping offices;
- Inspection of steamboats and boards of steamship inspection.
- Enquiries into causes of shipwrecks.
- Establishment and maintenance of marine and seamen hospitals, the care of distressed seamen and generally such matters as refer to the marine and navigation of Canada

Some of these matters now come under other departments, but the tasks performed by the Department of Fisheries and Oceans today are, apart from some technical aspects that were unheard of one hundred and fifty years ago, very much the same as those that were seen to be necessary during the first years of Canadian confederation. Most of them are still the responsibility of the present day Coast Guard.

Sovereignty and Northern Expeditions

On 1 September 1880, the British Government ceded to Canada all the territory from the continental land-mass to the North Pole and between longitudes 60 and 141

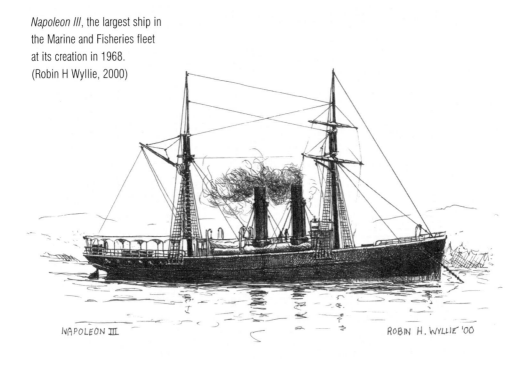

Napoleon III, the largest ship in the Marine and Fisheries fleet at its creation in 1968. (Robin H Wyllie, 2000)

NAPOLEON III.   ROBIN H. WYLLIE '00

West. The first official Canadian investigation of the region, conducted by the Department of Marine and Fisheries with scientific contributions from other government departments, was an expedition under Lieutenant A.R. Gordon in the chartered sealing vessel *Neptune* in 1884. In the two following years, additional exploration was carried out in the *Alert,* an expedition ship on loan from the British Admiralty. These voyages were to explore the route to Hudson Bay. In 1897 another sealer, the *Diana*, was chartered for survey and scientific research along the same route in an expedition under Dr William Wakeham of the Department of Marine and Fisheries. It was not until 1903 that investigation of more northern localities was attempted in the *Neptune*. This voyage was under the direction of Dr A.P. Low of the Geological Survey of Canada. After wintering at Fullerton, near Chesterfield Inlet in Hudson Bay, the ship proceeded further north to Cape Herschell on Ellesmere Island, where a cairn was erected and the sovereignty of the Crown in right of Canada was proclaimed. These were scientific expeditions, not voyages of exploration. For two hundred years these waters had been familiar to European whalers, and numerous expeditions by British and American explorers from Davis to Peary had passed through the area.

While the *Neptune* was engaged in its voyage, the Department had purchased the German Antarctic expedition ship *Gauss* and renamed it the *Arctic*. From 1904 to 1911 the *Arctic*, commanded by Captain J.E. Bernier, made four voyages to Hudson Bay, northern Baffin Island and Ellesmere Island and gradually explored further to the westward. Bernier would go north in one summer and spend the winter with the ship frozen in the ice in a protected bay, while dog-sled expeditions carried out further explorations.

The *Arctic* would sail from Québec usually in July, and return south in October the following year. On 1 July 1909, Bernier erected a bronze tablet proclaiming the annexation by Canada of the entire Arctic Archipelago. Between 1922 and 1925 the *Arctic* made annual voyages north, after which government officials travelled in chartered vessels or ships of the Hudson's Bay Company. Bernier was never successful in transiting the Northwest Passage. In the western Arctic, Hudson's Bay Company trading schooners traversed the northern shore of the Northwest Territories, where the RCMP had their own patrol ship, the *St Roch,* completed in 1928. During the Second World War, the *St Roch* became the first Canadian ship to transit the Northwest Passage, which she did in in both directions

Icebreaking

Icebreaking was not specifically mentioned in the Department's mandate but the two largest ships of the pre-Confederation fleet, the *Queen Victoria* and *Napoleon III,* had additional plating at the bow for strengthening against ice. The first purpose-built ice-breakers were needed to provide a winter passenger and freight service to Prince Edward Island, as this was one of the terms under which that province agreed to join the Dominion in 1873. The unsatisfactory *Northern Light* of 1876 was followed by the *Stanley* (1888) and *Minto* (1899), which were much more capable ships based on designs used in the Baltic. Nevertheless, conditions were sometimes so severe that it was necessary to resort to the former method of using ice boats, rowed across the leads and manhandled across the ice.

CGS *Neptune* in winter quarters at Fullerton, Hudson Bay, 1904.
(National Archives of Canada PA209428)

Henry Wolsey
Bayfield, the father
of Canadian
hydrography.
(National Archives
of Canada C1227)

The government ships provided the link between P.E.I. and the mainland in the winter. In the summer, commercial ferries carried the passengers and freight and the icebreakers were employed on lighthouse supply or fisheries patrol. This system prevailed until the First World War when two of the passenger carrying icebreakers, the *Minto* and the newer *Earl Grey*, were sold to Russia. With the government service greatly reduced, a new large icebreaking rail, automobile and passenger ferry, the *Prince Edward Island,* took over the service in 1915.

In the St Lawrence the first major icebreaker was the *Montcalm*, completed in 1904. She was assisted by smaller icebreakers, and their most important task was to break up the ice in the spring to prevent ice jams that used to cause flooding along the river banks. It was found that the most effective method was to use a large icebreaker in the main channel while smaller ships widened the cut and worked in the tributaries.

The icebreakers built for the P.E.I. and the St Lawrence services were sometimes used for expeditions to Hudson Bay in the summer, but the early vessels were not suit-

Rear Admiral Charles Kingsmill, head of the Canadian Marine Service from 1908 as well as Naval Service from 1910. (National Archives of Canada PA42541)

able for operations in the high Arctic or for wintering over, frozen in the ice. Until after the Second World War that was still the province of the strongly built wooden ships like the *Neptune, Alert* and *Arctic*, which were fitted with sails and had small engines, not requiring great quantities of coal. They were built to survive in ice, not force their way through it, and were not much use as icebreakers in more southern waters.

The Hydrographic Service

From 1817 to 1856 the distinguished Admiralty hydrographer Henry Wolsey Bayfield had made the survey and charting of the Great Lakes, the St Lawrence River and Gulf, and the East Coast his life's work. After 1867 surveys became a Canadian responsibility but it was not until 1883 that a Canadian hydrographic service was founded. It was known at first simply as the Georgian Bay Survey (the task in hand) and headed by Commander J.G. Boulton, who was on loan from the British Admiralty but paid by the Dominion Government. On completion of his work in Georgian Bay and Lake Huron, Boulton moved on to Lake Superior. He returned to England in 1892, and this service became part of Marine and Fisheries. Its first Canadian head was William J. Stewart, Chief Hydrographer from 1893 to 1925, who was followed by a succession of notable hydrographers.

In 1904, the surveying sections of the departments of Public Works, Railways and Canals and Marine and Fisheries were combined, by Order-in-Council, into the Hydrographic Survey of Canada. In 1910 the branch became the responsibility of the Naval Service of Canada and continued under the Royal Canadian Navy until 1922, when it was returned to the Department of Marine and Fisheries. In 1936, the branch was transferred to the Department of Mines and Resources and there would be further changes to follow after the Second World War. In spite of being subject to these administrative changes, the Hydrographic Service quietly continued with its work of issuing charts of high accuracy and quality.

Wireless Telegraphy

In 1902, the first transatlantic radio station was established by Guglielmo Marconi at Glace Bay, Nova Scotia, with the aid of a subsidy from the Canadian Government. In 1904, the Department of Marine and Fisheries negotiated a contract with the Marconi Company for a chain of marine radio stations along the Gulf of St Lawrence to the Belle Isle and Cabot Straits, including stations in Newfoundland and Labrador, which were not part of Canada at that time. Four Marine and Fisheries ships, CGS *Canada, Stanley, Minto* and *Lady Laurier*, were fitted with wireless telegraphy in 1904 and 1905. In 1906, after the international Berlin Convention, Canada passed a Telegraph Act incorporating regulations and detailed licensing requirements.

CGS *Canada*, fishery patrol vessel and training ship for the new Naval Service. (National Archives of Canada PA206972)

As the government did not want to be completely tied to Marconi, Marine and Fisheries built and operated seven stations on the West Coast in 1907–08. These had different equipment (the Massie system). The Marconi Company itself installed other stations on the upper St Lawrence. In 1910-1912 government-owned stations with Marconi equipment were built at five locations in the Great Lakes. It was now possible for messages to be exchanged with ships located across the Atlantic and up to the head of Lake Superior.

The London Convention in 1912 established international standards for radio watch-keeping and proficiency and assigned radio wavelengths and established the term "radio telegraphy" instead of "wireless telegraphy." It was followed by the appropriate Canadian legislation, the Radiotelegraph Act of 1913.

Responsibility for wireless or radio telegraphy was transferred to the new Naval Service of Canada in 1910. During the First World War, radio direction finding stations were installed by the Navy and used for military purposes, but after the war they were retained to transmit bearings to commercial ships on request. This was the first radio aid to navigation. Later, radio beacons allowed ships fitted with radio direction finders to take bearings themselves.

Control of the branch was relinquished by the Navy in 1922 and has remained with Marine and Fisheries and its successors to the present day. In 1924–1925, experiments with radiotelephone service were conducted on the West Coast and were extended to the East Coast in 1927. High-powered stations broadcast weather and ice reports, dangers to navigation, and even fish prices. In 1936, the new Department of Transport assumed responsibility for radiotelegraphy and broadcasts.

Fisheries and Customs Patrols

Fisheries patrols and the enforcement of fisheries regulations were an important task of the Department. Marine and Fisheries became separate departments in 1884, but were re-united in 1892. The Customs Preventative Service of the Department of Customs and Excise used similar patrol vessels and sometimes employment overlapped. Patrol vessels were armed with light quick-firing guns and carried small arms for use by boarding parties.

The Liberal government of Sir Wilfrid Laurier, Prime Minister from 1896 to 1911, favoured the establishment of a naval militia and saw the Fisheries Protection Service as the nucleus of such a body. Two ships ordered in 1903, CGS *Canada* and *Vigilant*, were miniature warships each armed with four automatic Maxim guns. *Vigilant* was stationed in the Great Lakes and *Canada* in the Atlantic. The latter was used train naval militia recruits, conducting voyages to Bermuda and the Caribbean where she exercised with Royal Navy units and her Commanding Officer, Captain Knowlton, exchanged the formal calls expected of a visiting warship, although she flew the blue, not the white ensign.

In May 1908, Rear Admiral Charles Kingsmill, a Canadian serving in the Royal Navy, was appointed to head the Canadian Marine Service. In the years before the

Top: GS *Arctic*, formerly the German vessel *Gauss*, acquired in 1904 for the Eastern Arctic Patrol. (National Archives of Canada PA207089)

Bottom: The RCMP vessel *St Roch* maintained a federal presence in the Western Arctic and transited the Northwest Passage both ways during the Second World War. (Royal Canadian Mounted Police)

Naval Service of Canada was created in 1910, he treated the Fisheries Protection part of it as a miniature Navy and when the infant Canadian Navy acquired its first ships— two old cruisers—he ran both services. CGS *Canada* was used to train junior officers. In 1911 her complement included a midshipman and six cadets, two of whom later became Admirals, together with their naval instructors. In 1912, three fisheries patrol vessels, CGS *Constance, Curlew* and *Petrel*, were fitted for minesweeping.

On the outbreak of war in 1914, responsibility for both fisheries and customs patrols was taken over by the Royal Canadian Navy, along with all the patrol vessels, some of which were commissioned and wore the white ensign while others continued their normal tasks. This only lasted for the duration of hostilities and the fisheries and customs patrol fleets reverted to their respective departments in 1920. The 1920s and 1930s saw other changes: in 1927, Marine and Fisheries became separate branches and, in 1930, separate departments. In 1932, the Customs Preventative Service became the Marine Section of the RCMP.

The Department of Transport

In 1936, the Department of Transport (DOT) was formed with responsibility for the regulation of land, sea and air transportation, but not cartography, so the Hydrographic Service and its ships went to the Department of Mines and Resources. As Fisheries was already separate, this left the DOT with a fleet consisting mainly of sturdy work-horse type vessels that were engaged in supplying the lighthouses and maintaining navigation aids; but the Québec agency operated icebreakers to reduce flooding and assist shipping in the spring. In the summer they visited Labrador and the south side of Baffin Island, with occasional diversions further north, and escorted ships on the route to the port of Churchill on Hudson Bay.

The Second World War

When the Second World War started in 1939, the Navy requisitioned the ships of other marine departments but not those of the DOT fleet, which continued its essential duties. In August 1940 Prime Minister Mackenzie King met with President Franklin D. Roosevelt at Ogdensburg, New York, resulting in an agreement for cooperation in continental defence. One result of this was the construction of airfields and radio and meteorological stations in Canada's north, and soon DOT icebreakers were engaged in missions to new bases in Labrador and Hudson Bay. After December 1941, following the Japanese attack on Pearl Harbor, this activity was greatly increased. Canadian and American personnel worked harmoniously together in pursuing the common aim of furthering the war effort, but the resources of the two nations were so disproportionate that the American presence could sometimes appear overwhelming. The need for a visible Canadian presence was understood in Ottawa, and the voyages of the RCMP vessel *St Roch* through the Northwest Passage during the war were an effort to demonstrate Canadian sovereignty at that critical time. These considerations would continue to be of concern after the end of hostilities in 1945.

Captain J.E.Bernier who commanded CGS *Arctic* on northern voyages between 1904 and 1925. (Bibliothèque Nationale du Québec 5042)

Captain J.E. Bernier

(1852–1934)

Joseph Elzéar Bernier was born at L'Islet, Québec on Jan 1st 1852. The Bernier family was prominent in an area known for its seafaring heritage. His grandfather, father, several uncles and cousins, and his two brothers were sea captains and many of them were also ship owners or held shares in the ships they commanded.

Joseph Bernier first went to sea in 1866 in his father's ship, the brigantine *Zillah*. At the age of seventeen he took command of this ship and subsequently commanded another of his father's ships, the *Saint-Michel*. In 1870, Certificates of Competency, issued after formal examinations, were instituted for Masters and Mates. Bernier was one of the first Canadians to obtain a Master's Certificate (in 1872). He then started working as master of large square-rigged ships for various Québec owners. At about that time, on a visit to Washington, he saw the *Polaris*, a vessel being fitted out for a polar expedition. Based on his experience of ice in the St Lawrence, he considered her (correctly as it turned out) to be unsuitable. From this time on he became interested in the efforts to navigate in Arctic waters and especially to reach the North Pole.

In 1887 he temporarily gave up seafaring to become Dockmaster of the Lorne Drydock at Lauzon, but returned to sea in 1890. From 1895 to 1898 he served as Governor of the Québec Gaol, This gave him time to continue studying the question of polar drift. In 1898 he gave an address to the members of the Québec Geographical Society outlining a proposed expedition to the pole by letting a ship drift in the ice from the Siberian islands to a position close enough to the pole to reach his objective by using dog teams or on foot. Special ladders were to be used to get over ice ridges, and at this early date he was already envisaging communication with the ship by the yet unproven wireless telegraphy. He vigorously promoted a Canadian expedition to the pole and requested government support and tried to raise money by giving, by 1902, more than a hundred lectures throughout Canada. The government of Sir Wilfrid Laurier was supportive, but not to the extent of providing the $100,000 asked.

Bernier also wanted to see Canadian sovereignty established over the Arctic islands, including any land yet to be discovered. In 1880, Britain had transferred title of the archipelago to Canada, but little had been done to consolidate our claim. Sovereignty in remote and unoccupied areas is not indisputable in international law. Eventually, becoming more aware of this, the Canadian Government in 1903 sent an expedition in the chartered ship *Neptune* under Dr A.P. Low, with the symbolic proclamation of sovereignty as one of its objectives. At the same time, the government decided to purchase a ship of its own and, on Bernier's recommendation, the German Antarctic ship *Gauss*, built at Kiel in 1900–1901, was bought for $75,000. The ship was renamed the *Arctic* and Bernier brought her back to Québec in May 1904.

Between 1904 and 1911 the *Arctic* under Captain Bernier would make four voyages to the north, departing Québec in the summer, over-wintering in the Arctic and returning the following October. The first expedition was to northern Hudson Bay. Before the ship sailed the Minister of Marine, the Honourable Raymond Préfontaine, reminded the members of the expedition of "the importance of the voyage ... to the remote territories of the North to enforce the laws of Canada and to affirm its rights to this territory." Bernier had to be resigned to the fact that his polar ambitions had to be put aside. He was convinced of the value of the expedition for establishing Canada's claims to sovereignty of the Arctic islands.

The 1904–1905 voyage was under the direction of Superintendent J.D. Moodie of the North-West Mounted Police, with Bernier commanding the ship, but during the subsequent voyages, those of 1906–1907, 1908–1909 and 1910–1911, Bernier was in full command of the expedition and was also appointed a Fisheries Officer. He issued licenses to Scottish and American whalers and took inventories of trade goods for the purpose of charging customs duties. As he explored, he surveyed the coasts, annexed islands, erected cairns and proclaimed the sovereignty of Canada. On Dominion Day, 1 July 1909, during his third voyage, Bernier erected a bronze marker and proclaimed Canadian sovereignty over the entire archipelago.

Bernier could not realize his earlier ambition to reach the North Pole. (Peary claimed to have done so in 1909). This did not appear to cause him distress: by the time he was put in command of the *Arctic* he was already in his fifties and had become focussed on the need to establish Canadian sovereignty in the region. Neither, in spite of several attempts during the 1908-1909 and 1910-1911 expeditions, did he manage to transit the Northwest Passage. Nevertheless, his four Arctic voyages were important for establishing the authority of the Canadian Government in the Arctic and the cairns, monuments and plaques he erected were the symbols of Canadian sovereignty, which otherwise could have been lost by default. Scientists accompanying his expeditions made valuable geological surveys and meteorological and tidal observations.

Bernier's success in four long and dangerous Arctic voyages was due to his careful planning and preparation. Although the 1904-1905 voyage was actually his first experience of the Arctic, he had made a study of all available literature and, during his voyages, befriended and questioned experienced Scottish and American whaler captains. He chose his overwintering quarters in time for the crew to hunt, fish and accumulate food for the winter. During the months of darkness, he gave lectures, organized games and dances, and made preparations for hunting and exploration by sled in the spring. When light returned, sports were played on the ice. National and religious festivals were always observed. In this way he was able to keep up the morale of his crew.

In 1911, at the conclusion of the fourth voyage, the Liberal government, which had supported Bernier, was out of office. Bernier, now 59, resigned his position with the Department of Marine and Fisheries but continued his interest in the Arctic. He had plans to establish a settlement at Pond Inlet and opened three fur trading posts in the area. Early in 1914 he purchased a small steamer, the *Guide*, with which he made two private expeditions in 1914-1915 and 1916-1917. In 1918 he had a narrow escape when a ship he was delivering to Britain sank in a storm. Bernier and all his crew were rescued by another ship of the convoy.

After the war Bernier again entered government service and resumed command of the *Arctic*, which in the interim had been employed as a lightship. He made four consecutive annual voyages between 1922 and 1925 in which he commanded the ship but not the expeditions, which were under the control of officials of the Department of the Interior. The *Arctic* was now old and in 1925 Bernier was 73 and ready to retire. Even so, in 1927 he was engaged as pilot on a tug towing barges to Hudson Strait. This was his last northern voyage, but he remained active and was often consulted on matters pertaining to the Arctic. Bernier died at his home in Levis on 26 December 1934. He is deservedly considered to be Canada's premier Arctic sailor.

The Banfield (later Bamfield) lifeboat, one of the few dedicated rescue craft existing in 1962. (Fisheries and Oceans Canada F169501)

Search and Rescue

In the House of Commons Debates (*Hansard*) the record of the announcement that created the Coast Guard is under the heading "Search and Rescue." Ever since the Second World War there had been public appeals from coastal communities and fishing and shipping interests for the creation of a Coast Guard. In the perception of a public that admired the United States Coast Guard and heard from time to time of its achievements is succoring Canadian vessels, sometimes even in Canadian waters, "Coast Guard" and "Search and Rescue" were practically synonymous terms.

The first proposal for the creation of a Canadian Coast Guard was a resolution by the White Ensign Club of Halifax, dated 16 June 1944, and addressed to the Prime Minister, the Speaker, the leaders of all political parties, and the relevant ministers. It stated: "To effect the complete and satisfactory rehabilitation after the war of personnel serving at sea, that a Canadian Government Coast Guard Service be established to carry out the pre-war functions of the RCMP Marine Section, the Department of Fisheries Protection Service, hydrographic survey, lifesaving and rescue and the DOT buoy and lighthouse service. To be conceived, like the United States Coast Guard, as a military service—the fourth arm of the Canadian Armed Forces." It was not until a year later, on 27 June 1945, that this resolution was addressed by the Acting Deputy Minister of Transport, who replied that in Canada there was little overlap of departmental responsibilities; that the main reason for the resolution by the White Ensign Club was to ensure employment for ex-service personnel, but provisions for that were being made anyway, and that there was no reason for an amalgamated service.

Nevertheless, on 28 January 1946 the Cabinet Defence Committee recommended that a conference be held to determine the need for a Canadian Coast Guard. This convened in February under the chairmanship of the Deputy Minister of Transport, C.P. Edwards. The meeting was attended by representatives of the RCN, the RCAF, the RCMP, the Departments of Transport, Public Works, Mines and Resources, Health and Welfare and the

CHAPTER 2

The Road Toward a Coast Guard Service

Canadian Legion. There were considerable differences of opinion. One suggestion, by Mr H.V. Anderson, Assistant Deputy Minister Marine Services, was that if an amalgamated Coast Guard Service was to be formed, it should be confined to vessels engaged in patrol (the prewar RCMP anti-smuggling patrols combined with fisheries patrols). The DOT would look after lifesaving. On 8 June 1946 Deputy Minister C.P. Edwards reported to the Cabinet Defence Committee that the recommendations of the Ad Hoc Committee were as follows:

1. That the establishment of a Coast Guard to provide new services offered no apparent advantages and was not recommended.

2. That the establishment of a Coast Guard consisting of a merger of the existing marine services was not desirable and was not recommended by a majority of the Committee.

3. The armed services, principally the Navy, disagreed with the second recommendation and wanted further study.

4. No major economies would be involved by the relocation of existing departmental functions.

The new Deputy Minister of Transport, H. F. Gordon, however, instituted direct contact between the marine Search and Rescue service and the RCAF Air–Sea Rescue branch to establish "intelligent direction, co-ordination and control of these facilities." (Since 1939, the RCAF Air–Sea Rescue service had provided fast rescue boats to aid aircrew forced down in the sea. They were also called upon to help small craft in trouble, but they operated only in local areas near coastal airfields.)

For the next fifteen years, regular demands for the establishment of a Coast Guard came from communities on both coasts and the Great Lakes—from Boards of Trade, Chambers of Commerce, newspapers, fishing and shipping organizations, labour unions and veterans associations. The towns of Annapolis, Yarmouth, and Lunenburg in Nova Scotia and Prince Rupert and Port Alberni in British Columbia all called for the creation of a Coast Guard. On 21 October 1948 the Victoria British Columbia Chamber of Commerce made a detailed recommendation for a Search and Rescue organization. It proposed that an operations centre be set up and that preventive as well as rescue measures be put in place. It went on to recommend the types of vessel to be used and the formation of two auxiliaries—one of yachtsmen and one of fishermen. In 1949, there was an eloquent appeal by twelve Vancouver business groups and societies and also by the Fisheries Council, recommending a Search and Rescue service for British Columbia. Newspapers in coastal cities supported these proposals.

While these appeals continued, a dissenting opinion came from Mr R.E.R. Chadwick, the President of the Foundation Maritime Company, which operated ocean-going tugs and salvage vessels. Mr Chadwick was clearly concerned that SAR vessels would not only save lives but tow vessels. In May 1950 he wrote: "Cost of salvage and towing is now borne by foreign underwriters. If a Coast Guard did this, the tug owners would lose income and ship brokers and taxpayers would shoulder the cost. The RCMP already does the anti-smuggling patrols ... With the cost of Government mounting, it is no time to saddle the country with an expensive Coast Guard that will duplicate the existing tug fleet and sacrifice U.S. dollars and sterling that it earns."

In October 1950, two fishing boats were lost off Woods Harbour, Nova Scotia. No government vessel was available (one was at the Lunenburg exhibition but did not sail). A freighter and a USCG cutter conducted a search without success. On 21 July 1951, probably as a result of this incident, Cabinet Directive No. 22 authorized RCAF coordination centres to task all government vessels to participate in a Search and Rescue operation until private or commercial salvage was available.

On 29 December 1953 the British Columbia Government passed a resolution requesting the establishment of a Coast Guard and recommended that voluntary life-saving by fishermen should be rewarded with payment for fuel and costs. In 1954, the Canadian Chamber of Commerce recommended the elevation of the current temporary arrangements for Search and Rescue to the status of a seagoing Coast Guard and the National Council of Women recorded its support.

On 19 March 1955 there was a detailed submission by the Naval Officers' Association of British Columbia. Its main points were:

1. Existing vessels are inadequate. The only good ones are lighthouse supply vessels but they are not equipped for towing and the crews are not trained.

2. Offshore vessels should be capable of operating from 50 miles south of Cape Flattery to 50 miles north of the Alaskan border and 100 miles off to sea

3. All personnel should be in the RCNR.

On 31 October 1955 Deputy Minister of Transport J.R. Baldwin reported on the state of marine Search and Rescue on the British Columbia Coast. His conclusions were:

1. There was a need for an improved helicopter service.

2. RCN vessels were not suitable and took too long to sail. (Note: Naval authorities would not agree with this opinion.)

3. RCMP and fisheries patrol vessels were too small and slow.

4. DOT ships were too slow and otherwise engaged. Most station-based vessels operated only by day.

5. There was a possibility of technical modifications to the design of future vessels.

This was the situation when the Conservative government of John Diefenbaker took office on 14 October 1957. George R. Pearkes became Minister of National Defence; George Hees, Minister of Transport, and Howard Green, Minister of Public Works. All had been advocates of the Coast Guard when in opposition, but two years after the election no action had been taken as "providing a fleet of special vessels solely for Search and Rescue would require a very expensive organization." (Statement by Minister Hees, 1 April 1959). But one month later the incident occurred that would change the way the subject of a Coast Guard, or at least the Search and Rescue component, was regarded. On 1 May at 4:23 p.m. the Norwegian freighter *Ferngulf*, when off Port Atkinson in the approaches to Vancouver, reported that she was on fire with injured on board. The first help did not arrive until 5:00 p.m., when an RCAF helicopter put a doctor on board. The Vancouver fireboat was not able to respond—later giving the reason, much criticized, that its activities were restricted to the harbour. Fortunately, two Canadian destroyers and a USN submarine were in port. Fire-fighting crews from HMCS *Saguenay* and *Assiniboine* and USS *Cavallo*, led by RCN Commander Ken Lewis, reached the *Ferngulf* at 6:00 p.m. and succeeded in bringing the fire under control. There were casualties among the freighter's crew, however, one of whom died in hospital. This event resulted in much publicity and further demands for action. From this time on, it is clear from internal correspondence that a Coast Guard would only be a matter of time.

On 1 June 1959 a memo from the Deputy Minister of Transport recommended that:

1. A Coast Guard should be a prestige service with a national pay scale.

2. There should be the possibility of transfer to shore jobs.

3. There should be a central marine school for officers and crews.

4. Some surplus ships of the same general layout as present vessels could be earmarked for SAR but it would not be feasible to provide fast dedicated SAR cutters.

5. Crews should be trained with a view to lifesaving but not salvage.

6. The service should have distinctive flags and symbols.

Other recommendations were that special fire-fighting and emergency equipment be carried, that standby vessels should be designated and all vessels should give daily reports of their locations, and that marine SAR coordinators be appointed to the RCAF rescue coordination centres. All these recommendations were eventually implemented except that, contrary to the comment about specialized vessels, dedicated Search and Rescue craft, both station-based and for offshore patrols, became an important part of the DOT fleet when the Coast Guard was eventually formed.

The Arctic, 1945 to 1962

While Search and Rescue was the issue in the public eye, the Government and the Department of Transport could not be blind to the implications of Arctic sovereignty. During the Second World War, the United States had built airfields and meteorological stations in the Canadian north and in Greenland to facilitate the aircraft ferry route

Top: The Eastern Arctic Patrol ship *C.D. Howe*, completed in 1950. (Fisheries and Oceans Canada F090102)

Bottom: The first post-war large icebreaker, the *d'Iberville*, completed in 1952. (Fisheries and Oceans Canada F100102)

to the European theatre. After the war, the threat of the Soviet Union caused an increase in installations of this type. Lines of radar stations were built: the Pine-Tree line, the Mid-Canada line and the Distant Early Warning (DEW) line. Ever since the Ogdensburg agreement of 1940 the two nations had worked together in matters of continental defence, but the United States had by far the greater resources. When a joint Canadian–American weather station was established at Resolute on Cornwallis Island in 1947, all the transport vessels and icebreakers used were American. (Another station was established at Eureka on the west coast of Ellesmere Island by American planes based at Thule in Greenland). The large U.S. presence in the North caused some misgivings in Ottawa, for sovereignty over remote territories is not unquestionable in international law and can depend on "effective occupation."

During the depression years of the thirties, strict economy was enforced by all government departments and no ships of any consequence were added to the DOT fleet. This period was followed by the Second World War during which ship construction in Canada was devoted to naval vessels and ocean-going freighters. By 1945 the Department of Transport fleet was quite out of date. The best icebreaker was the *N.B.*

The RCN icebreaker *Labrador* transferred to the Department of Transport in 1958. (Fisheries and Oceans Canada F100201)

McLean, completed in 1930, which was fully employed on the Hudson Bay route during the navigation season. It was necessary, both as a contribution to the alliance and to demonstrate the Canadian presence in our own territory, to do our fair share in the construction and supply of the new radar stations and airfields. Economic development of oil and minerals would be a possibility in the future and the government intended to bring improved medical support and modern facilities to the Inuit population. For this, it would be necessary to build suitable ships.

Starting in 1950, ice-strengthened vessels and icebreakers were built specifically for Arctic operations, and special craft were acquired to participate in the construction and re-supply of radar, radio and meteorological stations and Inuit settlements. A special Eastern Arctic patrol ship, the *C.D. Howe,* entered service in 1950. On her annual voyages she stopped at every coastal settlement and station in northern Labrador, the south coast of Hudson Strait, the south and east coasts of Baffin Island, and at points on Ellesmere Island. The *C.D. Howe* had accommodation for eighty-eight passengers which included employees of the Departments of Northern Affairs and National Resources and RCMP officers. Navigation aids were activated for the season and relief personnel brought to their stations. The ship had well equipped hospital and staff and dental facilities. A number of hospital berths were reserved for Inuit patients suffering from tuberculosis which was a severe problem at that time. They were taken south for treatment and, if this was successful, they were returned the following year. The second large ship for Arctic service was the powerful icebreaker *d'Iberville,* completed in 1952. She also had accommodation for additional personnel from other government departments.

In 1954, the Royal Canadian Navy also became interested in the Arctic and completed the icebreaker HMCS *Labrador*. For several years the *Labrador* was used in an active program of exploring, surveying and establishing a Canadian presence. It was a bitter disappointment to her crew and to those who believed that this was an important mission for the Navy when she was transferred to the Department of Transport in 1958. Her last naval commanding officer, Captain T.C. Pullen, felt that the DOT ships in the early days "drifted about," escorting ships when necessary but not adding much to our knowledge of Arctic waters. In fact, exploration was not, at that time, part of the Department of Transport's mandate, but this would change. As more icebreakers were built and as traffic increased and mineral extraction began, civilian government vessels, hydrographic ships as well as DOT icebreakers, and technical personnel became increasingly active and innovative in Arctic endeavours and projects and would find their way into ever more remote inlets and fjords.

During the years 1957 to 1960, the Department of Transport added several important ships to its fleet. When the *John A. Macdonald* was completed in 1960, four large icebreakers (counting the *N.B. McLean*) were available for deployment to the Eastern Arctic during the navigation season. Between 1957 and 1959, four smaller icebreakers joined the fleet on the East Coast (plus two ice-strengthened ships that only occasionally went north). Nine former British landing craft (LCT) were employed supplying the

CGS *d'Iberville* leading in St Lambert Lock, opening navigation in the St Lawrence Seaway, 25 April 1959. (Fisheries and Oceans Canada MP500103)

DEW line sites and in other construction work. These flat-bottomed craft could take advantage of the large tidal range to go aground and then unload into trucks at low water. They could also unload bulk fuel to tank storage ashore in a short period of time (one of their greatest operating assets). In the western Arctic, another approach was taken. From 1959, one small icebreaker, the *Camsell*, deployed annually from Victoria to set and service navigation aids. Most of the cargo delivery was via tug and barge traffic down the Mackenzie River. Materials for the DEW line were then taken along the western Arctic coasts by landing ships and tankers on loan from the United States Navy, but operated by the Northern Transportation Company and crewed by Canadians.

The Growth of Maritime Trade

Another incentive for the creation of the Coast Guard was the great increase in maritime trade and the use of the waterways that developed after the Second World War and especially after the opening of the St Lawrence Seaway. The St Lawrence Seaway Authority was constituted by an Act of Parliament in December 1951. The vast project, jointly undertaken by Canada and the United States, was finally commenced on 10 August 1954 and the Seaway opened for business on 29 April 1959, the first day of the navigation season. The first ships to transit the St Lambert lock at Montreal were the CGS *d'Iberville* and CGS *Montcalm*. Two months later, Queen Elizabeth and Prince Phillip were joined by President and Mrs. Eisenhower on board the Royal Yacht. When HMY *Britannia* broke a ribbon stretched across the canal, the Seaway was declared officially open.

As trade increased on both coasts and ships got larger, the work of the Department of Transport required more resources and central control. Channels had to be dredged to accommodate the larger ships and marked to prevent disasters that could block essential waterways. New ports were built in British Columbia and on the north shore of the Gulf of St Lawrence to handle mineral exports. The Mackenzie River became a major water highway for barge traffic and ocean-going ships were penetrating to the heart of the continent via the Seaway. The whole system had grown and assumed national importance. New electronic positioning methods, developed during the war, were in use on both coasts by 1962. The sheer size of the system called for national standards set by a body such as a Coast Guard.

These three imperatives—the demand for better Search and Rescue facilities, considerations of Arctic sovereignty and development, and the need to respond to technical advances and the growth of shipborne traffic—were the influences that led to the creation of the Canadian Coast Guard. The mission of the Coast Guard has been officially described in various ways but its core commitments have never changed: the Coast Guard exists to provide safe conditions for those who use the sea and to facilitate trade and commerce. As Canada has the longest coastline of any country in the world, this is no mean undertaking.

Aerial view of the Canadian Coast Guard base at St John's, Newfoundland. (Dan Pike, Fisheries and Oceans B010105)

As related in Chapter One, the Canadian Coast Guard was officially created with a simple announcement by the Minister of Transport in the House of Commons, on 26 January 1962, but it did not spring to life as a complete entity on that date. The process of developing its identity and establishing its presence was gradual and some progress had already been made. In 1958, Dr Gordon W. Stead, who had been one of the Secretaries to the Treasury Board, was appointed to the new position of Director General, Marine Services and Assistant Deputy Minister, Marine. The Deputy Minister was J.R. Baldwin, who gave full support to the reforms which were to come.

Dr Stead found a small and ineffective headquarters organization, eleven marine agencies and fifteen other marine services offices, all independent of each other. Yet the fleet had already been through its first postwar expansion and was about to grow again with a number of large modern vessels already planned. His first task was to establish an efficient central administration and to that end, he recruited Captain E.S. Brand from the Maritime Commission, and appointed him Director of Marine Operations. Mr Stead made a point of touring the agencies and going to sea in the ships and found much that needed to be improved. As a start, he re-christened the fleet "the Canadian Marine Service" and gave the ships the prefix CMS. But "marine" in French means "navy" so this was not a good title. As the politicians, influenced largely by the Search and Rescue public demands, came around to the idea of a Coast Guard, these three senior officials, Baldwin, Stead, and Brand, were already laying the foundations for an effective national service and were planning the founding of a Coast Guard College to provide officers of the highest calibre.

The next step was to organize the regions. The Maritimes Region was formed under a Regional Director in 1966. It was comprised of three districts: Dartmouth, Saint John and Charlottetown, with headquarters in Dartmouth. A year later the Western Region was established and was made responsible for the British Columbia coast, the western Arctic and the northwestern rivers and lakes, notably the Mackenzie River. Its headquarters was located in Vancouver and its three district bases were Victoria and

CHAPTER 3

Regions and Branches

Aerial view of the Canadian Coast Guard base at Hay River. (Ross Macdonald, Fisheries and Oceans Canada B040101)

Opposite top: Aerial view of the Canadian Coast Guard Base at Dartmouth, Nova Scotia. (Fisheries and Oceans Canada B020201)

Opposite bottom: Aerial view of the Canadian Coast Guard Base at Québec City, Québec. (Gilles Poirier, Fisheries and Oceans Canada B030101)

Prince Rupert, British Columbia, and Hay River, Northwest Territories. The other regions followed. Newfoundland stood on its own with its base at St John's. The Laurentian Region included Québec, Hudson Bay and the eastern Arctic. It had bases at Québec City and at Sorel. The Central Region, with headquarters in Toronto, had district offices at Prescott and Parry Sound, Ontario and looked after Ontario's inland waterways and Lake Winnipeg as well as the Great Lakes.

Coast Guard Headquarters also grew in importance and effectiveness. A major step was taken in 1975 when William A. O'Neill was appointed to the post of Commissioner of the Canadian Coast Guard. Mr O'Neill, together with his deputy, Ranald Quail, spent considerable time and effort to establish a consistent national policy and program direction from Ottawa.

Aerial view of the Canadian Coast Guard base at Prescott, Ontario. (Fisheries and Oceans Canada B040201-003)

In 1983, a new Northern Region was created. A headquarters office was already in existence to manage the annual northern sealift and other Arctic activities, including developing anti-pollution regulations and the Polar Icebreaker project. In March 1983 this group was reconstituted as a regional headquarters, and it later took over responsibility for the Hay River district. During the northern navigation season, the Northern Region exercised operational control of all the ships from other regions that were on Arctic deployment.

The 1970s were an active period in organizational growth and change. This was an era of increased spending to support national goals and broad-based administrative experimentation. The late 1980s, however, were characterized by recession and reductions, but these were minor compared to those of the early 1990s which placed virtually all government programs under scrutiny. One outcome of this was the final major organizational change for the twentieth century: the transfer of the Coast Guard from Transport Canada to the Department of Fisheries and Oceans (DFO). With this came also some adjustments to the regions. The Northern and Central Regions were combined with headquarters at Sarnia, Ontario, and the Western Region was renamed the Pacific Region. This conformed to the previous DFO organization. In 2002 the Laurentian Region was renamed the Québec Region.

Aerial view of the Canadian Coast Guard base at Victoria, British Columbia. (Fisheries and Oceans Canada B050101)

The Regions

Each region has its own characteristics and problems, which are the inevitable con-sequence of geography and climate. Newfoundland is our eastern bastion, where the traditions of fishing and sealing are an inescapable heritage and are as much part of the culture of the "townies" of St John's as of the people of the outports. The terrible deple-tion of the fish stocks has not yet changed the outlook of the population. The new oil and technical industries may replace some of the lost income but are not likely to imprint their characteristics on the people in the way that four hundred years of rely-ing on the sea's hard-won bounty has done. The Grand Banks stretch to the eastward for over 200 miles and are the hunting grounds of fishing vessels, although they are fewer in number than in the past. Exploration and production oil platforms spread over the oil producing areas. On its boundaries hang the foreign fishing fleets with fishery patrol vessels, Canadian and European, keeping watch. The Newfoundland Region is the first to be entered by shipping from Europe. From here they send their information messages to ECAREG, the traffic information authority. These ships may be bound for the St Lawrence through the Strait of Belle Isle or Cabot Strait, or to Newfoundland or Maritimes ports. They will encounter fog, icebergs and, in some seasons, pack ice. Coast Guard ships provide ice escort to merchant ships and fishing vessels and are on

A Maritime fishing harbour, Lunenburg, Nova Scotia. (Town of Lunenburg L-4-8)

patrol or stand-by for Search and Rescue duties. Navigation aids must be serviced around the island and in Labrador.

The Maritimes Region looks after a complex coastline with many inlets and fishing ports as well as commercial harbours with the major ports of Halifax, Nova Scotia, and Saint John, New Brunswick. They were once approximately equal in traffic volume but by the 1990s Halifax had grown as a container port. Icebreakers, offshore Search and Rescue cutters and navigation aids vessels operate out of the Coast Guard base on the Dartmouth side of the harbour. The Bedford Institute of Oceanography is home to the fisheries patrol and scientific vessels. Halifax is also the location of Maritime Command's East Coast naval base. Saint John was the major shipbuilding port with facilities for the construction of large ships. Buoy tenders of the Saint John District looked after the Bay of Fundy with its fierce tides and small craft serviced the aids on the Saint John River. A third district at Charlottetown, P.E.I., takes care of the southern part of the Gulf of St Lawrence and the Northumberland Strait between Prince Edward Island and Nova Scotia. This area and Cabot Strait are covered in ice in the winter.

The Gulf of St Lawrence is a narrowing sleeve channeling shipping into the St Lawrence River towards the ports of Québec, Trois Rivières and Montréal and on to the Seaway and the Great Lakes. Other ports are found on the north shore, at Port

Lake freighters early in the navigation season. (Fisheries and Oceans Canada FC010002)

Cartier, Sept Iles and the Saguenay River, but the main preoccupation of the Laurentian Region is keeping traffic moving in the Gulf and River. Depths of water must be constantly monitored by special sounding vessels to maintain channel depths that are mandated by legislation. Ice must be prevented from blocking the channels or causing flooding. This is done by hovercraft as well as by icebreakers. Navigation aids must be serviced on the long and sparsely populated shores of the Gulf. In winter, icebreakers from all the eastern regions work together in the Gulf of St Lawrence to provide vessel escort. The Laurentian Region has a history and tradition of icebreaking dating from the last century. It provided nearly all the ships that sailed north to Hudson Bay and the Arctic until the expansion of the Department of Transport fleet in the late 1950s.

The Central Region is active from April to December. (From January to March it is ice-bound). The volume of traffic in the Welland Canal and the Soo (Sault Ste Marie) locks exceeds that of any other waterway, the Suez and Panama canals not excepted. Endless processions of long, distinctively shaped lake boats carrying ore and grain cargoes have been joined, through the Seaway, by "salties" from all over the world. Navigation aids are constantly monitored and icebreaking is required in the spring and in certain harbours during the winter. The concentration of pleasure boats here is the greatest in Canada. In 1995, its headquarters was moved from Toronto to Sarnia, Ontario, and it was renamed the Central and Arctic Region, assuming the duties that were formerly allocated to the Northern Region's headquarters in Ottawa.

The reputation of British Columbia as an area with an ideal climate is well deserved and the crews of ships working in the Strait of Georgia and the inside passages as far as Prince Rupert could enjoy unparalleled beauty and ideal summer conditions, as well as challenging navigation among strong currents. This is not the case on the outer coasts of Vancouver Island or in the Hecate Strait, north of the Queen Charlotte Islands. The scenery there is even more impressive and rugged, but storms moving in from the Pacific can devastate fleets of fishing vessels and drive large ships ashore on inaccessible coasts. The Pacific Region has great numbers of fishing vessels and pleasure craft. Navigation aids vessels and Search and Rescue cutters and hovercraft are always busy. A stream of large bulk carriers comes to the port of Vancouver for grain and coal and to various smaller ports for ore, lumber and paper. There is no ice, but a light icebreaker goes every year to the western Arctic. For most of the period covered by this book, the Western Region was responsible for the northwestern rivers. A shallow draft buoy tender was operated on Lake Athabaska and the Peace River and up to four were based at Hay River to maintain the navigation aids on Great Slave Lake, the Mackenzie River, and along the coastline of the Northwest Territories. The Western Region was re-named the Pacific Region in 1995.

The Arctic was a region on its own for only twelve years, from 1983 to 1995, but Coast Guard ships and personnel from all the others have served there. Canada defines itself as a northern nation and we Canadians think of the Arctic, which most have seen only in paintings and photographs, as one of the most important characteristics of our country. Service in the Arctic is a definitive experience for the members of the Coast Guard. The captains and crews who go north every year have a job to do and are not there to seek records for furthest north or earliest or latest voyages. Each trip has a practical purpose but remarkable feats of navigation and scientific investigation are accomplished nevertheless, and those who have achieved them know it, even if the record is one familiar only to their peers. The crew of a Canadian Coast Guard icebreaker lives in very different conditions from the crews of the ships that took part in the expeditions of the nineteenth century, so vividly described by Pierre Berton in *The Arctic Grail*. The early explorers shivered in unsuitable wool clothing in the dark lower decks of unheated wooden ships and their expeditions might take several winters. Many succumbed to cold and starvation or died of lead poisoning from the solder in their canned provisions. A modern ship is a haven of light and warmth, with excellent food, ready communication with home, and electronic entertainment. True, it can be holed and sunk, and if the generators fail, the cold will soon penetrate the steel hulls, but the Canadian Coast Guard has never lost a ship in the Arctic. For those who have been there, the Arctic voyage, more than any other mission, exemplifies the Coast Guard experience.

The Branches

Integrated into the regional organizations were other branches of the Coast Guard, some of which had already been in existence in Transport Canada. The Aids and Waterways Branch developed the general policy for navigation aids—lighthouses, beacons, buoys, electronic aids and ship channels. The Ship Safety Branch, formerly the Board of Steamship Inspection, was responsible for applying the regulations made under the Canada Shipping Act. Ship plans and specifications had to be approved. Inspections were carried out during construction and completed ships were regularly inspected at specified intervals that depended on their type. Foreign ships arriving in Canada are also subject to inspection to ensure conformity with Canadian and international regulations. The inspectors are known as marine surveyors and include naval architects, marine and electrical engineers, master mariners and radio experts. The district offices of the Ship Safety branch were placed where they had the most convenient access to the ships that had to be inspected and were not connected with fleet bases. When the Coast Guard was transferred to the Department of Fisheries and Oceans in 1995, Ship Safety, renamed Marine Safety, remained in Transport Canada.

Under the Coast Guard, an effective Search and Rescue was created. Coast Guard officers were appointed to positions in the RCAF Search and Rescue Coordination Centres, located at Halifax, Nova Scotia, Trenton, Ontario and Esquimalt, British Columbia. New offshore Search and Rescue cutters joined the fleet and were operated under regional authority, while new station-based lifeboats were positioned at strategic locations around both east and west coasts and the Great Lakes. The crews of these self-righting craft are, for the most part, local mariners who are familiar with their area. An emergency response organization came into being in 1970 after the wreck of the tanker *Arrow* in Chedabucto Bay, Nova Scotia.

The Harbours and Ports also came under the Coast Guard but will not be covered in this book, which is concerned principally with operational matters. In the reorganization of 1995, the Harbours and Ports directorate, like the Marine Safety Branch, remained with Transport Canada. The most notable activities since 1962 of the branches mentioned above are described in subsequent chapters.

Dr Gordon W.
Stead.
(Fisheries and
Oceans Canada
P060001)

Dr Gordon W. Stead, DSC and Bar, LLD

(1913–1995)

Gordon Wilson Stead was born on 4 February 1913, the son of Major and Mrs. Frank Stead of Vancouver. When still a teenager he worked as a purser's writer on the RMS *Niagara,* a passenger ship on the Vancouver to Australia run. He attended the University of British Columbia, graduating with a B.Com. and a B.A. in 1934, and then worked for the Geodetic Survey of Canada, and later for Straits Towing, a tugboat company.

When the Second World War started in 1939, the Canadian Forces had more volunteers than they could absorb and train. Stead had attempted to enlist immediately but was not accepted by the army or air force. A year after the war started, he was able to join the Navy and, because of his age, he was commissioned as a full lieutenant RCNVR. After basic and technical training in England he was appointed to command one of the 112 ft.

Fairmile motor launches in a Royal Navy flotilla based in Falmouth. In June 1941 his flotilla was sent to the Mediterranean and was based at Gibraltar, being transferred to Malta in early 1942. This was the period of the siege of Malta by Axis forces and Stead, now senior officer of his group, was almost continuously in action, while the MLs proved their worth as minesweepers and antiaircraft escorts.

Stead and his flotilla took part in the invasions of Sicily and Italy, minesweeping and leading landing craft into the landing beaches. For his service in the Mediterranean, Gordon Stead was awarded the DSC and bar (i.e. two DSCs). He did not return to Canada until the end of 1943, having been promoted to lieutenant commander. After some leave he joined the new destroyer HMCS *Iroquois* and completed his war service in RCN ships.

In October 1945, after demobilisation, he was awarded an honorary Doctorate of Laws by the University of British Columbia. He became a lecturer in economics at the University and then joined the Federal Department of Finance. In 1956 he was appointed one of two Assistant Secretaries to the Treasury Board. Then, in 1958, he was given opportunity to draw on his nautical as well as his administrative experience when he was appointed to head the Marine Services of the Department of Transport with the titles of Director General Marine Services and Assistant Deputy Minister, Marine.

In this position, which he held until 1970, he was concerned with raising the standards of operation of the fleet, which had commenced an unprecedented expansion, and welding what was essentially a number of locally oriented agencies into a national body. To do so he recruited, first, Captain Eric Brand and then Rear Admiral Tony Storrs, as Directors of Marine Operations. (See biographies following Chapters 4 and 7). His efforts were successful, as demonstrated by the formation of the Coast Guard in 1962 and the founding of the Coast Guard College in 1965.

After retiring from the federal service, Dr Stead returned to UBC as a professor in the School of Community and Regional Planning. His book *A Leaf upon the Sea: A Small Ship in the Mediterranean, 1941-1943* was published in 1988. It is a fascinating first-hand account of active naval operations in a critical theatre of the war. Gordon Stead passed away in Vancouver on 19 October 1995. He is remembered as having played a vital part in the creation and early development of the Coast Guard.

The ice-strengthened navigation aids vessel *Edward Cornwallis*—the first ship of the postwar program, completed in 1949. (Fisheries and Oceans F131703)

The Canadian Marine Fleet in 1945 and 1962

In 1945, at the end of the Second World War, the Canadian Marine fleet of the Department of Transport was a rather insignificant collection of twenty-three small, mostly elderly, vessels. Only one, the icebreaker *N.B. McLean,* exceeded 3000 gross tons. The newest was the small icebreaker *Ernest Lapointe,* completed in 1941. Two, the *Druid* and the *Lady Laurier,* had been built in 1902. The average age of the ships was 24 years. By 1962, when the formation of the Coast Guard was announced, the fleet had increased to forty-nine ships, thirty-nine of which had been postwar additions. Some of these were former naval vessels, but twenty-three were new-construction ships, specially designed and built in Canada for the Department of Transport. (These figures exclude small craft, they are for vessels over 100 gross tons). Some old-timers were still in the list, notably the veteran West Coast lighthouse supply vessel and buoy tender *Estevan,* which would continue in use until 1969, having served faithfully for 57 years. Others were the *Grenville* built in 1915 and the St Lawrence channel sounding vessel *Detector* which would last until 1978, beating the *Estevan's* record by serving for 63 years. But most of the ships were modern. The most impressive was the new large icebreaker *John A. Macdonald,* completed in 1960.

Ship Design

Organizations such as the Coast Guard and its predecessors employ their own naval architects, on a permanent basis or on contract, to formulate design requirements for future vessels, based on the tasks the vessel is expected to perform and the environment in which it will be obliged to operate. In many cases, experience with existing ships helps greatly in the definition of such requirements. Once this work is done, the general requirements must be translated into detailed plans and instructions to the shipbuilder, including lists of all the equipment needed on board. This is done by naval architecture firms that specialize in such work.

Although the major Canadian shipbuilders—Davie Shipbuilding Limited, Canadian Vickers and Burrard—all had naval architects on staff, the Montreal company of

CHAPTER 4

The Fleet: 1962 to 1978

The very successful triple-screw diesel-electric icebreaker *John. A. Macdonald* completed in 1960. (Fisheries and Oceans F103016)

German and Milne, (originally Lambert and German and for a while Milne, Gilmore and German), was the pre-eminent ship design firm in Canada. It had been established in 1922 and was responsible for a number of innovative designs suited to Canadian conditions. In the immediate postwar period, the Department of Transport was starting to build a totally new fleet and it was only natural that German and Milne should become its principal designer. Eventually they would be responsible for more than thirty ships for the Departments of Transport and Fisheries and Oceans as well as many for the Navy. Ships designed by one firm tend to have a family resemblance, influenced both by the designer and by the fleet's parent. It is quite easy for the initiated to recognize a German and Milne ship designed for a Canadian government department. They are the ones that look like a "proper Coast Guard ship," somewhat traditional in profile and with appearance clues that are noted by ship lovers and enthusiasts. From the *Edward Cornwallis* of 1949 to the *Henry Larsen* of 1987 and from the large icebreaker *Louis S. St Laurent* to the little buoy tender *Verendrye,* the resemblance is there.

In examining the design specifications provided by the firm, it is immediately apparent that the postwar fleet before the 1970s was a fleet of samples. The maximum number of identical ships was two. Each ship was designed for a particular agency.

The *J.E. Bernier*, a light icebreaker and navigation aids vessel, completed in 1967. (Fisheries and Oceans F130702)

Specifications read: "a buoy tender and supply vessel for the Bay of Fundy and Maritimes." (This became the *Walter E. Foster*). "A buoy tender supply vessel and light icebreaker for service in British Columbia and the Arctic" (the *Camsell*). In language that had become standard, the instructions to the builder demanded that "the ship be constructed in a strong, seaworthy and high class manner," and "all material and work-manship to be the best of their respective kind."

The First Postwar Ships

The first three ships of the post Second World War building program were the navigation aids vessel *Edward Cornwallis* of 1949, the Eastern Arctic patrol vessel *C.D. Howe* of 1950 and the icebreaker *d'Iberville* of 1952. All were important in their own way. The *Edward Cornwallis* set the pattern for a long series of successful navigation aids vessels. The *C.D. Howe*, on the other hand, was unique. Her main purpose was to provide a Canadian government presence in the eastern Arctic. Both the *Edward Cornwallis* and the *C.D. Howe* were ice-strengthened but the *d'Iberville*, (5678 gross registered tons), was Canada's first modern full icebreaker. All these ships were fitted with Skinner uni-flow steam engines. The uniflow engine may be considered as the final development of the reciprocating steam engine. Its use resulted in a more manoeuvrable ship, more suitable for icebreaking and buoy work than either a steam turbine or the direct drive diesel engines of the time, and was considered superior to the more common triple expansion engines used in the corvettes, frigates and Fort and Park class merchant ships of the Second World War. Six Department of Transport ships had uniflow machinery, ranging from 2000 IHP in the *Walter E. Foster* to the 10,800 IHP of the *d'Iberville's* two six-cylinder engines. (*d'Iberville* attracted considerable attention at the Queen's coronation review in 1953, where she joined naval vessels in representing Canada, as icebreakers were seldom seen in British waters). From the 1960s on, electric drive became the preferred means of propulsion because it also gave flexibility while manoeuvring.

Icebreakers

In 1954, the Royal Canadian Navy completed an icebreaker of its own. She was HMCS *Labrador*, built by Marine Industries Limited, Sorel, and was practically identical to the United States Coast Guard's Wind class. After two history making Northwest Passage voyages under Captains O.C.S. Robertson and T.C. Pullen, the Navy decided to discontinue Arctic operations, which did not fit into its NATO mandate of specialization in antisubmarine warfare. This decision was a bitter disappointment to her crew and to those in Naval Headquarters who felt that Arctic sovereignty and capability was a vital interest of the Canadian National Defence Department. However, it was decided that the Arctic was the domain of the Department of Transport and *Labrador* was transferred to the Canadian Marine Service in 1958. The next icebreaker was the *John A. Macdonald*, (6186 GRT and 15,000 shp). Like the *d'Iberville*, she was built by Davie Shipbuilding Ltd. at Lauzon, Québec. During her construction in 1959 the yard was visited by Soviet officials who seemed very interested in her design. It may have been a coincidence but the next class of Russian icebreaker, the five ships of the *Moskva* class bore a distinct resemblance to the *Macdonald*, although somewhat larger and more powerful. The *John A. Macdonald* had three screws and diesel-electric propulsion. She was generally considered by all who sailed in her to be our finest icebreaker and it was regrettable that no sister ships were built.

By the mid 1960s, the major powers had nuclear powered submarines, the Russians were working on nuclear icebreakers, the United States had a nuclear powered aircraft carrier, USS *Enterprise*, and other surface ships, and two experimental nuclear powered merchant ships had been built, one in the United States and one in West Germany. It was natural that the Coast Guard would consider nuclear power for their next ship and this concept was the origin of the design of the *Louis S. St Laurent*. In the end, a more cautious approach was adopted. The ship was completed in 1969 as a triple screw turbo-electric vessel with steam for the turbines generated in conventional oil fired boilers. She was a large and powerful vessel, nearly 11,000 tons gross measurement and 14,000 tons displacement with engines of 27,000 Shp, but the propulsion system was expensive in fuel. When working in the most severe ice conditions she was capable only of ten days continuous operation before refueling was necessary. Nevertheless, she was our most powerful icebreaker and did good work up to 1988, when she was taken in hand for a major reconstruction and conversion to diesel electric drive, which made her a much better and more useful vessel. The other icebreaker of the period, also completing in 1969, was the *Norman McLeod Rogers* (4200 tons), which was intended to double as a large buoy tender capable of handling offshore buoys. In this ship, electric drive was combined with both diesel and gas turbine driven generators. This combination was used successfully in several navies but in the Coast Guard the gas turbines were not a success and were replaced by diesels in 1982.

Navigation Aids Vessels and Light Icebreakers

The *Edward Cornwallis* was followed by a series of navigation aids vessels of the same general design and size, about 2000 tons gross. The *Montcalm* and *Wolfe,* completed in 1957 and 1959, had uniflow engines of 4000 IHP. The *Camsell, Sir Humphrey Gilbert* and *Sir William Alexander* were diesel electric ships of 4250 Shp. All were completed in 1959. The *Alexander Henry,* built for the Great Lakes, was a bit smaller, 1674 tons, and had ordinary direct drive diesel propulsion, 3550 BHP. Two other ships were built later: the *J. E. Bernier* of 1967 and the *Griffon*, not completed until 1970, were somewhat larger at 2475 and 2212 tons and were diesel electric vessels of 4250 and 4000 SHP respectively. All these ships were classed as light icebreakers. Ships considered to be merely ice-strengthened were generally not as large and had a smaller power to displacement ratio. They included two pairs of sister ships: the *Tupper* and *Simon Fraser* of 1959/60 and the *Bartlett* and *Provo Wallis,* both completed in 1969, all four around 1300 tons. Propulsion methods in this group included steam uniflow, (*Walter E. Foster*); diesel, (*Montmorency* and *Thomas Carleton*); diesel with controllable pitch propellers, (*Bartlett* and *Provo Wallis*); and diesel electric (*Tupper, Simon Fraser, Simcoe* and *Tracy*). The *Narwhal,* which had been built as a Northern Depot Ship, had fixed and later variable pitch propellers.

Smaller tenders of less than 600 tons were of varied design. The *C.P. Edwards* was a wartime standard design "China" coaster, taken over at the end of the war. The *Alexander Mackenzie* and *Sir James Douglas* on the West Coast and the *Montmagny* and *Verendrye* in the St Lawrence River and the Great Lakes were reduced versions of the larger navigation aids vessels. The *Kenoki* was a barge with legs that could be lowered to steady her and hold her in place. However, in the raised position they affected stability, and first one pair and then the other was removed. The *Skidegate* and *Robert Foulis* were very small vessels. In 1977 the former was cut into four pieces and then enlarged in every dimension.

Northern Patrol and Supply Vessels

The *C.D. Howe,* launched in September 1949 and completed in 1950, was built to provide supplies and services to Inuit settlements in the eastern Arctic. She was a hospital ship, carrying two doctors, two nurses, and a dentist, as well as law enforcement

The *Rider*, one of six coastal Search and Rescue cutters, completed in 1963, based on a USCG design. (Fisheries and Oceans F160603)

officials and weather observers. She carried cargo to the settlements and installed and maintained navigation aids. Coast Guard ships, even icebreakers, are not very large compared to an average merchant ship. The *C.D. Howe* measured 3628 tons gross. In 1967 her port of departure for the Arctic was Montreal. A nurse, joining for the first time, was unable to find the ship, which was docked at the passenger ship terminal. Eventually, she looked down from the quay and saw what seemed, compared to the Cunard and Canadian Pacific liners at the adjacent berths, a very diminutive vessel. However, in the harbours of the north the *C.D. Howe* came into her own and her arrival was the most important event of the year at the Inuit settlements.

Between 1957 and 1961, Transport Canada had taken delivery of nine war surplus tank landing craft. Six of them (Type LCT 8) were used as supply vessels, going to the Arctic every season. They received new or modified bows and cranes or derricks were fitted. Tides in the Arctic have a range of 10 or 12 metres and the flat-bottomed landing craft could sail in on the high tide and unload their cargo onto trucks, which could drive up to the ship when the tide receded. (This method is still used by barges and by commercial coastal freighters, built for the purpose). Four of these vessels had tank space to carry fuel to supply the settlements. They were all given the names of birds.

The large offshore Search and Rescue cutter *Alert*, completed in 1969.(Fisheries and Oceans F160705)

Two others, *Mink* and *Marmot*, were smaller, (Type LCT 4). They retained their bow doors and were used principally as lighters, bringing cargo in from ships that could not beach. Another LCT 8, the *Nanook*, had accommodation for the stevedores who went north every year to unload the cargoes. In 1963 she was replaced by the *Narwhal,* which was classed as an Arctic Depot Ship. In other seasons the *Narwhal* could be employed as a navigation aids vessel and, when commercial ships took over cargo delivery at practically all the northern destinations, she reverted completely to that role.

The LCT 8s also proved very useful in southern waters as they, along with the *Narwhal,* were fitted with 40-ton derricks. They were used for lighthouse supply and construction as well as buoy work. However, in the mid to late 1970s all the landing craft types were discarded as Arctic cargo delivery was taken over by private companies.

The Cable Ship

In 1965 the *John Cabot* was added to the fleet. A state of the art cable ship, her equipment was continuously updated and she was always at the forefront of cable technology. She serviced the cables of the Canadian Overseas Telecommunications Corporation in the Gulf of St Lawrence, Atlantic Canada and the eastern Arctic. She was also frequently on charter to the U.S. Department of Defense and NATO to lay or repair cables carrying sensitive military information. Her exploits in a dramatic undersea rescue in 1973 and in gathering evidence after the Air India disaster in 1985 are described in a later chapter. She was also an icebreaker and was so employed in the ice season when not on charter. In 1993 she was sold to Teleglobe Canada, a crown corporation and subsequently sold to a British company, eventually ending up under the Italian flag.

Weather Ships

In the post Second World War period, propeller driven aircraft crossing the Atlantic and Pacific oceans needed accurate weather forecasting and navigational guidance. From 1945 to 1950 the Royal Canadian Navy operated weather ships. A corvette alternated with a USN ship in the Pacific in 1945–46 and the frigate HMCS *St Stephen* alternated with a USCG ship at Station "Bravo" in the Atlantic from December 1947 to June 1950.

In 1950, Canada withdrew from the Atlantic station and became responsible for Station "Papa" in the Pacific. Two frigates, *Stone Town* and *St Catharines* were converted for the purpose and turned over to the Department of Transport. They alternated on station starting in December 1950. The *St Stephen* was later acquired as a spare ship. In 1966, two purpose-built scientific and weather ships replaced the old frigates. The *Quadra* and *Vancouver* were the largest and most sophisticated of their type employed by any nation. They carried out oceanographic and fishery research simultaneously with their meteorological duties and acted as a navigational beacon and aid for aircraft crossing the Pacific. They had limitations. Their turbo-electric drive was not economical in fuel and additions to the original design during constructing resulted in a loss of stability that was compensated by filling some fuel tanks with concrete, so they returned after each mission with nearly empty bunkers. A huge radar dome made these ships readily recognizable.

Search and Rescue Cutters

As soon as the Coast Guard was founded in 1962, work started on creating an effective marine Search and Rescue component. Six 95-foot (29-metre), R class cutters, based on a U.S. Coast Guard design, were built and delivered in 1963. One served initially with the Department of Fisheries but was returned to the Coast Guard in 1969. They served on both coasts and on the Lakes. Two fast ex–RCAF crash boats operated out of False Creek, Vancouver. On the Great Lakes, three 70-ft. (23 metre) S class boats came into service in 1964. They were of double-diagonal wood construction and could launch an inflatable dinghy from a stern ramp. A much larger vessel for offshore patrol was the *Alert*, built in 1969 at Davie Shipbuilding Ltd., Lauzon, Québec. She was 234 feet (71 metres) long and measured 1752 tons gross with a speed of over 18 knots. She was the first of the offshore Search and Rescue cutters and was joined after a year by the *Daring*, (657 tons), a former RCMP patrol vessel, which was acquired as a direct result of the loss, on 20 April 1970 in the Cabot Strait, of CN ferry *Patrick Morris*. The

The *Nicolet*, a specialized sounding vessel for the St Lawrence ship channel. (Fisheries and Oceans F134401)

ferry had been looking for a fishing vessel in distress, but capsized and was lost with all hands. It was immediately decided to obtain a large SAR vessel for the Cabot Strait area. The *Daring* had a rather ironical end. After being sold in 1986 and passing through the hands of several owners, she was arrested in Belize as a drug mother ship. In 1967, a United States Coast Guard 44-foot self-righting lifeboat was acquired for evaluation. This boat, CG *101*, would be the first of a large class built by various small shipyards in Canada. They were stationed around the Atlantic and Pacific coasts and became well-known and trusted by fishermen and other mariners.

Offshore Supply Vessel Conversions

A joint Treasury Board, DND and Transport Canada Task Force study of marine Search and Rescue was established in 1976. In accordance with its findings, the Search and Rescue was to be improved. The Maritimes Region already had two offshore cutters, the *Daring* and *Alert*, but a primary SAR vessel was needed in Newfoundland. In 1977 the *Cathy B.*, an offshore oil-rig supply vessel was time chartered and approval was given to acquire vessels of the type, if she proved satisfactory. She did, and the *Grenfell*, ex *Baffin Service*, was purchased in 1978. In 1980 a sister ship, *Jackman,* ex *Hudson*

Service was bought, and so was the *Cathy B.*, which was sent to the Pacific in 1981 and renamed *George E. Darby.*

River and Lake Navigation Aids Vessels

Sounding vessels had always been necessary on the St Lawrence River, where the government has undertaken to provide and maintain certain minimum depths of water. The oldest ship in the Coast Guard, the *Detector* of 1915, was in use for sixty-three years. In 1960 and 1966 she was joined by two newer ships, the *Beauport* and *Nicolet.* Originally, the method was to tow a bar at a certain depth, resulting in a symbol on charts that has now disappeared: a number with a square bracket under it meaning "swept to (a certain depth)." Today, echo sounders and transducer booms to extend the swept width, precise short-range electronic navigation systems and computers to process the information have long superseded earlier methods. On the St Lawrence River and Lake Athabaska, the Great Slave Lake and the Mackenzie River, shallow-draft vessels were employed. The names of these ships: *Miskanaw, Dumit, Eckaloo,* and *Tembah,* are terms associated with navigation and travel in various native languages. Two more specialized vessels were added to the fleet. The *Nahidik* is a shallow-draft navigation aids ship that is much larger than her Mackenzie River consorts. Her area of operation is the Mackenzie delta and along the coast of the western Arctic. The task of the *Namao* is to service the navigation aids on Lake Winnipeg.

The Fleet in 1978

The year 1978 saw the Coast Guard approaching a peak in terms of the number of ships in service. A new icebreaker, the *Pierre Radisson* was completed, and her sister ship, the *Franklin* (renamed *Sir John Franklin* in 1980) was under construction. All of the prewar veterans had gone to a well-deserved ship Valhalla and the *C.D. Howe* had been dispensed with, but there were now ten large ships between 4000 and 11000 tons: seven icebreakers, the cable ship and the two weather ships. Thirty-five navigation aids and sounding vessels included eleven medium-sized ships of 1600 to 2500 tons, eight of which were classed as light icebreakers and the remainder as ice-strengthened. Ten of the smaller vessels were specially constructed for working on rivers and lakes. The Search and Rescue vessels included five offshore cutters, nine coastal types (not all in commission), three 70-foot (21m) craft on the Great Lakes, fifteen self-righting lifeboats and smaller craft. Counting only ships over 100 tons, there were now 57 ships compared to 49 in 1962 and 23 in 1945.

Admiral Anthony
H.G. Storrs.
(Fisheries and
Oceans P060201)

Rear Admiral Anthony H.G. Storrs, DSC and Bar, RCN

(1907–2002)

Anthony Hubert Gleadow Storrs was born at Overton, Hampshire, England in 1907. His family moved to Rhodesia where both his parents died before he was 15. He returned to England to Weymouth College and then joined the training ship *Worcester*, where he was sponsored by the P&O Company. He was on the *Worcester* from 1923 to 1925, and graduated as Chief Cadet Captain with two first class extra certificates. He had the rare distinction, in the post First World War era, of starting his seafaring life in sail: his first ship as an apprentice was the *William Mitchell*, owned by John Stewart & Co., one of the last two British-owned sailing ships engaged in deep-sea trading. Two years later the ship was sold and Storrs served in P&O ships until 1932. With the financial depression making sea-going jobs scarce, he joined the Chinese Maritime Customs Service, where he commanded patrol vessels.

In 1940, with Japan and China at war, Storrs and his wife, whom he had married that year, escaped by sampan, junk and blockade runner to Shanghai where they were able to find a ship bound for Canada. On arrival he joined the Canadian Navy, was commissioned as a Lieutenant, RCNR and appointed to command the naval trawler HMCS *Armentières*. After Japan attacked Pearl Harbor he commanded the corvette HMCS *Dawson* and participated in operations with the USN in the Aleutian Islands. In 1943 he commanded the corvette *Drumheller* at the height of the Battle of the Atlantic. By June 1944 he was senior officer of the 31st (Canadian) Minesweeping Flotilla which cleared the channels to the Normandy beachhead prior to D-Day. He was awarded the DSC and Bar and, for his services leading up to D-Day, the American Legion of Merit and the French Legion d'Honneur and the Croix de Guerre. At the end of the war, Commander Storrs transferred from the reserve to the regular force. He was promoted to Captain RCN and commanded the air station HMCS *Shearwater* and, in 1955–1956, the aircraft carrier HMCS *Magnificent*. He was promoted to Rear-Admiral, the first ex-reserve officer to achieve flag rank, and retired in 1962 as Commandant of the National Defence College of Canada.

In 1963, after briefly managing the Hydrographic fleet of the Department of Mines and Technical Surveys, Admiral Storrs accepted the position of Director of Marine Services of the Canadian Coast Guard, succeeding Captain Eric Brand. The Coast Guard had only recently been created from the Marine Services Fleet of the Department of Transport. Admiral Storrs held this position for ten years, during which he made a lasting impression on the Coast Guard's personnel. With his background in the merchant service and in China as well as naval service, he was especially qualified to guide the new organization. He worked to improve standards in the fleet, which reached a peak in numbers of ships during his tenure. In particular, the Search and Rescue element was greatly expanded, the large ice-breaker *Louis S. St Laurent* and other major vessels were completed and the Canadian Coast Guard College was founded at Sydney, Nova Scotia. When he retired in 1973 he was awarded the title of Honorary Commodore of the Coast Guard.

Admiral Storrs was then employed by a firm of consultants and worked for two years in Iran, before settling in Victoria, British Columbia. For some years he was active on the Board of Governors of the Canadian Corps of Commissionaires. He died in Victoria on 9 August 2002, aged 95.

The Fleet Capital Investment Plan

In 1978, it was seen that many of the ships in the fleet, including the first postwar additions, were approaching thirty years of service and were becoming obsolescent. A long term plan was developed to provide the fleet with new ships and equipment that met the operational requirements. Each type of ship would be designed to meet the specific needs of the programs assigned to the Coast Guard. The various fleet missions were identified and a series of vessel classifications were assigned: 700 to 1500 for navigation aids vessels and icebreakers and 100 to 600 for Search and Rescue (see Appendix III for type definitions). This initiative was known as the Fleet Capital Investment Plan (FCIP). It was to be carried out in two phases : 1979–84 and 1984–88.

The Later Icebreakers

As mentioned above, new icebreakers had already been ordered to replace the oldest ships and to cope with increased traffic. Two twin-screw, diesel-electric vessels, classed as Type 1200 Medium Gulf/River icebreakers (5910 GRT, 13 600 SHP), were ordered from Burrard Drydock Ltd., Vancouver. These were the *Pierre Radisson*, to replace the *N.B. McLean* and the *Franklin,* soon renamed *Sir John Franklin*, added to the Newfoundland Region fleet. They were completed in 1978 and 1979 and proved to be excellent vessels in the Gulf. They also performed well in the Arctic in the summer and fall seasons. A third ship of the same class was built by Port Weller Drydock in Ontario. This was the *Des Groseilliers*, which replaced the *d'Iberville* in 1982. The *Henry Larsen*, a modified version of the same successful design (6172 GRT, 16 320 SHP), was included in the second phase and built by Versatile Pacific in Vancouver. She was delivered in 1987 and replaced the *Labrador*. Under the FCIP all of these ships were classed as Type 1200.

As part of the second phase, the *Louis S. St Laurent* (now designated Type 1300) was given a mid-life refit. This was much needed: the ship's performance had always been hampered by her high fuel consumption and lack of endurance, and her age was beginning to be felt. It was intended to convert the propulsion system from steam to diesel-electric, give the ship an icebreaking bow of modern design and

CHAPTER 5

The Fleet: 1978 to 2002

Top: The *Sir John Franklin*, completed in 1979, was one of four twin-screw Type 1200 icebreakers. (Fisheries and Oceans F100707)

Bottom: The Polar 8 would have been the largest and most powerful icebreaker in the world, but was never built. (Fisheries and Oceans F101001)

improve the accommodations, removing asbestos insulation. The contract was also intended as a financial shot in the arm for the Halifax shipyard where the work was done, and a portion of the funds came from outside the normal Coast Guard budget. The ship had reached a point in her life when her operating and maintenance costs were such that she had to be either replaced or modernized and this was the opportunity. Krupp MAK diesel engines were ordered and new generators provided, converting the ship not only from turbo electric to diesel electric but also from a DC/DC to an AC/DC system. The electric propulsion motors were rebuilt. A new design of icebreaking bow was to be fitted and the crane and hangar arrangements changed.

All did not go well: serious problems arose and extended delays were experienced. Steelworkers had to be brought from Japan to shape and fit the high tensile steel plates of the new icebreaking bow. The company that was supposed to assemble and test the German-built diesel engines at a new plant at Sheet Harbour, Nova Scotia, proved unable to do so, and they had to be sent to Montreal. Nevertheless, the machinery was ready before the hull was able to receive it, for when the ship's interior was stripped, the inner plating was found to be corroded and had to be replaced. When the job was eventually completed the refit had become practically a reconstruction. She had been out of service for nearly five years and the cost had escalated enormously. However, she was a much improved, powerful icebreaker with increased capabilities and endurance. In 1993 in her first year of operation, she transited McClure Strait westbound, the first surface ship to do so.

With the *Louis S. St Laurent* out of service and the *John A. Macdonald* at the end of her life, the powerful icebreaker/supply tug *Terry Fox* was leased from the Gulf Oil subsidiary, Beaudril, in 1991. A number of excellent icebreakers had been built for Beaufort Sea operations and became available when exploration came to an end. With 23 200 BHP (17 300 kW), she was second only to the *Louis S. St Laurent* in power. Her design was quite different from the Coast Guard icebreakers. She had diesel propulsion with controllable pitch propellers, while the Coast Guard used electric propulsion and fixed propeller blades. In consequence, different icebreaking techniques were needed. The ship proved satisfactory and was purchased in 1993. An icebreaking tug, the *Arctic Ivik* was bareboat chartered for western Arctic service in 1993. She was employed intermittently until 1996.

The Polar 8

In the type definitions under the FCIP, the Type 1200 Medium Gulf/River icebreaker was defined as being capable of summer and fall Arctic operations, as well as large vessel escort in southern waters in winter. Only one existing vessel, the *Louis S. St Laurent*, could be placed in the Type 1300 Heavy Gulf icebreaker class, capable of large vessel escort in the most severe Gulf operations and extended season operations in the Arctic. Provision was made in the definitions for Type 1400, defined as a Sub-Polar icebreaker and Type 1500, a Polar icebreaker. The former would be suitable for Arctic operations year round, except in the most difficult ice areas: McClure Strait and among the Queen Elizabeth Islands; and the latter would be capable of year round operations in all Arctic waters. Among the world's icebreakers, only the Russian *Tamyr* and *Arkitka* class nuclear powered ships can be considered in these categories. Nevertheless, for nearly thirty years, successive Canadian governments contemplated such a vessel, and Coast Guard personnel worked on a succession of proposals. Type 1400 designs, (at that time designated Polar 7), were commissioned from foreign and Canadian companies and received by 1975. Next, feasibility studies for a nuclear powered Type 1500 or Polar 10 were completed. (These designations mean that the ship should be capable of continuous progress at a rate of three knots through uniform ice seven or ten feet thick, respectively). In 1981 a contract was awarded for a Polar 8 design, which was completed in 1983, but still no construction order was given.

In 1985 the U.S. decision to send the USCGC *Polar Sea* through the disputed Canadian Northwest Passage, with the reluctant and conditional approval of Canadian authorities, gave temporary impetus to the Polar 8 project, which by now involved many design and shipyard interests. The last initiative came in 1987 when it was announced that the ship would be built by Versatile Pacific Shipyards in Vancouver, to a design developed by a new consortium. There was now a further delay as alternative models based on the Beaufort Sea type icebreakers like Gulf Oil's *Kalvik* and *Terry Fox* were considered. Then, in a dramatic turnaround, the February 1990 budget contained an

The *Arktos-Beta* was conceived as an emergency evacuation vehicle for the Polar 8, but proved to have other uses. (Fisheries and Oceans FT010201)

announcement that the whole project was cancelled as an economy measure. The effect on people who had worked for twenty years or more on the various polar initiatives can be imagined.

The Polar 8 would have been by far the largest and most powerful icebreaker in the world. Displacement would have been 39,000 tonnes and power 107,000 SHP, (80 mW) compared to 23 500 tonnes and 67 500 SHP, (49.6 mW) in the Russian nuclear powered Arktika class. No final decision had been made on the propulsion system which would have been either diesel electric or diesel direct drive. Maximum sea speed was to be 19 kts. She was to be capable of uninterrupted progress in 2.44 metres (8 ft) of 10/10 pack ice. The hull was to be built of steel tested to retain its ductility down to -60°C. She would have carried 13 000 tonnes of diesel fuel and 875 tonnes of aviation fuel in tanks separated from the outer hull to minimize the possibility of pollution. Comprehensive laboratories, deck fittings for equipment, and a "moon pool" would be available for scientific expeditions and projects. The ship would have carried two or three helicopters. (Her proposed employment is described in Chapter 9). Naturally, the Coast Guard was disappointed not to have the use of such a magnificent ship but was unable to justify the cost, especially in a period of waning activity in the Beaufort Sea, and while DND was seeking approval for their frigate program. In the political climate of the time, her cancellation was perhaps inevitable.

An Arctic Amphibian, The *Arktos-Beta*

The Polar 8 icebreaker was expected to spend most of its life in ice-covered waters. When the normal ice navigation was over, no other vessel could be expected to be in the vicinity or even in the same part of the Arctic, and taking the whole crew off by helicopter could not be completely relied on. What if some event made abandonment imperative? If the ship was in an area of smooth ice and if there was time, a landing strip for aircraft could be built, but hummocked ice or a mixture of ice and water would preclude this. A special type of rescue craft to cope with these conditions, the *Arktos-Beta* was developed by the Coast Guard in conjunction with Watercraft Canada in Vancouver. It was an amphibious vehicle consisting of two units each tracked for propulsion on land or ice and each with water jets for use when afloat. Between them, they could carry 50 people in the evacuation mode. The length overall was 15.3 metres and the speed on ice was 21 kph and in the water 5.25 knots. Endurance at cruising speed was 48 hours. The total unit weighed 11 tonnes.

Although the Polar 8 was cancelled, the *Arktos* would have been useful in many Arctic applications. It could cross distorted ice such as ridges and rubble. It could crawl into the water and back onto floes, each unit pushing or pulling as required, and was equally at home on beaches and swamps. The prototype was completed in 1988 and its trials were technically and operationally successful. Development continued and in 1993/94 the water propulsion system was improved; but neither government nor private industry in Canada found a need for its unique capabilities. The developmental unit was sold in

1997, but the success of the trials in the end resulted in eight improved versions being constructed and sold by the manufacturer to a subsidiary of an American oil company involved in arctic oil exploration in Russia. One Russian use was in getting supplies ashore over the ice using hover platforms. A supply ship would unload offshore onto a platform which was then towed to land by a group of snowmobiles. If cracks developed between the offloading area and the destination, the snowmobiles could go no further and the hover platform was marooned on the ice. If *Arktos* vehicles were used this was no longer a problem as they could tow it over water. An additional order for twelve units has been received so this unusual vehicle has finally found its proper niche.

Icebreaker Hull Design

The first icebreakers had sharp bows designed to cut the ice. Later, riding up on the ice and breaking it by the weight of the vessel was seen to be more effective. Recent developments have been concerned with hull design, bow shape, low-friction coatings and bubbler systems.

A new shape of bow was tried in CCGS *Wolfe* in 1975. It incorporated an ice knife at the forefoot which struck the ice while the weight of the upper part of the bow was still on it. This design, modified, was used in the Type 1100 and 1200 classes. Starting in the 1960s, the Finnish firm of Wartsila developed a bubbler system. Compressed air was pumped through underwater apertures and rose to the surface, reducing friction of the ice against the hull. This was tried in Canada in the *Sir Humphrey Gilbert* when she was modernized in 1986, and also in the P.E.I. ferry *Abegweit*. The *Henry Larsen* (1987) has an air bubbling system and the latest bow design. So does the *Louis S. St Laurent* as refitted in 1988–93. The Polar 8 would have had a bubbler system.

Five ice navigation capable Coast Guard ships: the Search and Rescue cutters *Mary Hichens* and *Sir Wilfred Grenfell*, the two navigation aids vessels: *Samuel Risley* and *Earl Grey*, and the icebreaker Ter*ry Fox,* have hull shapes derived from offshore supply-tug designs, incorporating hard chines in the midship section and, in the case of the *Terry Fox,* bow and stern shapes developed for supporting Beaufort Sea drilling operations. Another feature of the *Terry Fox* is the strength of her controllable pitch propellers which have comparatively small blades on a large boss. This has avoided problems experienced by other vessels with the same type of propulsion.

Classification of icebreakers

The terms used to classify icebreakers have changed over time and can be confusing. As mentioned above, Polar 6, 8, 10 and so on meant that the ship should be able to cope with smooth ice of that thickness (in feet). They are quite different from the Arctic Class numbers used in the Arctic Waters Pollution Prevention Act and the Arctic Shipping Control Zones Order, which are related to specific construction criteria. Nor should they be confused with the Ice Class criteria in competing classification societies and national systems, like Det Norske Veritas, Lloyd's Register, the American Bureau of Shipping and the USSR/Russian Register of Shipping. These various systems have

Vessels based on offshore supply vessel designs, like the Search and Rescue cutter *Mary Hichens*, proved to be suitable for use in the Coast Guard. (Fisheries and Oceans F161207)

proved difficult to reconcile and efforts are now underway under IMO auspices, led by Canada, to harmonize polar ship rules. The new "Polar Code," (The International Code of Safety for Ships in Polar Waters), will specify classes from Polar Class 1 to Polar Class 7, with the PC1 having capability for year-round operation in polar waters.

Although Canada may be taking the lead in the regulation of shipping and navigation in the Arctic, we can no longer claim to be leaders in ship design. No major icebreaker has been built in Canada since 1987. In Finland, new hull shapes have been developed that break ice more economically and efficiently while using less power and hence less fuel. They also have enhanced ability when going astern. These designs are most likely to be the type of icebreaker hull that will be built in the future.

More Search and Rescue Cutters

Under the Fleet Capital Investment Plan, the offshore SAR cutters were designated Type 600 and the existing ships of the type were placed in this class. In the smaller SAR categories, four fast 21-metre Type 400 vessels were built in Nova Scotia and distributed around the regions, two in Western, one in Central and one in Laurentian. The self-righting lifeboats were given a Type 300 designation and four more were built, and a number of small, very fast, Type 100 craft were acquired for use in sheltered waters.

For the second phase of the program, a specification for a very capable patrol vessel was prepared by Coast Guard Headquarters. It was envisaged as a combined SAR, Fishery, and Sovereignty patrol vessel, lightly armed like Fishery Patrol vessels and

The supply vessel design was also used in the navigation aids vessels *Earl Grey* and *Samuel Risley*, completed in 1985/86. (Fisheries and Oceans F130903)

capable of 22 knots. In essence, this was an updated corvette. However, the various departments, the Coast Guard, DFO, and DND were not ready for this, and the final resolution was to take over two more ships of the offshore supply type under construction at the Marystown shipyard in southern Newfoundland. They were the *Mary Hichens* which replaced the *Daring* and the *Sir Wilfred Grenfell* in place of the *Grenfell* itself. In 1990, two new-construction intermediate Type 500 vessels, the *Gordon Reid* and the *John Jacobson*, took over rescue patrol duties in the Western Region from the smaller "R" class cutters. In Newfoundland, two small ice-strengthened vessels built on fishing boat lines, the *Harp* and *Hood* (Type 200) were put into service to support fishermen and sealers. They proved to be most uncomfortable seaboats as well as being slow, but their ice capability was necessary.

New Type 300A self-righting lifeboats were of the British designed *Arun* class. The first was built of fibreglass in the United Kingdom. Nine more were built in Canada of aluminum. They are larger (52 ft. or 15.8 m.) and have a greater range and are faster than the Type 300s. The latest boats are 47-foot (14.6 m.) craft of U.S. Coast Guard design, slightly modified. The first, *Cape Sutil*, was delivered in 1998 and seven were in service in the Great Lakes and Pacific by the end of 2002. A continuing procurement program will result, eventually, in the replacement of all the original 44-foot boats plus the establishment of eight new lifeboat stations by 2005.

Search and Rescue cutters and other Coast Guard ships carry Fast Rescue Craft (FRCs) to recover survivors from the water, and to go alongside distressed craft or into shallow or restricted areas. On the Type 400 cutters they are launched and recovered from ramps at the stern, while in larger vessels they are handled by special fast-acting cranes. The same type of craft are used in the Inshore Rescue Boat program. Originally these were simple 15-foot inflatable craft but over the years new and larger models culminated in seaworthy 24-foot rigid hull inflatable boats, (RHIs) with impressive electronic and communications equipment.

From 1984 to 1995, the superstructures of all SAR vessels and hovercraft were painted orange-yellow. This not only served to identify them as dedicated SAR units but also made them more visible. This paint scheme was discontinued when multitasking became the general policy and all the ships of the expanded fleet, including the former DFO vessels, adopted the usual red and white Coast Guard livery.

Navigation Aids Vessels

One of the benefits of the FCIP was that the Coast Guard for the first time was building ships in classes. As mentioned above, three identical icebreakers had been ordered and now six Type 1100 Light Icebreaker/Major Navaids Tenders were put in hand for delivery in 1986/87: two for the Western Region, two for the Maritimes Region and one each for Laurentian and Newfoundland Regions. The Maritimes ships differed in having their buoy handling cranes fitted at the break of the forecastle instead of aft of the well deck and the bridge structure had one less level. Otherwise, they were identical. It is the policy of the government to foster industrial development, and for this reason the ships were provided with a state of the art diesel-electric AC/AC propulsion system. Like all new technical steps, the control system gave some trouble at first. The Type 1200 icebreaker *Henry Larsen* also had AC/AC propulsion with three main diesel-generators providing power for all internal electrical needs as well as for propulsion. In these ships, if the control system failed, so did all power, including lighting. It could take up to twenty minutes to set matters right. Fortunately this never happened at a critical time and before long the bugs were detected and the system became reliable. In the Type 1100s the 20-tonne speed crane that handled the buoys also gave trouble initially. The company that had built them had gone bankrupt and they cost a great deal of money to fix. Eventually, however, the Coast Guard had six effective and seaworthy ships. They were much larger than previous buoy tenders: 3800 GRT as opposed to about 2000. With 7000 SHP they were good icebreakers. The *Martha L. Black* and *George R. Pearkes* were built in Vancouver for the Western Region and the Sir *Wilfrid Laurier* at Collingwood, Ontario, for the Laurentian, now the Québec Region. These ships later exchanged their stations. The *Ann Harvey* was built at Halifax for the Newfoundland Region and the *Edward Cornwallis* and *Sir William Alexander,* built at Sorel, Québec, replaced the older ships of the same names in the Maritimes Region.

The success and availability of the offshore supply type of vessel led to an experiment in which a crane was temporarily placed on the afterdeck of the Type 600 vessel *Jackman* to see if this type of installation would be suitable for buoytending. In 1980/81 the *Jackman* visited all the principal bases in the Maritimes, Laurentian and Central Regions to test the concept in a variety of conditions. The results were satisfactory and in 1983 a contract was placed with Robert Allen Ltd. of Vancouver for a navigation aids tender design based on these concepts. The resulting ships, *Samuel Risley* and *Earl Grey*, were classed as Type 1050. They were diesel ships with controllable pitch propellers. The 15-tonne capacity crane was motion stabilized for safe buoy handling. With over 8500 BHP, they could be classed as light icebreakers. The *Samuel Risley* was built in Vancouver and proceeded through the Panama Canal to the Great Lakes and the *Earl Grey* was built at Pictou, Nova Scotia and was stationed at Charlottetown P.E.I. Both were delivered in 1985.

Another class of identical vessels were the four Type 800 small buoy tenders built in 1985/86 at Port Hawkesbury, Nova Scotia. They followed two slightly smaller versions built in Ontario in 1980. They are useful work boats, capable of handling the smaller buoys in rivers and sheltered waters.

Two other ships built under the FCIP are the Type 700s *Dumit* and *Eckaloo*, completed in 1979 and 1988 for the Mackenzie River to replace the original craft with the same names. They are much larger than the originals but smaller than the *Nahidik*. With a length of 49 metres, their draft is only one and a half metres.

The Integrated Fleet

When the Coast Guard and Fisheries and Ocean fleets amalgamated in 1995, (although in practical terms this was not really implemented until 1996), the work of all patrol and rescue type craft could conveniently be integrated. Offshore Fishery Patrol vessels and Offshore SAR cutters are essentially the same type of ship, and coastal and inshore Fishery Patrol craft correspond to the intermediate and small Coast Guard cutters. All are now classed as multi-tasked (patrol) cutters in categories based on their size and capabilities. The work of the hydrographic research and survey vessels and the fishery research vessels is unaffected by the merger of the departments, although ships' personnel now serve in any kind of vessel, which provides a wider variety of experience. The Fisheries and Oceans fleet on amalgamation in 1995 consisted of three offshore and six coastal research/survey vessels; six offshore and nine inshore fishery research vessels; and five offshore, four coastal and over fifty inshore fishery patrol craft. In the reduction of the fleet that was one of the purposes of the merger, several of the larger ships and about twenty of the inshore patrol craft have been retired and sold. In 2002, the Coast Guard Fleet includes twenty-three ships over 2000 gross tons, the largest still being the *Louis S. St Laurent*. There are six major icebreakers, ten large navigation aids vessels classed as light icebreakers, three offshore scientific ships; and four offshore patrol vessels. The total number of craft of all kinds is about 130.

The second *Dumit*, completed in 1979, is a shallow draft navigation aids vessel for the Mackenzie River. (Fisheries and Oceans F140603)

New Construction

As already mentioned, a program for the construction of new self-righting lifeboats is in progress in 2002, but only one other initiative is in the planning phase. Since 1998, a design for a class of shallow-draft multitasked utility vessels has been awaiting approval. These new Type 1000 ships would replace all the existing ice-strengthened vessels placed in this class, but are intended to be far more versatile. The design requirements imposed on the naval architects, both those who are part of the Coast Guard and who frame the construction specification, and the shipyard people who must meet them, are more detailed and demanding than in any previous class. These ships must be as capable buoy tenders as any previous vessel in their category and as effective ice-breakers as the best of them. They will have a shallow draft, yet be capable of operating offshore. Hydraulic machinery and deck fittings for scientific work will be provided. Ergonomic design of each part of the ship is intended to allow effective operation with the minimum crew. They will be diesel electric ships with an AC/DC system driving azimuth propellers. These are mounted on pods that can turn through 180 degrees in lieu of rudders. Exceptional manoeuvrability and reliability is expected.

The Bell 47 was the early workhorse helicopter carried on Coast Guard ships. (Fisheries and Oceans F240502)

Helicopters

Helicopters have become an essential mode of transportation when the need is for speed and direct delivery on-site of people or materials. They are used by the military, by civilian government departments and by industry. Navies use helicopters in the anti-submarine role and for surveillance, personnel transport, rescue work and replenishment at sea. They are essential to the oil industry both for prospecting on land and for transportation to and from offshore platforms. They are used in logging operations and as passenger carriers where no airfields exist.

Canadian Coast Guard helicopters are used for ice and pollution reconnaissance, for servicing navigation aids and for general transportation duties. In Canada, the air element of the Search and Rescue is provided by the Canadian Forces, which operates fixed wing aircraft and helicopters dedicated to those tasks. However, two of the Coast Guard's helicopter detachments, one in Prince Rupert, British Columbia and the other in Yarmouth, Nova Scotia, have a specific SAR role. The former has been long established, but the Yarmouth-based helicopter has only been stationed there since 1995. The public has not always been aware of the division of responsibility between the Armed Forces and the CCG and misconceptions have arisen. In fact, most Coast Guard helicopters are small, short-range, visual flight rules (VFR) aircraft and, with the two exceptions mentioned above, are not fitted with Search and Rescue hoists and equipment. That is not to say that they have not been used in rescue and medical evacuation roles when required.

The Arctic patrol vessel *C.D. Howe* was the first Department of Transport ship to have a helicopter deck. In 1950 on her first Arctic patrol she embarked a Sikorsky S51 helicopter for trials. Unfortunately, an accident on take-off destroyed the aircraft early in the voyage but in the following year a smaller Bell 47 was acquired and used successfully for ice reconnaissance. The first helicopters for the RCN, also Bell 47s, were delivered in 1951, so the Department of Transport fleet was as early as the Navy in its use of these aircraft.

In 1958, the Department of Transport had nine Bell 47s on inventory. At first, all were based in Ottawa but by the

CHAPTER 6

Helicopters and Hovercraft

time the Coast Guard was founded in 1962, two had been moved to Moncton to support Coast Guard operations in the Maritimes and three to Victoria. In the same year, a Sikorsky S62 was purchased and permanently based at Prince Rupert. This was a single-engine amphibious helicopter that could land and take off from the water.

By 1963 seventeen Bell 47s of different configurations and the S62 were in service. The Bell 47s were continually updated with modifications, including new engines. These changes altered the model designations. Later versions had a larger bubble and could carry an extra passenger. In 1964 and 1965 three Alouettes III were purchased from France. At first they were used on ships as well as from shore bases but eventually, all were moved to the Victoria base and employed on navigation aids servicing duties. The Alouettes remained in the fleet until 1987. In 1964, a twin-engine S62N large amphibious helicopter replaced the S62N, which was moved to Dartmouth, where it did not long survive, being scrapped after an accident. Also in 1966, the first Bell 206s began to replace the Bell 47s as the standard ship-borne helicopter but the last of the "bubble" type Bell 47s was not retired until 1978.

In 1971 a Bell 212, a medium sized twin-turbine helicopter, was acquired and found to be very suitable for servicing navigation aids. For over-the-water operation, the second engine was a safety factor and its ability to lift up to 3000 lbs or carry up to 9 passengers was needed for lighthouse re-supply and navigation aid construction work. By this time it was evident that, in certain circumstances, servicing navigation aids by helicopter was faster and often more economical than using ships. Over the next several

The Bell 206L replaced the Bell 47 during the 1960s and 1970s. (Fisheries and Oceans F241503)

years four more Bell 212s were bought and distributed one to each region. (On 10 May 2000, the fleet of five 212s was reduced by one in a tragic accident off the east coast of Newfoundland. The accident claimed the life of the pilot and totally destroyed the helicopter.) Also in 1971, another Sikorsky S62N had to be purchased to replace the first aircraft, which had crashed, fortunately without loss of life. The northern British Columbia coast has unique characteristics. Almost all lights and aids to navigation are inaccessible by land, and so the work of this large helicopter, stationed at Prince Rupert, includes transporting equipment and food, radio and power plant spares and personnel, including lighthouse keepers and their families as well as technicians. As it is amphibious, it can land on the water and launch an inflatable dinghy to allow technicians to service the smaller lights and beacons. (The aircraft has aged, and to minimize corrosion problems it no longer alights in salt water, but still will do so in fresh water lakes if necessary).

In 1975, the S62N was flown from Prince Rupert to Ottawa where it was fitted for Instrument Flight Rules (IFR) and night flying capability. It was used as a search platform in distress incidents and could drop an inflatable liferaft. Much later, in 1993, a hoist was fitted and crew members were trained as SAR technicians. This capability is extremely valuable because the northern waters of British Columbia are a very long way from Comox, where the Department of National Defence SAR helicopters and fixed-wing aircraft are based. It was the Coast Guard S62N that first sighted the upturned hull of the freighter *Lee Wang Zin* in 1979 and it played a prominent part during the multiple fishing boat disasters of 1983 and 1985 (see Chapter 10) and has participated in many SAR incidents.

In 1976, five Bell 206Ls were added to the CCG fleet. This aircraft was an improvement on the 206A and B types with somewhat longer range, slightly greater speed and ability to lift a considerably greater load. The 206Bs and 206Ls continued to be procured while the Bell 47s were phased out. By 1978 all the 47s had been retired and the Bell 206B or L was the standard ship borne helicopter. The earlier 206s were aging and the aircraft selected for their replacement was the Messerschmitt-Boelkow-Blohm BO 105, a twin turbine helicopter with good performance and great versatility. It has rear loading clamshell doors, removable seat combinations, space for a stretcher and good payload. The first two went into service in 1983 and a total of sixteen were eventually acquired, the last in 1988.

In the Yarmouth area of southern Nova Scotia, the Department of Fisheries and Oceans had contracted with a private sector firm to operate an all-weather helicopter for fishery patrol and secondary SAR duties. It had participated in a number of rescue incidents and there were protests when the contract was not renewed in 1995. Responsibility for the Coast Guard had just been transferred from Transport Canada to DFO so it was decided to use a specially equipped BO-105. In a month it was fitted with a rescue hoist and the crew were trained. However, unlike the Prince Rupert S62N, it is not an IFR capable aircraft.

The French built Alouette III helicopter. (Fisheries and Oceans F241001)

Ownership and Personnel

The system under which the helicopter fleet is managed is somewhat complex. The aircraft are purchased by the Coast Guard, which until 1995 was part of Transport Canada, although in the 1960s and 70s some units were owned by the Department of Fisheries and Oceans. These included aircraft that were based at Uplands Airport in Ottawa and for the most part were used for survey work in the summer and ice reconnaissance in the winter. In the late 1970s, DFO relinquished its ownership of specific helicopters in return for a joint funding arrangement and the use of helicopter hours when required. As the two organizations are now merged, it has now become just a matter of assigning helicopter facilities to the various programs.

Although, with the exceptions noted above, the aircraft are owned by the Coast Guard which was part of the Marine Administration of Transport Canada, the pilots and engineers who fly the aircraft and keep them running are employees of Transport Canada's Air Administration. Nevertheless they wear Coast Guard uniforms, whether embarked on a Coast Guard or Fisheries and Oceans ship or shore based. These arrangements have not been affected by the transfer of the CCG to the Department of Fisheries and Oceans and the amalgamation of the two fleets.

Deployment and Bases

Originally all helicopters were based in Ottawa at Uplands Airport and a detachment would be deployed to the ship or agency where it was needed. Beginning in 1962, aircraft were based in the regions, although some might be retained in Ottawa. The pilots and the engineers who maintained the aircraft were also moved to the area where they were based. The number of aircraft in service steadily increased to a peak of 37 in the 1970s and 1980s, (several of which were employed by DFO), and then declined to 28 by 1998. Much of the reduction has been in hydrographic work. No helicopters are now kept at Uplands airport in Ottawa, but major modifications and maintenance work are still carried out there. As already mentioned, the only large long-range helicopter, the S62N, is stationed at Prince Rupert, and originally all five regions had a medium sized Bell 212. These arrangements are of long standing and lasted until the tragic loss of the Newfoundland-based 212 on 10 May 2000. All other helicopters are small Visual Flight Rules (VFR) aircraft. The distribution of the Coast Guard helicopter fleet among the five regions in 1979 and 1998/99 is shown in Table 3, Appendix IV. The Hay River district, which covers the Great Slave Lake and the Mackenzie River, was originally part of the Western and later of the Arctic Region. It is now part of the Central and Arctic Region, but the Pacific Region's Victoria base still deploys a helicopter there in the navigation season.

Tables showing the characteristics of Coast Guard helicopters and the helicopter fleet at selected dates from the 1950s to the present are found in Tables 1 and 2, Appendix IV.

Ship Facilities for Helicopters

Almost all the major ships built for the Canadian Coast Guard, the heavy, medium, and light icebreakers, have helicopter platforms and hangars. (There are a couple of exceptions.) Others, including the larger river navigation aids vessels have platforms but no hangar, while types based on the offshore supply tug design have open after decks. As already mentioned, the first ship to have a flight deck was the *C.D. Howe,* completed in 1950. The *Edward Cornwallis*, completed the year before, had a flight deck added later. The icebreaker *d'Iberville* of 1953 had a large hangar as part of the superstructure and could stow two Bell 47s, as did the *Labrador* and the *John A. MacDonald*. The old icebreaker *N.B. McLean* was fitted with a deck and a hangar. The *Louis S. St Laurent* had a hangar below the flight deck connected by an elevator. This arrangement works in aircraft carriers but is not the best for ships with a flight deck aft. It was changed during her major refit to a conventional arrangement of a hangar on the same level as the flight deck. Had the Polar 8 icebreaker been completed, she would have carried two or three large helicopters. The EH-101, which was subsequently ordered for the Navy, only to be cancelled, was the helicopter envisaged for this ship.

Salt-water spray causes corrosion, which is always a major problem in aircraft carried on vessels. The buoy tenders completed in the late fifties had flight decks only, but

in 1964 a design for an aluminum telescopic hangar was accepted and added to these ships and formed part of the design of future vessels. Hangars were not considered necessary in the Alex*ander Henry* and *Griffon,* which normally operated in fresh water, but the quite small Tu*pper* and *Simon Fraser* each had a deck and telescopic hangar. The only offshore SAR cutter to have one was the *Alert.* The newer Type 1200 icebreakers have hangars with an extendable section and can carry a couple of Bell 206s or BO 105s. The big hydrographic ships *Baffin* and *Hudson* carried helicopters and found them invaluable during their historic Arctic survey voyages in 1970. The former DFO ship *John P. Tully* has a deck forward of the bridge. The fishery patrol vessels *Cape Roger* and *Leonard J. Cowley,* now classed as offshore cutters, have decks and hangars, while the *Cygnus* has a deck only. As was the case with the *Alert,* they seldom carry an aircraft. Helicopter capable ships engaged in icebreaking duties normally have a helicopter detachment on board but helicopters are only embarked on other vessels for particular purposes connected with specific missions.

Flight Operations and Navigation

Ships that are equipped to operate helicopters are, for the most part, also fitted with refueling equipment and all have fire-fighting facilities, including trained personnel (the Flight Deck Officer and Flight Deck Party), who are dressed in protective gear and on deck when helicopters are landing or taking off. The original Bell 47s did not operate far from the ship, and their navigation equipment was minimal but included Automatic Direction Finders (ADF) that gave a bearing to the ship's radio beacon operating in the medium frequency range, (410 or 413 kHz). Then came Distance Measuring Equipment (DME), which operated in conjunction with ADF could provide bearing and distance. Finally came NAVLINK, which automatically receives information from systems such as Loran C or GPS, and exchanges geographical positions between two units so that each knows where the other is.

Fixed Wing Aircraft

In 1968, a Cessna 337 aircraft, based at Ottawa, started pollution and ice patrols in the Great Lakes and the St Lawrence River and Gulf. In 1976, it was replaced by a longer range DC-3. In 1991 a second DC-3 was put into service from Vancouver and a smaller Twin Otter was based at Moncton, New Brunswick. In 1995, the DC-3s were retired. A DASH-8 replaced the Ottawa aircraft and the Twin Otter was re-deployed to

Top: The long range Bell 212 is a shore based helicopter used for servicing navigation aids. (Fisheries and Oceans F242509)

Middle: The versatile twin-turbine MBB BO-105 helicopter. (Fisheries and Oceans F243002)

Bottom: The Coast Guard's S62N helicopter, based at Prince Rupert British Columbia. (Fisheries and Oceans F243521)

Vancouver. At first, pollution surveillance was simply visual, but the DASH-8 aircraft now carries an ultraviolet/infrared scanner that can identify an apparent slick as being one caused by oil. Our coastal areas are so vast that from time to time oil and dead birds are found that prove that oil has been dumped or oily tanks have been illegally cleaned at sea. The patrols carried out by aircraft are a deterrent to these breaches of the anti-pollution regulations, which otherwise would be much more frequent.

Hovercraft

The first Air Cushion Vehicle, (ACV), usually referred to as a hovercraft, was acquired by the Coast Guard in 1968. It was an SRN5, a proven, fully amphibious vehicle built by British Hovercraft at Cowes, England and already in use as fast passenger ferries on such routes as Portsmouth to the Isle of Wight and by the British military. It was put into service as a Search and Rescue unit, based at Vancouver airport. Here the delta of the Fraser River leaves extensive tidal mudflats. Should an aircraft crash or a boat be wrecked there, a hovercraft would be the ideal rescue vehicle. Their main advantage, however, is the radius of effective operation conferred by their speed. The area in which a 55-knot ACV can respond within one hour is five times greater than the coverage of a 25-knot Type 100 Rescue/Utility craft or a rigid inflatable Fast Rescue Craft and nearly twenty times larger than a conventional 12.5 knot lifeboat. However,

SRN 6 hovercraft used on the West Coast were invaluable as Search and Rescue craft in the Vancouver area. (Mike Mitchell, Fisheries and Oceans F230401)

it was 1977 before the next ACV, a slightly larger SRN6, was acquired. In 1981, two more SRN6s were bought from Northern Transportation Ltd. Initially they were acquired for parts but one was soon put into service as a replacement for the SRN5. The other was gradually refitted on the initiative of the hovercraft unit at Vancouver and eventually also entered service as an operational unit. From 1984 to 1993, one craft operated out of Parksville on Vancouver Island and two from the Vancouver base.

In 1971 a very different type of ACV was being developed by Bell Aerospace Canada. The first unit of the *Voyageur* type ACV was made marrying the engines and rudders of two SK5s (a U.S.-built military derivative of the SRN5) to a modular hull that could be disassembled for shipment by road or aircraft. It was essentially a cargo and utility vehicle. Trials were conducted on the Mackenzie River and the Beaufort Sea and on the Great Lakes in both summer and winter. In 1972 the Coast Guard took delivery of the second prototype and a hovercraft development unit, managed by Coast Guard's ACV Division in Ottawa, undertook extensive testing. The ability of the hovercraft to break ice was discovered at his time. From 1974 it was based at Montreal and used to conduct various operational tests. An evaluation of the *Voyageur* in the regional work program resulted in the craft being accepted into full service for checking and replacing navigation aids, lighthouse re-supply and a variety of other tasks, and it was transferred to the regional fleet in 1980. The hovercraft base was at Ile des Soeurs in Montreal

After trials on the Great Lakes and in the Arctic, the large Voyageur hovercraft was used for servicing navigation aids in the St Lawrence River. (Fisheries and Oceans F230508)

The latest model of hovercraft—the diesel powered *Sipu-Muin*. (Fisheries and Oceans F230701)

Harbour. Twenty tonnes of buoys or supplies could be carried and a crane was fitted for buoy work or cargo handling. In the winter, it was employed breaking ice, especially in the wider areas of the waterway, to prevent jams occurring at the exits to Lac St Pierre, Lac St Francis and similar areas. Most importantly, it was also used to break ice in nine tributary rivers between Beauharnois and Trois Rivières and was successful in substantially reducing the incidence of flooding in the area. In the summer of 1982, the *Voyageur* was lent to the Maritime Region for a construction project on Miramichi Bay, New Brunswick. It completed the 600-nautical-mile journey at an average speed of 35 knots. The hovercraft was able to move heavy loads of construction material without damage in the vulnerable marshy terrain.

In 1987 the *Voyageur* was replaced by the *Waban-aki*. In this ACV, diesel engines were used in place of the gas turbines of previous craft and the lift and propulsion engines were separated which significantly improved control. The success of this concept led to the construction of two units of an improved larger version that were delivered in 1998. The *Sipu Muin* is based at Trois Rivières in addition to the *Waban-aki*. (The hovercraft base was transferred there from Montreal in 1996.) It has replaced a buoy tender with a much larger crew. The second unit, the *Siyäy*, was sent to Vancouver (on the afterdeck of a large offshore supply vessel) and will undertake navigation aids servicing as well as Search and Rescue. Canada pioneered the use of hovercraft for these duties.

(Specifications of helicopters, helicopter inventory and distribution at selected dates and specifications of hovercraft are given in Appendix IV).

The personnel employed in Department of Transport ships, at the time of the foundation of the Coast Guard were drawn from the general seafaring population in the regions in which the ships were stationed. They were individuals who were willing to accept perhaps less remuneration than they might have received in commercial ships for the chance to do challenging work in their home areas and to enjoy the benefit of the comparative security that comes from government service. There was also a measure of prestige in belonging to an organization that operated well maintained, long lived vessels doing the useful work of ice-breaking and maintaining navigation aids.

The officers on the ships were recruited from the coastal merchant marine and from crew members who sat the required examinations and obtained the requisite certificates.

They made up for their lack of formal education with extensive local knowledge, but the new large ships coming into service required higher qualifications. As the fleet expanded in the years after the war, some British officers with foreign-going certificates had been recruited, while another source of experienced and well-qualified officers and engineers was Canadian National Steamships (CNS), the government-owned line of passenger and cargo ships trading to the Caribbean. The Canadian Marine Service was in the midst of its postwar expansion when CNS ceased operations in the 1950s and many of its best personnel joined the DOT.

From 1963, the executive head of the Coast Guard was the Director of Marine Operations, Rear-Admiral Anthony (Tony) Storrs, RCN (Ret'd) who had taken over from Captain Eric Brand, who had retired. Dr Gordon Stead continued in the post of Assistant Deputy Minister Marine until 1970. His successors took on the additional title of Administrator, Marine Services.

In 1975, the office of Commissioner of the Canadian Coast Guard was instituted with William O'Neil, (who had already been serving as Deputy Administrator, Marine Services) as the first incumbent. By then the Coast Guard had expanded to include the operational branches of the Marine Services Administration, including Aids and

CHAPTER 7

Personnel and Training

Top: The Coast Guard College, established in 1965 at the former Point Edward naval base at Sydney Nova Scotia. (Fisheries and Oceans Canada FX010000)

Bottom: The new Coast Guard College buildings, at Westmount, opened in 1981. (G Langille, Sydney Nova Scotia 344-24)

Opposite: The Transport Canada Training Institute at Cornwall, Ontario. (Nav Canada Training Institute FX010101)

Waterways and the Ship Safety Branch. As time passed, administrative levels were added and titles changed. After Admiral Storrs, the Ottawa head of the fleet was successively called the Commandant of the Coast Guard, the Director Fleet Systems and the Director General Fleet Systems, and became one senior administrator among several. With the merger with the Department of Fisheries and Oceans in 1995, the former responsibilities of the office were further diffused. The names that are mentioned here are some of those, who guided the Coast Guard in its formative years. Many others should be included, as it is very difficult to mention some without leaving out others of equal importance. However, the following should be noted: Carole Stephenson, who headed the Polar 8 project for many years and was the first Director of the Northern Region, Captain Dave Johns who became the Coast Guard's trusted liaison with the United States Coast Guard, Captain Art Mountain who was involved with many important projects including the Fleet Capital Investment Plan in the late 1970s and the 1980s, and Michael Turner, a long time Deputy Commissioner and often acting Commissioner, whose dedicated service in senior positions until 1999, had given him a uniquely comprehensive perspective on the Coast Guard and its many challenges.

Positions and Levels in the Coast Guard Fleet

In the Coast Guard, the captain of a ship is officially termed the Commanding Officer, rather than the Master as in the Merchant Service. Certificated ships officers, including commanding officers, deck officers, and engineering, radio, electrical and logistic officers are classified as Marine Operators (MAO). The level (and pay) of var-

Bridge of the *Pierre Radisson* during an Arctic voyage. (Fisheries and Oceans Canada F100601-001)

ious positions on the ships is determined by classification standards that have not changed much during the last thirty years. Ships are divided into categories depending on tonnage and horsepower, and this governs the classification level of the commanding officer and all certificated personnel. Non-certificated crew members are classed as DED, ERD, STD (deck, engineering, and stewards, including cooks), SPT (special trades–cable technicians and some specially qualified electrical technicians), and EQO, (equipment operators). There are several levels in each category and the classification depends on the ship and the job. Rescue specialists and divers are not separate categories but qualifications that entitle the holder to extra pay.

Uniforms

The Coast Guard is a uniformed service. Dress uniforms, work clothing and special safety equipment such as hard hats and flotation suits are issued free of charge to all personnel serving on ships and in certain positions on shore. The officer's dress uniform is the traditional eight-button navy blue uniform with a maple leaf above the stripes; (rather to the envy of the Navy which, after spending many years in unification green, reverted to a six-button navy blue jacket with neither the traditional curl nor a maple leaf). The badges of rank worn by officers are similar to those in other nautical services: one, two, two and a half, three, or four stripes, depending on the position held and the class of ship, (to which is tied the MAO level as described above). Officer

Replacing navigation buoys. (Fisheries and Oceans Canada MP150501)

cadets wear a maple leaf on the collar or, in their last year, a thin stripe. Commanding officers who wear three or four stripes also wear a cap with the peak embroidered with maple leaves. Helicopter and hovercraft pilots and engineers wear two, two and a half, or three stripes depending on their position, and pilots have wings on the left breast of the jacket. The dress prescribed for shore based uniformed personnel, including Coast Guard College instructors, follows the same principles.

To distinguish the branches, deck officers and helicopter and hovercraft pilots wear the gold stripes directly on the uniform. Colours between the stripes distinguish other branches: Engineers–purple, Electrical or Electronic–dark green, Logistics–white, Radio–emerald green, Meteorologists and Ice Observers–light blue, Medical–scarlet, Nurses–maroon, Instructors–royal blue, Boating safety and the inshore rescue units–orange. Most of these colours were traditional in Commonwealth navies up to the 1950s and have been retained in the Canadian Coast Guard and the Canadian and British Merchant Services.

Non-certificated crew members wear qualification badges to distinguish their branch: a wheel surmounted by a maple leaf for deck, a propeller and maple leaf for engineering, and a star and maple leaf for supply. These are worn on the right sleeve. Petty Officers, (coxswains of small vessels, boatswains, engine room supervisors, chief cooks, senior storekeepers), also wear crossed foul anchors on the left sleeve. There are cap badges prescribed for the various levels.

Management/Personnel Relations

Coast Guard fleet officers belong to the Canadian Merchant Service Guild, which also represents certificated personnel who sail in Canadian flag merchant ships. Uncertificated personnel and employees in non-seagoing categories belong to the Public Service Alliance of Canada, which represents the vast majority of federal government employees. Coast Guard pay is generally somewhat lower than that provided by the larger shipping companies but most people would say that greater (although not absolute) job security and more interesting work compensates for that, along with opportunities to move to various positions on shore. The Guild and the PSAC have participated in efforts to adapt civil service work rules to the realities of a seagoing service. Up to 1976, each position on a ship was competed for in a civil service competition and an individual was officially in that job; but the demands of running a fleet frequently resulted in officers being placed in acting status in another position in another ship and perhaps several steps above his or her substantive level. The ease of transferring people in this manner dissuaded management from running competitions that were expensive and time consuming, yet still did not result in stable manning. In 1976 a pilot program of competitions for "promotion to level" was tried in the Laurentian Region. In 1979 it was introduced in the Central Region and in 1981/82 to the Maritimes and Newfoundland, but Western Region held out until 1989. This greatly reduced the number of competitions and officers could be moved between any of the positions, throughout the Coast Guard, that required a given pay level, while acting in higher posts was still possible.

Coast Guard crews are members of the Union of Canadian Transport Employees, which is a branch of the Public Service Alliance of Canada. During this period there was one strike, in November and December of 1989. This was the first time in 22 years that a strike had been called with no safety and security designations, which meant that no ship could operate even with minimal crews. Only one icebreaker was at sea at this time, the *John A. Macdonald*, escorting MV *Arctic* on a late trip to Nanisivik. However, the crews had agreed to return to work in cases of life-threatening emergencies and did so on two occasions. On 4 December the *Samuel Risley* was alongside in Thunder Bay when news was received that the U.S. Coast Guard cutter *Mesquite* had run aground near Keweenaw Point on the south side of Lake Superior. The crew returned and the ship sailed to the *Mesquite's* aid, although on arrival they found that the crew had already been rescued. A few days later the *Earl Grey* sailed from Charlottetown when two ships were in danger in the Gulf of St Lawrence. (This incident is described in Chapter 10.)

Although the entire fleet was tied up, the effect in most of the regions was not long lasting. The exception was the Laurentian Region. In the St Lawrence River, the buoys that should have been lifted for the winter were caught by an early freeze-up. Some were dragged by the ice into water deeper than their moorings allowed for. Others capsized and were pulled under the ice, and in some cases their anchors caught under power and telephone cables. The pilotage authority notified the Coast Guard that navigation was no longer safe. As a result, on 1 December the St Lawrence from Les Escoumins to

Québec City was temporarily closed, by authority of the minister on the advice of the Coast Guard. Meetings were held in Montreal between the Coast Guard, port authorities, the Canadian Shipping Federation, the Canadian Shipowners Association, the pilots and other interested parties. As a result the channels from Montreal to Les Escoumins were opened on a limited basis on 5 December. Traffic, under escort, was allowed in daytime only and in a way that prevented too high a concentration of ships at the end of the day's movements. The permitted draft to which vessels could load was also reduced by three feet or one metre.

On 15 December the government legislated an end to the strike. This did not mean that navigation returned to normal. Buoys that could be found were lifted and some winter buoys placed, but traffic restrictions continued until the ice cleared in the spring. The Shipowners Association and the Shipping Federation sued the government for financial losses: the Coast Guard for not ensuring safe navigation and the Treasury Board because there was no list of exclusions (from the right to strike) of ships' crews. This lawsuit continued for ten years. In the end the Coast Guard was not held to blame. For the crewmembers, one successful result of the strike was the achievement of pay parity between the East and West Coasts, although this was not implemented until 1991. The difference had reflected the higher pay customary in commercial vessels on the British Columbia coast. The ships' officers also gradually achieved parity in a series of steps.

The Lay Day System

Few initiatives have improved the efficiency and morale of fleet personnel more than the introduction of the Lay Day system of manning. Under previous arrangements, (still in use on some ships), the ship runs on a three-watch system and the work day is eight hours, after which overtime is paid. Leave is accumulated at a comparatively slow pace and, if a relief is not available, the crewmember must remain on board, sometimes only learning this at short notice. With the Lay Day system, each ship has two crews who relieve each other at 28-day intervals. While on board, everyone works for twelve hours a day (what else is there to do at sea?) for seven days a week. At the end of each period on board, there are four weeks to enjoy the family, work on the house or take a vacation, while pay continues at a steady rate. Some additional leave accumulates so eventually there is a complete trip off–twelve free weeks. Time off/on schemes had previously been used on lightships and on SAR cutters, but for larger ships it was first tried in the Newfoundland Region in 1983 in the *Sir Humphrey Gilbert*. It was a success from the start. With a smaller crew, everyone felt more essential to the operation. The commanding officer's report included the following comments: "The introduction of the Lay Day system has precipitated an unexpected effect on the administration of this vessel. Major reductions in shipboard staff mean each has a greater role to play. This, coupled with the twelve-hour day, appears to be fostering an attitude of co-operation and professionalism throughout the complement. Individual performance is much enhanced and discipline problems practically non-existent."

Student in a radar simulator. (Fisheries and Oceans Canada FX010502)

After the trials, the system was extended to all regions, but not to all ships. It is particularly suited to offshore SAR cutters and buoy tenders and icebreakers working in areas away from their home port, but is not best in every case. Other two-crew methods are used for lifeboats and inshore SAR cutters where the on-duty crew lives in a house or trailer ashore. Navaids vessels on the Mackenzie River work a twelve-hour day for five to six months, then have the rest of the year off. The Laurentian Region, where ships often work the river from a base or location not far from home port to which they return each night, was slow to accept the system. Many crewmembers felt that it would cut down on overtime pay, but when overtime was restricted anyway because of budget restraints, the Lay Day system became more attractive. Today, only a few ships still use the three-watch system. Chartered aircraft are used to change the crews of ships deployed to the Arctic: usually two ship's crews are changed at the same time. Some former Fisheries and Oceans ships are on the "averaging" system, which is essentially the same.

The Coast Guard College

It was recognized by Captain Eric Brand, Director of Marine Operations and by Dr Gordon W. Stead, Assistant Deputy Minister of Transport, 1958–1970, that a college for the training of future officers would be an essential part of the new organization. Commander Douglas J. Williams, an RCN instructor officer with high qualifications and great experience, was asked to plan the syllabus and Captain Gerard Brie, former

Students in marine diesel engineering simulator. (Fisheries and Oceans Canada FX010501)

head of the Québec Provincial Marine School at Rimouski, was appointed the first director. The course of instruction was to last four years. The graduates would receive a Coast Guard College diploma but not an academic degree. The college was and is bilingual with instruction given in the students' primary language but with courses in the second language forming an important part of the syllabus. The College trains both deck officers and engineers, but initially the first year of instruction was common to both disciplines. The faculty was divided into four departments: Navigation, which provided instruction not only in navigation but in all the professional subjects required by a deck officer; Engineering, which performed a similar function for engineering students; Science, which provided both navigators and engineers with theoretical basis for their professional studies; and Language, which embraced first and second language instruction and other liberal arts courses. Practical instruction in seamanship and small boat handling was provided and a well-equipped machine shop ensured that engineers acquired hands-on skills essential to their trade. Qualified former armed forces physical education instructors were part of the staff and a quasi-military regime was instituted from the start. The college was at first located in the former naval base at Point Edward, near Sydney, Nova Scotia. Numerous buildings provided accommodation, classrooms and offices as well as a machine shop, gym, library and chapel. A boat shed accommodated the small craft and a large wharf area gave more than enough berthing space for training vessels and visiting Coast Guard and other craft, including commercial shipping. In 1983, the college moved to a new campus with impressive and attractive buildings and facilities, not far from the original location.

The first class of forty-three officer-cadets was enrolled in September 1965 and eighteen graduated in 1969. (One, O/C M. Purney, was killed in a tragic marine accident off St Pierre just two months before graduation). The students followed a normal academic year with practical sea training in the summer and fall months (July to October). At the end of the course, the newly graduated junior officers were awarded a Coast Guard College diploma. After further seatime, with the recommendation of their commanding officer, they returned to the college for examinations and practical training and on successful completion of this phase they were issued with a Coast Guard Watchkeeping Certificate. Engineers graduated with a Fourth Class Engineering Certificate but both disciplines had received instruction to much higher levels, which made future qualifications easier to obtain. The entries from 1965 to 1972 (Classes '69 to '76), followed the first four-year program. The academic and behavioural standards were rigorous. During this period the average number in the entry class was about 46, half of whom graduated. The losses were about 25% because of academic failure and 25% from voluntary withdrawal and other reasons. This ratio has remained nearly the same throughout the college's history.

There were inevitable cultural adjustments from the introduction of officers under training into a fleet that had not been accustomed to a cadet system, but most of the young officers found that their reception was positive. In their first sea training phase, the classes would embark together in one or two large ships with a college instructor in charge. The *C.D. Howe,* the *Labrador* and the *Louis S. St Laurent* were all used for this purpose. In subsequent years, the cadets were distributed among smaller ships where they had to work particularly hard, the more so when chief officers discovered they were available labour that did not have to be paid overtime! Nevertheless, the cadets responded with enthusiasm and a remarkable number are still in the Coast Guard or in other government service or in the marine industry, while many have reached high positions in the civil service and other endeavours.

In 1973 the course was shortened from four years to three and the intake increased to meet the requirements of the expanding fleet. This scheme was in force for the next seven years (Classes '76N to '82). Intake during this period averaged 76, with roughly the same success rate as before. In 1977 the first female graduates–four navigators–completed the course. They had suffered the same pressures as other women entering formerly male-only occupations and earlier female entrants had dropped out before completing the program; but from now on there would always be women on the graduating list.

In 1980 a new program was introduced known as the "sandwich" scheme. This brought a change to the certification of deck officers. The qualification levels obtained by Coast Guard College navigation graduates were similar to those used in the

Canadian Navy: a Watchkeeping Certificate and, later in their career, a Command Certificate. Originally these had no validity for service in commercial ships, although graduates could, when they had amassed the required seatime, take the exams set by the Ship Safety Branch of the Coast Guard and be issued with a commercial certificate. Under the new program, however, navigation cadets graduated with a commercial Watchkeeping Mate Certificate, as well as credits towards the higher commercial qualifications. An Operations Endorsement provided the qualification specific to the Coast Guard. In order to meet the sea time requirements for the commercial certificate and also to find sufficient berths for an increased cadet intake, the sea training periods were arranged so that some cadets were with the fleet at all times, rather than just from July to October. The staggered classroom instruction phases also allowed the same instructional staff to teach a greater number of students. In the five years that this system was in force, the intake was again raised to an average of 105 (Classes '83 to '87).

Forecasting the number of people that will be needed in an organization like the Coast Guard is a very difficult task. Statistical analysis based on a previous year's figures lead to decisions that may take another year to implement. Then, if it takes three or four years to train a class, six or seven years have passed by the time they graduate and requirements may have changed. In the late 1970s large numbers of officers, both navigators and engineers, were leaving to join the booming offshore oil projects and other industries. By the mid 1980s the bloom was off and they started to return. Berths in the fleet were hard to find and some officer cadets went to Fisheries and Oceans ships for their sea phase. The graduating class of '87 could not all be accommodated in the fleet and many were distributed among regional and district offices and headquarters to learn by shadowing key personnel. It was a convenient time for the restoration of a four-year program. This occurred in 1984 and meant that there would be no class of '88 and the intake was reduced. The "sandwich" principle was continued. The first summer was spent at the college learning seamanship and practical engineering skills. Language training was enhanced and the opportunity was taken to restore some of the liberal education courses that had been lost when the program was shortened. Nevertheless, the fleet was now in a period of reduction. From 1989 the intake was further reduced to a bare minimum (of engineers only) and in 1992 there was no recruitment at all.

The small navigation and engineer entries in 1993 and 1994 (Classes '97 and '98) benefited from an agreement between the Coast Guard College and the University College of Cape Breton and from courses provided by the latter. They graduated with a Bachelor of Technology in Nautical Science degree, jointly awarded by the two institutions. The next intake was in 1998 (the class of 2002), which followed the same curriculum. In the years of low officer-cadet population, the college had enlarged the scope of its programs and continued to be active, but it is a matter for satisfaction that there will never have been a year without some officer cadets undergoing training. The total number of graduates from 1969 to 1998 was 864. 661 followed the English programs and 203 the French. Of these, 464 were navigators and 400 Engineers; 750 were men and 114 women. A detailed breakdown is shown in the following table.

Table 7.1 Coast Guard College – Intake and Graduates, 1965-1998

Program	Intake	Grads	Navigators		Engineers		Male		Female	
Graduating Years			Anglo	Franco	Anglo	Franco	Nav	Eng.	Nav.	Eng.
First Four Year 1969–76 (8 years)	365	186	53	31	84	18	84	102	0	0
First Three Year 1976–82 (7 years)	532	258	121	30	92	15	123	100	28	7
Sandwich 3 year 1983–87 (5 years)	526	272	112	44	89	27	116	107	40	9
Sandwich 4 year 1989–95 (7 years)	216	121	37	16	53	15	37	62	16	6
Degree Program 1997–98 (2 yrs)	41	27	13	7	7	0	12	7	8	0
TOTALS 1976–1998	1680	864	336	128	325	75	372	378	92	22

With the fleet reducing and a surplus of officers, there were no entries in the years 1995-1997. One class of engineers joined in 1998 and thirteen graduated in 2002. Students in all categories will complete their course in subsequent years.

The graduates of the Coast Guard College have distinguished themselves in government and in industry. Although obstacles were placed in the way of those who wanted to leave too soon after graduation, it was never expected that all would be retained in the fleet or even in the Coast Guard, and the investment in their education was considered to be a benefit to the nation. They are to be found in senior positions in other government departments and in the marine industry. Many have acquired university degrees at the masters level and some have been awarded doctorates. Positions reached by graduates in government service include: Regional Director General, Fisheries and Oceans; Regional Director, Coast Guard; Director General, Fleet Systems; and Director General Marine Safety Branch, Transport Canada. In industry, the Superintendent of Marine Operations for Beaudril during the Beaufort Sea explorations was a Coast Guard College graduate and others have held high positions in Canadian and American shipyards. Among female graduates, Mia Hicks ('78) is the most senior in the fleet. She is Chief Engineer in large ships in the Newfoundland Region. Miriam van Roosmalen ('79) was the first women appointed to a command position (CCGS *Kenoki*), and later was director of the icebreaking program in Ottawa. These are examples of Coast Guard College graduates making noteworthy contributions in industry as well as government.

Two alumni of the college have, in turn, become directors of the institution. David Parkes, an engineering graduate of 1969, appropriately became its director in the twenty-fifth anniversary year, 1990. His successor was James Wheelhouse, class of '76. The directors of the Coast Guard College since its founding were:

Gerard L. Brie	1965–1969
James Y. Clarke	1970–1973
Hugh W. Plant	1973–1981
John A. Read	1981–1986
Edward J. Kelly	1986–1989
David G. Parkes	1990–1997
James Wheelhouse	1997–1998
Bernard Leonard	1998–

The Transport Canada Training Institute

In 1975, the main training activities of the Department of Transport were brought together in organizatioin known at first as the Ministry of Transport Training Institute and then as the Transport Canada Training Institute (TCTI). Until an impressive new facility was built at Cornwall, Ontario, about one hour by road from Ottawa, training activities were conducted at several sites in the Ottawa area. They included training for air traffic controllers, telecommunications technicians and meteorologists, and courses for intermediate and senior level managers. Although the Atmospheric Environment Service (weather forecasting) had been transferred from the Department of Transport to the Department of the Environment some time previously, Transport continued to be responsible for instruction in meteorology as a matter of convenience. Air traffic controllers also had to receive this type of training and meteorologists were embarked in some Coast Guard ships. Coast Guard involvement was limited: managers and ship safety inspectors attended some courses at TCTI's Heron Road facility in Ottawa. However, when the new TCTI building in Cornwall opened its doors in the fall of 1978, one of its principal components was the Maritime Training Centre (MTC), which took over responsibility for advanced courses for Coast Guard officers and, in 1983, Vessel Traffic Regulators.

Command Courses

After serving as ships' officers for a prescribed period, holders of a Coast Guard Watchkeeping Certificate (after 1983 an Operations Endorsement) can undergo further instruction and sit the examinations for the Coast Guard Command Certificate. These certificates are at the Master Mariner standard and meet the worldwide requirements of the relevant IMO conventions, but are not valid on merchant ships. However, in 1976 the Coast Guard Ship Safety Branch made important changes to the certification system and at the same time granted exemptions for examinations that were deemed equivalent. From 1980 on, the Coast Guard fleet exams were gradually made more compatible with the commercial certificates, so that eventually only a few papers and an oral examination were needed to obtain a Master Mariner's Certificate of Competency. Of course, the many Coast Guard officers who had not come through the college system had this type of certificate already, and for engineers there was only one system and no difference between government and commercial service.

The first Coast Guard Command Certificate was issued in May 1972 (to Fred Guse, Class of '69, who had also obtained the first Coast Guard Watchkeeping Certificate). The first five courses were held at the Coast Guard College. The venue was transferred to Ottawa until 1982, when the new Transport Canada Training Institute in Cornwall was opened. Between 1972 and 1998, 147 Coast Guard Command Certificates were issued.

Training for Engineers

The Marine Training Centre at Cornwall provided upgrading courses for engineers wishing to sit the examinations for third-to first-class certificates, including correspondence courses. Courses were also given in mechanical drafting, refrigeration, electrical engineering and electronics. When AC/AC electric propulsion systems were introduced in new construction ships, special courses in control systems were found necessary and were developed at the Coast Guard College by the engineering instructional staff.

Search and Rescue Programs

The Search and Rescue component of the Maritime Training Centre at TCTI Cornwall (since 1992 at the Coast Guard College in Sydney), developed courses in Search and Rescue techniques that have undergone continual development since their inception. Coast Guard ships' officers and Rescue Coordination Centre personnel and helicopter and fixed-wing aircrew members all take the same courses, so that in an actual operation each has confidence in the others. In 1983/84 a SAR Coxswain's training program was developed at the MTC and is continued today at the Coast Guard College. Courses have been conducted for overseas students in Canada and also on site in various locations in the Caribbean. The instructional staff maintains a close liasion with the USCG operators and researchers and participates in international forums The Canadian SAR Planning Program (CANSARP) is a product of the Search and Rescue Branch of the Coast Guard and has been incorporated into the training given at the school. It is a program that has received international recognition.

In 1990, as a result of the various reports that followed the loss of the oil drilling platform *Ocean Ranger* on the Grand Banks in 1982 (see Chapter 10), a Training Standard was prepared for a new qualification of Rescue Specialist. In 1992 funding became available for training equipment, and training commenced in 1993 in order to fill the 265 positions that had been identified within the fleet. The course included advanced First Aid, in two levels and training in the operation of Rigid Hull Inflatable rescue craft. They were conducted by the regions to a national standard and the

Newfoundland and Western (Pacific) Regions added In-Water Rescue Skills to the program. While other categories are not excluded, Rescue Specialists are primarily drawn from the deck crew (DED) classification, whose existing skills and nature of work (e.g. the operation of RHI craft) are complementary. The additional expertise and duties clearly deserve remuneration, but for legal reasons relating to the collective agreements in force, it was not until 1997 that it was possible to institute special allowances for Rescue Specialists.

Clearance and Rescue Divers

In the 1930s and before, Marine Service ships would sometimes embark hard-hat divers who could inspect wharves and moorings. In the 1960s, the crews of some Coast Guard ships included ships' divers who had been trained in the Navy's diving school. Their duty was to inspect the hull for damage or untangle lines caught in propellers, but from time to time they would assist in rescue operations. Some well publicized incidents in the southern Strait of Georgia in the early 1990s, notably the case of the *Arctic Taglu*, resulted in an initiative to train rescue divers. A pilot project was implemented at the Sea Island Hovercraft unit in Vancouver in the summer of 1995. It was intended to be a two-year trial but was extended through 1998 and subsequently to December 2000. It was then terminated, only to be re-instated in July 2001 after an accident occurred adjacent to the base. Although the Sea Island base rescue divers have returned to active duty, Coast Guard ships no longer carry divers and must rely on commercial diving companies when they are required.

Oil Spill Response Training

In 1990, the Public Review Panel on Tanker Safety and Marine Spill Response Capability in Canada (the Brander-Smith Report) recommended that response capability be improved. New initiatives, starting in 1994, resulted in new training programs being delivered at the Coast Guard College and across Canada by the college staff. These included Pollution Prevention Officer training (for Transport and DFO personnel), the Marine Spill Response Operations course, and an On-scene Commanders' course. Representatives from industry as well as Coast Guard personnel attend these courses. All this was in addition to oil spill response training that was already being delivered by regional personnel under the general direction of Coast Guard headquarters.

Other Marine Courses Held at TCTI
and the Coast Guard College

Between 1979 and 1992, the Maritime Training Centre at Cornwall provided the fleet with training in a number of areas in addition to the Command and SAR courses. These included an Administration course for ship's officers, Simulated Electronic Navigation (SEN) courses (which are a Ship Safety / Marine Safety Branch requirement), and courses and seminars on a variety of other nautical subjects. After 1992, the venue changed to the Coast Guard College at Sydney.

Officer Training for Ships' Crews

Deck and engineering personnel who obtained, on their own, the first level of certification, a Watchkeeping Mate or a Fourth-Class Engineering Certificate, could hold officer positions on an acting basis and compete for permanent positions. When the Coast Guard College was turning out large numbers of graduates, such opportunities became hard to find, although they were never completely cut off. With the reduction of new college graduates after 1995, a more organized system of selection was put in place. Serving crew members with basic qualifications can apply to join the Ships' Crew Officer Training Program. If selected, they undergo a practical shipboard training program that is based on the structured sea training program followed by the cadets and also take eight weeks of courses at the Coast Guard College. Successful candidates are appointed to positions where they can obtain their Coast Guard Operations Endorsement, and from then on they follow the general scheme of competitions and postings.

Logistics Officers

Logistics Officers were originally called Pursers and then Supply Officers. Apart from short special courses, they gained the knowledge for their position through training on the job. In 1981, the title was changed to Logistics Officer and a 24-week course was instituted at Heron Road, Ottawa, later moved to TCTI, Cornwall. Certificates of Competency were issued. After 1982, central stores management under the logistics officer was gradually introduced in Coast Guard ships. In recognition of this, the pay levels of logistics officers were raised by two steps in 1987. The last logistics officers' course was held in Québec in 1994. Qualification is now (2002) by correspondence course and examination.

Vessel Traffic Service Regulators

When Vessel Traffic Services centres were instituted, starting in 1967, operators were recruited from three main sources: air traffic controllers, certificated ships' officers and former naval radar branch personnel. As a former air traffic controller explained, monitoring seaborne traffic is no less onerous than air traffic, for although the actual speeds are much slower, the radar coverage area is much less and, to the operator, the relative movement across the radar screen is not very different. Furthermore, the air controller has the additional dimension of altitude with which to separate the aircraft. Regulator training was initially carried out in the regions, on the job, with some classroom instruction. The first formal VTS course was given in 1981 at the Maritime Training Centre at TCTI, Cornwall. A total of 106 regulators took this course. In 1986, amendments to the Canada Shipping Act and the implementation of the VTS Zone Regulations introduced requirements for the formal certification of regulators. Serving personnel were brought back in turn for enhanced training but there was also a Regional element involving local geography and regulations and familiarisation with local emergency services, which was conducted on site. The training methods and the equipment used were developed by the MTC staff. From 1987 to 1992, 265 new and existing regulators were certified in courses run at Cornwall, Vancouver, and other locations. Courses were conducted in both languages.

In 1992, the Maritime Training Centre moved from Cornwall to the Coast Guard College in Sydney. The first course in the new location was a 28-week *ab-initio* course for candidates without previous training or experience. There was then a major change. The integration of the Radio Operator and Vessel Traffic Regulator disciplines in 1994 required a major effort to cross train existing operators and regulators. A VTS simulator had been developed at TCTI, using available equipment and improvisation. It was not re-installed at Sydney; instead, a new VTS simulator was constructed that could provide automated inputs. It uses computers to represent "the outside world" and provide realistic messages for the operators to deal with. The specifications were developed by MCTS training staff and it is the first such simulator in the world. In fact, in all respects, Canada has been the world leader in the development of MCTS training. In addition to the longer courses, courses in distress procedures and the Global Maritime Distress and Safety System (GMDSS) are given. The latter is an international requirement and is normally provided by provincial schools and the private sector. The courses at Sydney are for fleet personnel.

Other Training

Marine Emergency Duties (MED) training is a requirement of ships' personnel of every branch and rank. This includes fire fighting, lifeboat, liferaft and survival suit drill, damage control and first aid. At first, Coast Guard crew members took these courses in naval facilities on both coasts, but when certification and crewing regulations demanded MED courses for all mariners, provincial schools built facilities of their own and took over all non-naval training, including that of Coast Guard personnel. On the West Coast, Canadian Coast Guard lifeboat coxswains learn heavy weather boat handling with the United States Coast Guard and, in turn, the Canadian Coast Guard provides other forms of SAR training to the USCG. On the East Coast, lifeboat coxswains train at the Coast Guard College, which maintains training craft for the purpose. SAR courses are also provided for Inshore Rescue Boat (summer) crews and Coast Guard Auxiliary members. Practice in the other Coast Guard responsibilities, such as the deployment of pollution prevention booms and equipment is carried out at the bases where the equipment is stored, as described in Chapter 11.

The Caribbean Program

Between 1982 and 1990, under the auspices of the Canadian International Development Agency (CIDA), the Coast Guard developed special courses and provided training for personnel from sixteen Caribbean Commonwealth countries, and Guyana, also a former British colony. The candidates were members of Coast Guards, Defence Forces (army), the Police, and civilian Harbour Board employees. The train-

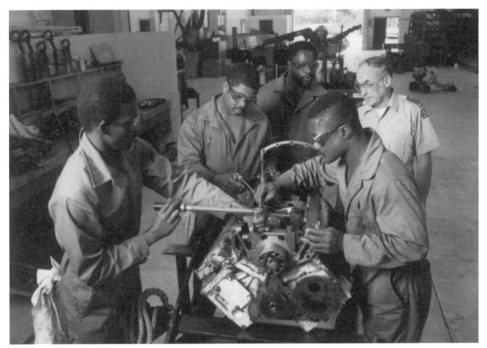

Foreign students in practical engineering training. (Fisheries and Oceans Canada FX020202)

ing for boat operators and engineers was tailored for the type of small patrol craft in use in most of the island nations. The courses varied from nine to twenty-six weeks, the longer courses also being suitable for navigation and engineering watchkeeping officers on the larger patrol craft operated by countries with significant Coast Guards (Jamaica, Barbados, and Trinidad). The islands that participated were: Anguilla, Antigua, Bahamas, Barbados, British Virgin Islands, Cayman Islands, Dominica, Grenada, Jamaica, Montserrat, St Kitts, St Lucia, St Vincent, Trinidad and Tobago, and Turks and Caicos, and the mainland countries of Belize and Guyana. In all, 517 people were trained at the Coast Guard College during the nine-year period and instructors from the Coast Guard College and the Transport Canada Training Institute conducted training in the Caribbean. In addition, eleven officers from Antigua (1), Barbados (1), British Virgin Islands (1), Guyana (2), Jamaica (3), St Lucia (2), and Trinidad (1), have completed the full officer cadet program.

International Training Initiatives

VTS training has been provided by Canada to traffic regulators from several countries. Courses were run for Hong Kong regulators in Canada and in Hong Kong in 1987 to 1989, and a marine communications training program, on site and in Canada, was provided for Vietnam. GMDSS training and VTS workshops have been put on in Taiwan. Perhaps the most interesting type of international involvement has been the

Marine Safety Colloquiums, held at the Coast Guard College in 1997 and 1998. These were, in effect, a type of Search and Rescue virtual exercise using the facilities of both the VTS simulator and the navigation simulator. They involved personnel from fourteen countries in the Middle East and the former Soviet bloc. Participants from countries that were hostile or at least guarded towards one another were placed in a situation where they had to co-operate. Techniques were invoked that had been developed by the USA and the USSR to avoid dangerous confrontation when warships met at sea. Even prior to this, in October to December 1995, nine Palestinian Police Officers had attended an unpublicized Search and Rescue course at the Coast Guard College, Sydney. These students were the first ever to travel on a Palestinian passport. The implications of this course and the later colloquiums reached far beyond the technicalities of Search and Rescue procedure. They were a Canadian contribution to the Middle East peace process and to encouraging regional cooperation.

Officer Cadet Training: Gulf States

In November 1998, following a year and a half of negotiations, government representatives of Kuwait and the United Arab Emirates and the Canadian Coast Guard signed agreements to enroll Kuwaiti and UAE nationals in the degree program at the Coast Guard College. After a spring and summer of intensive language training in 1999, they joined the new entry Canadian officer cadets for four-year courses for deck or engineering officers. Upon successful completion, each will be granted a university degree in Nautical Science by the University College of Cape Breton in conjunction with the Coast Guard College. The first group will graduate in 2004.

Ship Surveyors, Port Wardens, and Accident Investigators

The Ship Safety Branch, which enforces the regulations under the Canada Shipping Act, was a part of the Coast Guard until the latter's transfer to the Department of Fisheries and Oceans in 1995. The branch remained part of Transport Canada along with the corresponding air and surface regulating agencies. The duties of Ship Surveyors, Port Wardens, and Accident Investigators are described in Chapter 13.

It is fair to say that the Canadian Coast Guard has skilled and dedicated personnel engaged in every facet of its activities. This has come about as the result of staffing and training policies that are recognized by the International Maritime Organization and all seafaring nations.

Captain Eric
Brand. (Fisheries
and Oceans
Canada P060101)

Captain Eric

S. Brand OBE RN

(1896–1991)

The Canadian Coast Guard is fortunate to number among its founders an officer and gentleman of outstanding ability and humanity who contributed much to his adopted country in war and in peace. Eric Sydney Brand was born at Ipswich, England on 14 May 1896. He joined the training ship HMS *Conway* as a cadet in 1909. A year later he was accepted at the Royal Naval College, Dartmouth, where he was a classmate of the future King George VI. As a sub-lieutenant he was assistant to the gunnery officer of the battleship HMS *Valiant* at the Battle of Jutland and was Mentioned in Despatches. After the war he specialized first as a gunnery officer and then as a navigator (his chief interest). He was an exceptional instructor at the Royal Navy's navigation school, HMS *Dryad* and was appointed navigating officer and executive officer of several of the Royal Navy's largest ships. In June 1939, as a commander, he was loaned to the Royal Canadian Navy to serve as Director of Intelligence and Trade.

This was a most fortunate choice. Soon promoted to Captain, he worked indefatigably to organize the Canadian side of the convoy system, the control of ships in harbour and the naval boarding parties that inspected arriving ships. Finding that the conditions the merchant seamen worked under were intolerable, he improved their lot by arranging medical services and entertainment for them while in Canadian ports and encouraged volunteers to provide them with comforts such as sweaters, warm clothing and tobacco. When the United States entered the war in December 1941, he advised the USN on setting up their Control of Shipping organization. For this, he was made a Commander of their Legion of Merit. He was also invested as a Chevalier of the Legion d'Honneur of France and was awarded the Order of the British Empire.

Captain Brand was the naval member of the Canadian Shipping Board from 1942 to 1946. He retired from the Royal Navy in 1946 but continued to live in Canada. He held a number of civilian posts as an advisor to the Canadian government on merchant shipping and the transportation of immigrants to Canada. From 1949 to 1959 he was the executive director of the Canadian Maritime Commission.

In 1959 he was appointed Director of Marine Operations of the Canadian Marine Service, which, three years later, became the Canadian Coast Guard. Rather than be tied to a desk in Ottawa, he made frequent voyages in ships of the fleet. His aim was always to promote the concept of the Coast Guard as a national service and to forge bonds between headquarters, the regional bases or agencies and the ships. When commanding officers came to Ottawa for meetings, Captain and Mrs. Brand would entertain them in their Ottawa home.

Captain Brand retired in 1963 with the honorary rank of Commodore in the Coast Guard. However, in 1964 he was recalled to assist in setting up the Canadian Coast Guard College at Sydney Nova Scotia. He recruited Commander Douglas J. Williams, RCN, a very experienced instructor officer to assist in framing the curriculum, and Captain Gerard L. Brie to be the first director. In 1979, with the permission of Her Majesty the Queen, Commodore Brand introduced the Queen's Conway Gold Medal as the premier award to graduating officers and several of the *Conway's* trophies and traditions are maintained at the college. For many years, into his nineties, Eric Brand would attend the Coast Guard College graduation ceremonies, wearing his Commodore's uniform and his many decorations and exemplified to the Officer Cadets the continuity of our best maritime traditions. Commodore Brand died in Ottawa in 1991 at the age of 95.

Haut Fond Prince lightstation in the Saguenay River entrance. (Fisheries and Oceans Canada L500301)

The minister responsible for the Coast Guard (until 1995 the Minister of Transport and subsequently the Minister of Fisheries and Oceans), is responsible, under the Canada Shipping Act and also under the Oceans Act of 1996, for facilitating safe navigation by providing and maintaining lighthouses, beacons, buoys and radio aids to navigation. The act also requires the minister to establish compulsory traffic routes and other traffic controls considered necessary for safe navigation. Authority is given to the minister to enter into agreements with the United States with respect to navigation in shared waterways. Another responsibility is to verify and maintain the depth of water in main shipping channels and, under the Navigable Waters Protection Act, prevent unauthorised structures which might obstruct navigation.

Lighthouses

To the public at large, the most visible aid to navigation has always been the lighthouse. The tall tower with its lighted beacon, warning the shipmaster of sunken rocks or guiding the mariner to safe haven, has been celebrated in song and story for hundreds of years. Today, they still evoke nostalgia and romance and have inspired many writers and historians. However, only their technical features are discussed in any detail in this history. Many excellent books on the subject are available. *The Canadian Lighthouse* by Edward F. Bush. (Occasional papers in Archeology and History, No. 9), although published in 1977, is definitive. Other comprehensive descriptions of lighthouses and the life of their keepers (one for every region of the country), are listed in the bibliography.

By 1968 nearly all lighthouses had been converted to electric power. Those on land, except for some in very isolated locations, were connected to the normal power grid but had emergency diesel generators in case of power failure. Pillar lights (those built on caissons or on rocks just above or just under the water), and those on offshore islands provided their own power using main and backup generators. Major lighthouses were still staffed. The keepers maintained the equipment and grounds and were there in case any of the automatic functions failed. They also observed the weather and made regular reports and kept a general eye on traffic in the vicinity. In the past, life as a keeper usually meant isola-

CHAPTER 8

Navigation and Communications

tion, a poor diet and danger. With improvements in the aids to navigation program and new buoy tenders that could carry a helicopter, life for keepers and their families had become less onerous. Helicopter platforms were built at lighthouses; sometimes on the very top of pillar lighthouses—over the light itself. This allowed for more frequent staff changes, mail delivery and medical evacuation if necessary.

Many of the lights were still fitted with the elaborate dioptric Fresnel lenses, made up of many curved prisms, set in a bronze framework, with the original oil or gas lamp replaced by an electric bulb. In the 1970s, airport-type rotating lights and intense halogen light sources were being installed. Some of the impressive old lenses are exhibited in maritime museums and in the lobbies of Coast Guard office buildings.

The first battery powered minor lights had Edison cells; glass containers that were filled with an electrolyte on installation. From 1965, disposable batteries with solar switches that turned the light on or off in response to ambient light levels were in use. In 1980, power obtained from solar panels was introduced. These panels could keep the batteries of the smaller lights charged. Goudge Island in British Columbia was the first to be solarised and last a full year. The system was then extended to larger lights. At first diesel generators were retained where they were already fitted as a backup, but eventually solar charged batteries proved to be so reliable that the generators were removed.

Lightstation De-staffing

The most important trend over the last thirty years has been the gradual automation and de-staffing of lighthouses. Automatic systems have been developed which bring stand-by circuits or equipment into play, as well as simply switching equipment on or off. The next stage was to install computer technology and links, by landline, VHF, or microwave to a central location. The computers do the monitoring and alarms attract human attention if needed. In the mid-1970s there were 264 staffed light stations. Reductions occurred on an opportunity basis as people retired. By 1991, staffed lights had been reduced to 70: 32 in Newfoundland, 3 in the Maritimes, and 35 in British Columbia. In 1995 a second phase was commenced and incentives for early retirement of lighthouse staff were provided. By 1998, 52 staffed light stations remained: 24 in Newfoundland, 1 in the Maritimes, and 27 in British Columbia. On the Pacific coast, there was a lot of opposition to de-staffing. Lightkeepers there often performed other duties including guiding tourists and providing first aid to hikers, for example on the West Coast the "shipwrecked mariners trail" along the southwest coast of Vancouver Island. There was a public perception that the eyes of the lighthouse staff and their families provided additional safety for pleasure boaters, and some incidents in which keepers used the station boat to rescue yachts or sports fishermen in distress reinforced this view. In Newfoundland, keeping the lights staffed also had great public support. In the Great Lakes and the Laurentian Region, de-staffing was completed without any great protest. In the Maritimes, the sole remaining staffed station, Machias Seal Island, is occupied for reasons of sovereignty: the United States has never recognized it as Canadian territory.

Lightships

Lightships were once a common method of marking dangerous turning points and the entrance to important harbours. They were small, crewed ships, self-propelled to go to and from their station, where they secured to exceptionally strong permanent moorings. As well as a flashing light, they were fitted with a powerful fog signal and, frequently, with a radiobeacon. Several have been run down and sunk by ships homing in too accurately on the beacon's signal in thick fog. By 1968 they had been replaced: in the St Lawrence by pillar lights and in other regions by large offshore buoys. *Lightship No.4*, stationed on the Lurcher Shoal off the southwest coast of Nova Scotia, was the last of them. After modifications, it became the Coast Guard College training ship *Mikula.*

Buoys and Beacons

The buoyage system is the other important visual aid to navigation. Lighted buoys are powered by large batteries located under a watertight hatch in the body of the buoy. A four-bulb device automatically rotates to the next good unit in case of failure. The crews of navigation aids vessels regularly check batteries, bulbs and the exact position of each buoy. In the 1960s, light buoys had already progressed from gas to 6-volt dry cell batteries. In the 1970s, buoys and beacons were converted to 12-volt batteries, which would last 400 days. Solar panels are fitted to light buoys to recharge the batteries, which extends their life even more. These panels could be horizontal, which makes them subject to fouling by birds, or on the sides, where reflected light from the sea makes up for some of the loss of direct sunlight. Wind recharging systems were tried from 1975 to 1980 but maintenance costs were found to make them impractical. Other buoys have whistles or bells actuated by the motion of the buoy in the waves. Many have radar reflectors.

Commencing in April 1983, the Canadian buoyage system was changed to conform with the IALA System "B," which would be in force in the Americas, much of the Pacific, the Philippines and Japan. Two years were required to complete the changeover. Extensive changes were made to the colours that buoys were painted and some patterns new to Canada were adopted. Port hand buoys, previously black, were painted green. Fairway buoys at the entrance to channels changed from black and white to red and white, and black and yellow cardinal buoys with special light characteristics were introduced. The IALA System "A," which is used in Europe and most of the rest of the world, is similar, except that the colours of the port and starboard hand buoys are reversed.

Research and development on the buoys themselves has been continuous and directed to reducing costs and the amount of service needed. Fast water buoys have been designed that remain in position despite strong currents. Other developments include better moorings, better paint and plastic buoys with built-in colour, so that no repainting is needed.

Beacons are small fixed navigation aids on land. They are usually powered by landline with battery backup. Those situated on rocks or islets are battery powered, usually with solar charging. Some buoys and beacons are fitted with radar transponder beacons (RACONS) which provide positive identification of the radar echo to the observer on a ship.

Estevan Point lighthouse, British Columbia. (Fisheries and Oceans Canada L500501)

Technicians arrive by helicopter to service a light. (Mike Mitchell, Fisheries and Oceans Canada MP150502)

Fog Signals

A New Brunswick engineer, Robert Foulis, invented a steam foghorn that was used at light stations in the nineteenth century. By 1968, compressed air was the method employed at large stations; electric horns were used at smaller lights. Fog sensors, which measure the light backscatter from water particles in the atmosphere and automatically turn the foghorn on, were also in use.

Electronic Navigation Aids: Direction Finders

The first electronic aid to navigation was the medium frequency direction finder, operating in a frequency range of 285 to 325 kHz. A ship could ask a shore station for a bearing or it could take a bearing of a radio beacon that transmitted a morse code identification at listed intervals. These were great circle bearings that had to be corrected for plotting on mercator projection charts. In Canada, these beacons were arranged in groups, all using the same frequency, so that plotting cross bearings was simplified. In the Arctic, radio beacons were activated for the navigation season and closed down as the last Coast Guard ship departed the area. As other systems, particularly the Global Positioning System (GPS), became more popular, radiobeacons were used less and less. From about 1993, their number diminished. By 1996 only four, at Cape Spear, Sable Island, Halifax and Point au Père were still continuously transmitting. Ships can tune in to aero beacons or ask a shore station to transmit while they take a bearing, but by 1998 MFDF was no longer a widely used marine navigation aid. VHF DF equipment is mostly used to obtain bearings of another vessel or aircraft and is useful in Search and Rescue situations.

Hyperbolic Systems

Electronic systems that transmit from pairs of stations, in most cases referred to as "master" and "slave" or "secondary" stations, generate lines of position in the form of hyperbolae. These hyperbolae are shown as coloured lines on navigational charts and two or more readings provide the observer with the ship's position. A group of stations, located to give optimum accuracy, is termed a chain. Hyperbolic systems include Omega, Loran, Decca and some close-range systems.

Loran A was developed in the United States during the Second World War. It operated on a frequency of about 2MHz and measured the time difference between receiving signals from a master and a slave station. Its range was about 800 miles by day and 1400 by night. In 1968 Loran A coverage included both coasts of Canada, the Davis Strait and Baffin Bay. Loran A was being replaced by Loran C in the early 1980s and the last Canadian Loran A station closed in December 1983.

The Decca navigation system was developed by Britain, also during the Second World War. It transmits in the frequency band of 70 to 130 kHz and operates on the principle of comparing the phase difference between signals from a master station and slave stations, usually three per chain. It was more accurate but shorter ranged than Loran A. By 1962 the Canadian East Coast had full Decca coverage with the completion of the

Cabot Strait chain. Decca was never installed on the West Coast. In 1982 Decca began to be replaced by Loran C and in March 1984, Decca was discontinued in Canada, although it remained in use in Europe and other parts of the world.

Loran C, operating on a frequency of 90 to 110 kHz, was an improvement on Loran A with slightly greater range and was able to match the accuracy of Decca. The first Canadian Loran C station was erected at Cape Race as early as 1965 as part of a United States military network. The other stations of the chain were in Caribou, Maine and southern Greenland. In 1977 a station was put in at Williams Lake, British Columbia to operate in conjunction with stations in Washington State and Alaska. When it was found that the Strait of Juan de Fuca was in a blind spot, another was built in 1980 at Port Hardy at the north end of Vancouver Island. Loran C was by then in general civilian use and by 1982 the East Coast had full coverage. The Great Lakes are served by an American chain, operated by the USCG but the Arctic is not covered. Loran C soon became the standard electronic navigation system for commercial ships, fishing vessels and yachts. Display units were put into production that gave the position in latitude and longitude and the true course made good, and could be programmed with pre-determined waypoints and route information.

Omega was a Very Low Frequency (VLF) world-wide hyperbolic system designed by and for the United States military, chiefly for use by submarines. In the late 1960s it was experimental and in the mid 1970s, four stations were in use, which grew to eight by 1982. It could have been valuable in the Arctic, which was out of range of Loran chains, but it was subject to errors, especially when the signal had to travel across the Greenland glacial ice. In 1981 the USCG installed ground stations at Inuvik, Resolute, Frobisher (Iqaluit) and St Anthony to measure the position differences: it was assumed that other receivers on ships in the area of a station would have the same errors. The Coast Guard telecommunications branch conducted a study on differential Omega in the Gulf of St Lawrence in 1981, but Omega never became very widely used and it was discontinued in 1997.

Various types of short-range hyperbolic systems are used to provide precise navigation in narrow channels or for hydrographic surveys. These are installed temporarily for the duration of a task.

Satellite Systems

The U.S. Navy's Transit satellite navigation system, referred to as "Satnav" was released for commercial use in July 1967. It relied on six satellites in polar orbits. By 1981 eleven Canadian Coast Guard icebreakers were fitted with this equipment. It was replaced in the 1990s by Navstar GPS.

The Navstar Global Positioning System, usually known simply as GPS, is a worldwide system operated by the U.S. military. It was declared operational in December 1993. A constellation of satellites provides position (and altitude) information continuously, anywhere in the world. Receivers are compact and can be battery powered and hand held and can be used on land as well as at sea. At first, the accuracy was deliberately degraded, for civilian users, to the order of 100 metres. This measure was deliberately subverted in the USA as well as in other countries by the use of Differential GPS. A shore station transmitted a correction that improves accuracy to about 10 metres. From 1995, the Canadian Coast Guard operated DGPS stations, located at some of the former MFDF sites, but in August 2000, President Clinton announced the removal of the accuracy errors applied to the transmissions and GPS is now very precise, world wide.

Arctic Navigation

Navigation in Arctic waters poses special problems to the navigator in addition to the expected hazard of ice. Charts do not show the mass of soundings or contour lines found on charts of well surveyed southern waters. Instead, lines of soundings, with blank areas on either side, attest to the scarcity of depth information. The usual destinations of shipping have been surveyed in some detail and ships try to follow the established routes for which information is available. In the western Arctic, many pingoes, which are steep pyramidal shoals, seen as hills on land, were only discovered in the 1980s during exploration for oil. When in proximity to land, radar is a much used aid and visual coastal navigation can be practiced in clear weather. Radiobeacons that were activated by the Coast Guard at the start of each season were the chief electronic aid. The Transit Satnav system could provide a correct latitude and longitude of the ship, but the problem was that the coordinates of the land shown on the chart were often in error. In the days when the surveys for many Arctic charts were made, finding accurate positions in those latitudes was difficult. On the other hand, the various features on the chart were correctly plotted in relation to each other. In such circumstances, radar is usually the best method of navigation as it correctly locates the ship in relation to the land and other dangers. Loran A, when it was in operation, did not extend beyond the southern part of Baffin Bay and no Decca or Loran C chains were ever established. Had they been available, they would have suffered from the same disadvantages as Satnav in respect to the charts, but in the last decade, great strides have been made in reproducing accurate charts. GPS is therefore a useful aid, but navigation in the Arctic must always be conducted with particular caution.

Electronic Navigation Transmitters

In Canada, the funding, construction and maintenance of electronic navigation transmitters was the responsibility of the Telecommunications and Electronics Branch of the Department of Transport, which maintained both air and marine systems. In 1977 there was a split into air and marine sections, the latter becoming part of the Coast Guard. Navigation system stations were staffed by technicians and usually by a diesel mechanic but many are now highly automated. They may be at the same location as radio or meteorological stations and have a combined staff. When Loran A and C were first installed, Canada provided the site and buildings and the United States the equipment. Decca stations were wholly Canadian, Later, all equipment and sites including Loran C and DGPS were Canadian. In all cases, the Coast Guard staffs the station and maintains the equipment. While remote sensing has been installed, the de-staffing of electronic sites has not been as extensive as at lighthouses. All stations still have a staff that works

A light buoy with solar panels. (Fisheries and Oceans Canada L030302)

by day; but at night computers at a remote location monitor all functions. For the Loran C system, this is located at St Anthony, Newfoundland. If a malfunction occurs at, say, Port Hardy in British Columbia, it is noted in St Anthony on the other side of the continent! The Port Hardy technician is then alerted, by telephone, to go to the site and repair the defect.

Radio Stations

In 1968 a new department, Communications Canada, assumed responsibility for administering all radio regulations, including those that applied to ships and aircraft. The radio operators and technicians who worked at marine radio stations, at airports and on board ship were Transport Canada employees and belonged to the Telecommunications and Electronics Branch. In 1978, there was a further split into two divisions that served the Air and Marine Transportation Administrations, respectively.

In 1995 the Marine division moved to the Department of Fisheries and Oceans, along with the rest of the Coast Guard.

In the 1960s and 70s, many radio stations were very isolated and operators and technicians lived on-site in housing that was provided. Some were co-located with lighthouses and weather observing stations, in which case a small village of government employees with their families would be found in remote, often spectacularly beautiful places. One example was Estevan Point in British Columbia, where about seventeen families lived. The only way to the station was a trail from a nearby First Nations village and over a beach that was often wave swept. Access was never easy until a helicopter pad was built. There were other stations of this type on both coasts and some near large cities and populated areas. In the Arctic, the operators and technicians were brought in only for the navigation season.

The Coast Guard publication *Radio Aids to Marine Navigation* gives details of all radio stations and transmissions, including electronic navigation systems, for which the Coast Guard is responsible. Different volumes cover the Atlantic/Great Lakes and the Pacific. The 1973 issue shows 49 stations providing communications with shipping, two of which, Halifax and Vancouver, were international stations with world-wide coverage. Twenty-one of these stations were on the East Coast and the Gulf and River St Lawrence, nine on the Great Lakes, nine on the West Coast and ten in the Arctic and Hudson Bay. Only eight of these had extended range subsidiary stations. In addition there were VHF stations at canal entrances and for harbour control and at the Vessel Traffic Services centres.

The principal changes that occurred over the next two decades can be considered from two viewpoints, ship and shore. Morse key communications died a long slow death, with the last transmission from a Canadian Coast Guard station being made from Station VCO (Sydney Nova Scotia) on 28 July 1999. With improved radio telephone, both VHF and HF and, especially, satellite communication (SATCOM), it was no longer necessary for the Master of a ship to pass a telegram type message to "Sparks" (as the radio operator was called), or at least call him to tune a recalcitrant HF radio telephone. On shore, the ability to control distant subsidiary transmitter/receiver sites reduced the number of staffed stations. In 1997 there were fifteen in the East, five in the Great Lakes (with a remote site at Churchill on Hudson Bay), four on the Pacific Coast and only three in the Arctic, each controlling several extended range facilities. This was less than half as many as in 1973. More detailed studies of the history of radio communications in North America can be found in other publications, most recently *Come Quick Danger. A History of Marine Radio in Canada*, by Stephan Dubreuil.

Vessel Traffic Services

The first Vessel Traffic Regulating scheme was in the St Lawrence River, where the first stations had been opened in 1967 at Québec City and Montreal. At first it was a reporting system but later radar coverage was added and the system extended. The last VTS centre for the area was installed at Point Escoumins in 1974. In the Great Lakes,

Comox MCTS Centre. (Mike Mitchell, Fisheries and Oceans Canada MP350503)

similar methods were used. Halifax Harbour had a radar set at its entrance from an early date and by 1973 a set of routes and calling in points had been designated and shown on charts. Chedabucto Bay, where the tanker *Arrow* had gone aground in 1969, had a control centre and routing system. Saint John and the outer part of the Bay of Fundy was also built in 1973 with two (later three) radar stations covering the main shipping rotes. In 1974, Vancouver Traffic was established and over the years the West Coast coverage was extended until a station at Tofino, with its radar and communication antennas on a high mountain, could see and talk by VHF to ships 60 miles off the coast. Conception Bay in Newfoundland followed when the Come-by-Chance refinery was built. (Preventing oil pollution was a primary reason for the expansion of Vessel Traffic Services). In the early days, not all ships had VHF radio and when a ship entered a VTS zone it was obliged to rent a portable set which was brought out by the pilot. The annual edition of the Coast Guard publication *Notices to Mariners* has complete instructions for vessels entering the various traffic regulation schemes.

In the mid-1970s, the Coast Guard also introduced an offshore advance reporting system (ECAREG) for ships coming to Eastern Canada. This "low level" information system requires ships to report their condition, including any defects, and their estimated time of arrival at a position where "high level" reporting would be required and radar surveillance is provided. A similar system on the West Coast is operated in conjunction with the United States Coast Guard.

In 1994, the Radio Communication and Vessel Traffic Services were united under the designation Marine Communication and Traffic Services (MCTS) and the operating personnel were cross-trained. With the ability to remote both radio and radar coverage, both facilities could be combined in one operations room fitted with the latest computers and equipment. A ship approaching Canada would come under the area regulation scheme (ECAREG or CVTS, the West Coast Cooperative Vessel Traffic Services), pass its obligatory information messages, report its position and, eventually, enter a traffic scheme and come under radar coverage until it reached its destination. This is a practical union of the navigation and communication functions that keep ships and their crews safe and shores unpolluted.

Ships arriving in Eastern Canadian waters in winter and ships voyaging to the Arctic must expect to encounter ice. Although some merchant ships from Russia and the Scandinavian countries have experienced crews and are very ice-capable, most other vessels have no special strengthening and the masters and officers may never have navigated in such conditions. In accordance with its mandate, a principal task of the Coast Guard Fleet is to assist vessels through ice filled waters. It does so by providing advice, routing information and icebreaker assistance when required. (See map, page xii) The Coast Guard publication *Ice Navigation in Canadian Waters* has this advice for mariners:

CHAPTER 9

Icebreaking and the Arctic

> The first principle of successful ice navigation is to maintain freedom of maneuver. Once a ship becomes trapped, the vessel goes wherever the ice goes ... The long way round a difficult ice area whose limits are known is often the fastest and safest way ... Experience has proven that three basic ship handling rules apply: keep moving, even very slowly, but keep moving; try to work with the ice movement and not against it ... excessive speed means ice damage.

Ships being escorted by an icebreaker normally follow in its track. The distance between the ships should be close enough so that the ice does not close in but far enough to avoid running up to the icebreaker if it has to come to a halt. This is usually done by veering off to the side so that the ship is stopped by the ice, and/or by going astern. If a ship does become beset, that is, stuck, the icebreaker may back up and try to clear the ice on either side of the bow of the vessel. Another technique is to cut a parallel channel to ease the pressure, then angle across the ship's bow. A special set of signals and lights is used and all ships navigating in ice or being escorted must have on board the publications required by the regulations. It is common for foreign ships to engage Canadian ice navigators to advise the master and act as a liaison with the Coast Guard and Canadian shore authorities.

The St Lawrence River and Gulf

The normal winter working season for a Canadian Coast Guard icebreaker starts in mid-December or early January, depending on the area and the actual ice conditions. The original purpose of icebreakers, dating from the 1890s and still of major importance, was flood control in the St Lawrence River. Large rafts of shore-fast ice or "battures" can break off and jam across the stream or against bridges forming effective dams. These must be broken up by icebreakers working from downstream which is, in any case, the best way to keep the channel clear. The smaller icebreakers are used to break out harbours and in shallower water. In areas with less rafting or piling up of loose ice, air-cushion vehicles (hovercraft) have proved to be very effective for this task, especially where the tributaries join the main river. Besides flood control, the main and most prominent mission of the icebreakers is to facilitate the movement of shipping to and from ports in the Gulf of St Lawrence and up the river as far as Montreal.

At the beginning of the season, Regional Ice Operations Centres are activated in Sarnia, Québec, Dartmouth (formerly at Sydney) and St Johns. They maintain ice charts and issue forecasts and routing advice to shipping through the ECAREG traffic advisory system. They respond to requests for assistance from merchant ships and direct the icebreakers under their control. Generally, the job of the larger icebreakers is to assist traffic along the main routes while light icebreakers keep traffic moving in the smaller ports, but tasking is flexible and governed by the prevailing conditions. The ships come under the control of the Regional Operations Centres for the area they are in. Typically, in January, the larger Laurentian Region icebreakers are stationed between Québec and the estuary of the St Lawrence, light icebreakers at the Saguenay and on the north shore of the Gulf, while the outer Gulf is covered by Maritimes-based heavy icebreakers. Other Maritimes Region vessels keep traffic moving in P.E.I., and northern New Brunswick ports. In Newfoundland, a large icebreaker usually starts the season on the northeast coast while icebreakers from the Gulf cover the western ports. Above Québec, smaller vessels and the hovercraft are used, but units are switched as required.

The Great Lakes

As winter sets in, shipping continues to move in the Great Lakes until early January, when the Seaway and the Welland canals are closed. The Soo locks between Lake Superior and the St Mary's River, leading to Lake Huron, usually close in mid-January. Coast Guard icebreakers may be called on to assist harbour movements as ships are loaded with grain or ore in anticipation of the coming navigation season. Some commercial fishing continues in Lakes Erie and Huron when winds clear a section of the St Clair River, Lake St Clair, the Detroit River and near the entrance to the Welland Canal at the eastern end of Lake Erie. When it is anticipated that the Central Region ships will need assistance, Laurentian icebreakers are moved up through the Seaway to help and operate under Central Region control. Ice conditions vary from year to year and occasionally very heavy ice delays the opening of the navigation season, while in other years icebreaker assistance is hardly needed. Ice management in the Great Lakes and their interconnecting channels is carried out under the provisions of a partnership agreement between the Canadian and United States Coast Guards. Icebreakers of both nations operate in the waters and harbours of the other whenever necessary.

In April 1984 an exceptional ice event occurred. The navigation season had just opened and large numbers of ships were attempting to pass between Lakes Erie and Huron. The USCGC *Mackinaw* and four smaller icebreakers were unable to cope. The CCGS *Des Groseilliers* (Captain Pat Toomey), was stationed in Lake Erie and came to assist and CCGS *Griffon* arrived later. Six cargo ships had been driven ashore by the ice and later eighteen ships had become stuck in one and a half miles of river. The *Des Groseilliers* arrived on 11 April and worked practically non-stop until 29 April. By then 300 ships had been passed through the once congested stretch. The operation had become a spectator event with thousands of people from both sides of the river watching the ships of the two Coast Guards work together. Amateur radio enthusiasts kept track of progress by monitoring the VHF traffic on scanners. There had been heavy ice years before but this one was dubbed "the ice jam of the century." Conditions just as severe have subsequently occurred but both the icebreakers and the freighters have learned to deal more efficiently with the ice in this congested area. The most effective measure is to hold the traffic back until the icebreakers have had a chance to clear the channel. This was the lesson learned in 1984. The late 1990s have been marked by a series of light ice years, attributed to "El Niño," the Pacific warm water phenomenon which affected North America's climate in several ways, some beneficial.

Icebreaking with Air Cushion Vehicles

Air cushion vehicles (hovercraft) are very effective icebreakers when the ice is in smooth continuous sheets. This type of ice is common in the St Lawrence River where it forms in Lakes St Pierre and St Francis and the other wider sections. If a large ice sheet breaks loose from the shore and is swept down river it will drive any ship in its path before it. If it jams on a narrow section, it will cause flooding, so it must be broken up. Hovercraft based in the Laurentian Region achieve this in the following manner. At slow speeds a hovercraft generates waves like an ordinary vessel. The hovercraft starts in clear water and then moves onto the ice, taking its wave system with it. The ice then falls into the trough between the bow and stern waves and breaks of its own weight. If the wave system is lost, the craft must return to clear water, generate another wave and start again. Successive passes can peel strips off sheets of first-year ice, each three or more times the width of the hovercraft. The system does not work when there is heavy ridging or where the ice is too thick. Consequently, hovercraft are not of much use in the Arctic.

In 1976, CCGS *Alexander Henry* experimented with an air-cushion platform that was attached to the ship's bow and pushed ahead of the vessel. It had a notch fitted with flexible skirts that could adapt to any shape of bow. In the *Alexander Henry* trials, the

Top: The CCGS *Des Groseilliers* leads a convoy in the Gulf of St Lawrence. (Fisheries and Oceans Canada F100807)

Bottom: Icebreakers and freighters. (Fisheries and Oceans Canada MP100301)

device worked effectively in certain conditions, but it needed a lot of fuel, made an enormous noise and could have provided a serious impediment to the ship in case it went off hover in the event of a breakdown. The plan to attach similar platforms to freighters was found not to be practical.

The Arctic

When the traffic lanes in the Gulf and the Great Lakes are clear, the icebreakers return to port to prepare for the summer navigation season in the Arctic. Like the winter season in the Gulf, most of the missions are routine. They always include activating and servicing navigation aids, escorting merchant ships, delivering supplies and cargo to locations not serviced by commercial vessels, and carrying out hydrographic and scientific work. Marine commerce in the Canadian Arctic is restricted to summer and early fall. This is as true today as it was in 1967, although some special ships like the MV *Arctic*, built with Canadian government assistance, can undertake some early or late trips.

Extensive planning is needed so that the Coast Guard can provide effective assistance to all agencies and commercial interests. Before each season, government and private scientific interests define their programs. Shipping companies are contacted to ascertain their proposed voyages, some of which are, in any case, under government contract. Voyages for hydrographic survey are planned. These used to be undertaken by the Department of Fisheries and Oceans' own vessels and by hydrographic personnel in Coast Guard ships, but since the merger in 1995 these two fleets are one. Responsibility for the program now lies with the Central and Arctic (formerly with the Northern) Region Headquarters. Each year an Arctic Operations Order is issued specifying when ships from the different regions are to sail and their program through the season as far as it can be forecast. A pre-sailing conference is held in Ottawa attended by the icebreaker captains, DFO scientific and hydrographic personnel and representatives of the shipping companies and various interests. Normally, all the available heavy icebreakers and some light icebreakers are needed for the program, including one Victoria-based ship for the western Arctic. Departure dates for the icebreakers vary from late June to mid July but ships on special missions may leave as early as May or as late as August. Once in the Arctic they came under the control of Northern Headquarters in Ottawa, but since 1995 and amalgamation with Fisheries and Oceans, control is exercised by Central and Arctic Region in Sarnia. During the season, generally in August for ships on a normal manning regimen, the ship's crews are changed as needed. Ships return when their tasks are complete, usually between the end of September and the end of November.

These measures have been perfected over many years, starting in 1950 when the *C.D. Howe* made her first northern voyage with government officials and supplies for the settlements. The *N.B. McLean* made her usual annual voyages to Hudson Bay and Labrador. In 1953 the new *d'Iberville* made her first northern trip and in that year the *d'Iberville* and *C.D. Howe* carried Inuit families from Port Harrison (Inukjuag) on the eastern side of Hudson Bay to Ellesmere Island for resettlement there, an event which is still considered controversial.

Some Notable Events

Canada assumed the task of re-supplying the joint weather stations in the far north in 1954. The RCAF assumed responsibility for the airlift and the Department of Transport coordinated supplies by sea. The *d'Iberville* was in charge of the convoy of supply ships and was joined by the *N.B. McLean* for the trip to Resolute. In that year the *d'Iberville* reached Eureka through heavy ice and unloaded her cargo. The *Edward Cornwallis* assisted in Hudson Bay and would do so in future years until stronger ice-breakers were built. Also in 1954, the Navy's new icebreaker HMCS *Labrador* became the first large ship to transit the Northwest Passage and went on to circumnavigate North America by returning to Halifax via the Bering Strait and the Panama Canal. She continued exploration and survey work each year up to 1957, but was transferred to the Department of Transport in 1958. In 1957 the light icebreaker *Montcalm* joined the fleet, and by 1960 the large icebreaker *John A. Macdonald* and four new light icebreak-ers provided northern operational capability. The Northern Supply Vessels (the former LCTs) became available and were suitable for cargo delivery in tidal harbours.

In 1962, the year the Coast Guard was created, the ships ranged over a greater area of the Arctic Archipelago than ever before, according to a Department of Transport press release. That year the *John A. Macdonald* set a "farthest north" record by reach-ing the northern tip of Tanquary Fiord, which is at 81° North latitude, only 1000 km from the Pole. Coast Guard ships and chartered ships delivered 90,000 tons of cargo to various Arctic destinations.

Although ice conditions in 1963 were reported as being "the worst on record," Coast Guard ships successfully carried out supply and other operations, delivering 112,000 tons of cargo with chartered and commercial vessels. Ice conditions were again relative-ly poor in 1964 but 96,000 tons of cargo were delivered. The reduction from the previ-ous year was a result of a number of projects having been completed. Ten Coast Guard ships, in addition to the "Bird" class LCTs, participated in these operations.

In 1965, the *d'Iberville* and the USCG icebreaker *Westwind* assisted the *John Cabot* as she repaired a vital cable link to the United States air base at Thule, Greenland. 1966 was a relatively routine year with fifteen Coast Guard vessels deployed to the Arctic.

In 1967, the *John A. Macdonald* transited west through the Northwest Passage to assist the *Camsell* in the western Arctic. It was a heavy year for ice and the *Camsell* could not cope with all the calls for assistance she was receiving as the Arctic pack closed in on the mainland. The *Macdonald* went through Victoria Strait, the first large ship to do so—only the *St Roch* had preceded her. After three weeks working in the Beaufort Sea another call for help came from the USCGC *Northwind*, beset in the polar ice 500 miles north of Alaska. In company with the USCGC *Staten Island*, the *John A.*

Macdonald fought to reach the *Northwind*. At times it seemed that the efforts of the two ships would be unsuccessful and that the *Northwind* would have to be left in the polar pack for the winter; but suddenly there was a wind shift and the trio was able to rendezvous and proceed south to open water. The eastern Arctic was now frozen and the only way back was via the Bering Strait and the Panama Canal. Transport Minister Paul Hellyer met the *John A. Macdonald* on her arrival in Vancouver and congratulated the crew. At Seattle the ship had been given a civic reception and Captain Paul Fournier received a citation from the commandant of the United States Coast Guard.

In 1968 some thirty ships, including thirteen Coast Guard vessels, delivered cargo to seventy northern destinations.

The Voyages of the *Manhattan*

In the late 1960s oil had been discovered on Alaska's north slope and it was necessary to decide how it would be shipped to the "lower forty-eight" States. Eventually this turned out to be by pipeline to the south coast of Alaska and then by tanker. This method was not without problems, for example the pollution caused by the *Exxon Valdez* grounding, in 1989, but was judged to be more reliable and less ecologically dangerous than other routes. However, in 1968 this was not so apparent and the Humble Oil Company elected to test the feasibility of using large icebreaking tankers to bring oil through the Northwest Passage to the U.S. East Coast. They chartered the *Manhattan* (built by Bethlehem Steel, Quincy, Mass. in 1962), which was particularly suitable as she had a better power to displacement ratio than other contemporary tankers. The ship was then extensively modified and given a completely new icebreaking bow of novel design and an ice belt extending nearly to the stern. The new bow section was 20 feet (6 metres) wider at its maximum than the original ship's beam and the icebelt, at its upper edge, 8 feet (2.4 metres) wider. From the side, the profile of the bow was concave rather than the convex shape of conventional icebreakers. This technique of breaking the ice was different as it relied on the great mass of the loaded or fully ballasted tanker. As modified, the *Manhattan* was 1015 feet (309.5 metres) long, 148 feet (45 metres) wide at the belt and had a deadweight capacity of 124,000 tons. For the trials she was ballasted to 52 feet (15.8 metres) forward and 48 feet (14.6 metres) aft. She was a twin-screw turbine vessel, 43,000 SHP and had twin rudders. New high strength propellers were fitted as well as an ice protection pad to guard the rudders. The whole ship was instrumented to record hull stresses, accelerations and hull movement. Communication and navigational equipment was comprehensive.

The plan was to send the *Manhattan* through the Northwest Passage and return during the 1969 season. The Canadian Coast Guard provided ice reconnaissance and an escorting icebreaker, the *John A. Macdonald*, commanded by Captain Paul Fournier, who would later be awarded the Order of Canada for his achievements during these trials. On 31 August the *John A. Macdonald* met the *Manhattan* at the south end of Davis Strait. At Resolute on 6 September they were joined by the USCG icebreaker *Northwind*

The supertanker *Manhattan* is escorted by the CCGS *John A. Macdonald* through the Northwest Passage. (Fisheries and Oceans Canada F100312-004)

and the three ships made the transit in company. For the *Manhattan* the icebreakers' assistance was essential. For all her bulk she had limitations. Her power, although high for a tanker was not quite adequate and her shape made reversing and turning very difficult. Her mass kept her moving well, but once stopped she was hard to restart. Canada monitored the experiment closely. Captain T.C. Pullen, RCN (Ret'd) was the Canadian government representative in the *Manhattan*. He had commanded the *Labrador* in 1956 and had taken the ship through Prince of Wales Strait, following Larsen's 1944 route in the *St Roch*, and conducted a running survey using the ship's helicopter to set up shore triangulation stations. Rear-Admiral Anthony Storrs (RCN Ret'd), Coast Guard Director of Marine Operations, joined the *John A. Macdonald* at Resolute. The ships arrived at Prudhoe Bay, Alaska, on September 19th. They had come via Prince of Wales Strait, the only practical route as the other deep-draft channel, McClure Strait was practically always impassable because of the Arctic ice pack at its western entrance (although it was speculated that the very large and very high powered super-tankers of the future might be able to use it).

For the return voyage, the USCGC *Staten Island* replaced the *Northwind*. The objective on the return trip was not simply to make the passage but to carry out tests in various types of ice. The ships were often stopped while measurements of the ice were taken, before the *Manhattan* attacked the pack. Scientists on the *John A. Macdonald* also carried out experiments of their own. On 26 October 1969 the eastward transit had been made and the *Manhattan's* trials for that year were officially completed.

In the spring of 1970, the *Manhattan* returned to the Arctic to complete her trials. The objective was to establish power requirements for future tankers, by steaming through ice of even thickness and not under pressure. Ice of this nature was found only in Pond Inlet at the north of Baffin Island. If enough data could be collected, requirements for larger ships could be calculated. (Humble Oil's concept at this time was for a fleet of over thirty ships capable of steaming at a steady speed through eight feet of ice). The *Manhattan's* escort in 1970 was the new CCGS *Louis S. St Laurent,* the most powerful non-nuclear icebreaker in the world. Captain Paul Fournier was in command, but fell ill early in the voyage and was replaced by Captain George Burdock. Various officials visited the ships during the trials, including Mr Nixon, the U.S. President's brother, and then Minister of Northern Affairs, the Hon. Jean Chretien. Following this, by the vagaries of the ice movement, the ships became jammed together and could not be separated without endangering both vessels. Finally after six days they got clear of each other and were able to proceed. These trials lasted from 5 April to 3 June 1970. They provided valuable data, but the concept of huge icebreaking tankers on regular passages through the Arctic has remained theoretical. Fears of the consequences of a major spill of crude oil in the Arctic have led to a preference for shipping by pipeline as being safer and more reliable. This does not rule out tanker traffic in the future. Several oil cargoes have been shipped in the *MV Arctic* (the only capable ship), from Bent Horn on Cameron Island. The use of liquid natural gas carriers is another possibility and perhaps will precede further exploitation of oil.

The Arctic Waters Pollution Prevention Act

Even though the type of traffic envisioned by the *Manhattan's* sponsors never materialized, the experiment initiated Canadian legislation to protect the Arctic environment. The Arctic Waters Pollution Prevention Act was proclaimed by the Government of Canada on 15 July 1970. The Arctic Shipping Safety Control Zones Order established in 1970 divided the Arctic into sixteen zones, based on previously observed average ice conditions. The Arctic Shipping Pollution Prevention Regulations classified fourteen categories of ship, based on hull strength and design, engine power and crew qualifications. These orders dictate the time of year during which a given type of ship may enter a particular zone. The rules have some flexibility to allow for conditions that may vary from season to season. (Only the large Russian nuclear powered icebreakers fulfill the criteria for the top three categories of ship: those capable of operating in the highest zones for all or most of the year.)

The Arctic Canada Traffic System (NORDREG), established in 1977, covers the waters of Ungava Bay, Hudson Bay and James Bay and Canadian waters north of 60 North Latitude, to all of which the Arctic Waters Pollution Prevention Act apply. It is administered from an office in Iqaluit. NORDREG issues clearances in accordance with the orders and regulations associated with the act. Shipping entering the area report their position and intentions, receive ice information and routing advice and may request icebreaker assistance.

Events in the Arctic from 1969 to 1984

In 1969 the Eastern Arctic Patrol vessel *C.D. Howe* made her nineteenth and last voyage to the Arctic. In her early years she had re-supplied settlements and carried out administrative and legal duties as well as being the principal provider of medical services to remote settlements. Later she was used for survey and scientific work in addition to her medical mission; but improved air transport and other facilities had made her service unnecessary.

In 1970 the veteran icebreaker *N.B. McLean* made her fortieth annual voyage to Arctic waters. She would be used for icebreaking in the Gulf and sometimes the Lakes for some years more. The addition of the *Louis S. St Laurent* and the *Norman McLeod Rogers* to the icebreaking fleet significantly increased the Coast Guard's ability to provide escort service and deliver cargo. Coast Guard and chartered vessels delivered 127,000 tons of cargo.

In 1971, the *Louis S. St Laurent*, carried out a combined program for the Defence Research Board and Danish hydrographers in the Robeson Channel between Greenland and Ellesmere Island and then penetrated to 82°56' N in the Lincoln Sea, the farthest north ever reached by a Western surface ship at that time.

In 1972 the Louis *S. St Laurent, d'Iberville* and the *J.E. Bernier* escorted seven cargo ships to Mokka Fjord and Eureka in the high Arctic, the largest convoy ever to penetrate such remote waters (79°35'N).

In 1973 the MV *Helga Dan*, assisted by the *Labrador,* took the first cargo of lead-zinc ore from Little Cornwallis Island to a U.S. port.

In 1974 the Lo*uis S. St Laurent, John A. Macdonald, Norman McLeod Rogers* and *Labrador* all carried out hydrographic work in addition to their normal escort duties. The *Rogers* investigated the possibility of a gas pipeline from Bathurst Island, but no suitable route was found.

In 1975 the little 26.5 metre buoy tender CCGS *Skidegate* sailed from Tuktoyaktuk for Sydney, Nova Scotia, manned chiefly by Coast Guard College cadets. Ice conditions on the north Alaska coast prevented her westward passage, but there were good conditions to the east and she proceeded through the Northwest Passage unassisted, including a transit of the narrow Bellot Strait. In the Western Arctic, the *Camsell* was seriously damaged by ice and nearly lost. The *Beaver Mackenzie,* a commercial dredge was damaged and beset by ice off Herschell Island. The *John A. Macdonald* went west to assist and extricated the dredge and brought it back to the Mackenzie River. The *Camsell* was patched up by divers and made it back to Victoria but was out of service the following year.

In 1976, the *Louis S. St Laurent* escorted the drill ship *Canmar Explorer II* westward to commence drilling operations in the Beaufort Sea. The *J.E. Bernier* was transferred

The icebreaking bulk carrier MV *Arctic*. (Fisheries and Oceans Canada FC010101)

to the West Coast via the Panama Canal to replace the damaged *Camsell* for operations in the Beaufort Sea. Conditions north of Alaska were very severe. The *Bernier* assisted CGS *Parizeau*, but that ship finally elected to turn back. The *J.E.* Bernier carried out a crew change at Cambridge Bay instead of Tuktoyaktuk as planned. Then both propellers were damaged. She returned across the north, assisted by the *d'Iberville* and the *Louis S. St Laurent*, thus circumnavigating North America. This was not the first such feat, as the hydrographic ships CGS *Baffin* and CGS *Hudson* had done so in 1970, as had the civilian diving research vessel *Pandora II* in 1975. The keel of the world's first icebreaking bulk carrier, the MV *Arctic* was laid at Port Weller Drydocks, St Catharines, Ontario in this year.

In 1977 the *Louis S. St Laurent* left Dartmouth on 17 May for an early season probe of the Eastern Arctic islands. The vessel gathered data for government and industry on the feasibility of lengthening the Arctic shipping season. The first yacht to make the transit, and the only one to do it in one season, was the Dutch ketch *Williwaw*. Its skipper, the very experienced sailor Willy de Roos, accomplished much of the passage single-handed. A Canadian yacht, the ketch *J.E. Bernier II*, Skipper Réal Bouvier, made the east to west passage over three summers in 1976–78. (This boat is preserved at the Bernier museum at L'Islet sur Mer, Québec).

The new icebreaker *Pierre Radisson*, built in Vancouver, was completed in 1978. She supported shipping activities in the western Arctic and then carried out trials in various conditions while on passage to the eastern Arctic and her home port of Québec.

While still in the western Arctic, she assisted the *Camsell* which had again been badly damaged by ice. The new specialized icebreaking cargo vessel MV *Arctic*, entered service. She was managed by Canarctic Shipping Ltd., a joint venture between Transport Canada and several shipping concerns. In her first season she took three cargoes of zinc concentrates from Nanisivik in Strathcona Sound to Antwerp and then a cargo of grain to Europe from Churchill, Manitoba. The *John A. Macdonald* was chartered to Dome Petroleum Ltd. for one year. She spent the winter of 1978-79 laid up in the north and returned to Coast Guard service in 1980.

The *Franklin*, completed on the West Coast in 1979, attempted to follow the same program that her sister, the *Pierre Radisson* had accomplished in the previous year, but lost a propeller in Viscount Melville Sound. The *Louis S. St Laurent* was sent to the rescue and escorted the *Franklin* westward. Both ships proceeded to the East Coast via the Panama Canal. In 1979, the MV *Arctic* made several trips to Nanisivik in Strathcona Sound to load zinc concentrates for Europe as well as a very late trip to Churchill, Manitoba, leaving on 17 November escorted by the *Pierre Radisson*. The *Labrador* searched for the wreck of the *Breadalbane* sunk in 1853. She had been a supply ship for one of the expeditions looking for Sir John Franklin.

In 1980, the *J.E. Bernier* again circumnavigated North America. She first went through the Panama Canal to replace the *Camsell*, which was still out of service. On 14 August at Cambridge Bay, Victoria Island, she was visited by Governor-General Edward G. Schreyer, who presented the ship with a copy of a vice-regal proclamation commemorating the Arctic Islands' centenary: the transfer of the Arctic archipelago from United Kingdom to Canadian jurisdiction in 1880. Conducting the ceremony on this ship was most appropriate, as it was Captain J.E. Bernier, then in command of the CGS *Arctic*, who on 31 July 1909 had reiterated Canada's sovereignty by formally proclaiming all the islands and territories within 141° and 60° West Longitude as Canadian territory. Continuing eastward, the *J.E. Bernier* assisted the research vessel *Pandora II*, both ships transiting the passage to the East Coast. The *John A. Macdonald*, with researcher Dr Joe MacInnis on board, returned to the site discovered by the *Labrador* the previous year and confirmed that it was the *Breadalbane* wreck. The *Louis S. St Laurent* conducted a late data-gathering voyage, researching ice pressure and ice impact on ships' hulls.

In 1981 the *John A. Macdonald* escorted a factory barge to the Polaris lead/zinc mine site on Little Cornwallis Island. The barge was beached and the area around it filled with rock and earth to incorporate it into the land. The *Sir John Franklin* (name changed from *Franklin* at the request of the crew) was used to conduct an experimental oil spill exercise known as the "Baffin Island Oil Spill." The *Pierre Radisson* conducted hydrographic surveys in Tanqueray Fjord on the west side of Ellesmere Island and landed cargo and fuel for the British Transglobe Expedition. The *Pierre Radisson* conducted further research at the *Breadalbane* wreck site. (Coast Guard's involvement in Dr Joe MacInnis' search for this ship is dealt with more fully in a later chapter). The *d'Iberville* made her last Arctic voyage.

In 1982, the MV *Arctic* arrived at Nanisvik in northern Baffin Island on 30 June, a record date for the earliest docking of any vessel. On her second voyage she arrived at the Polaris mine on Little Cornwallis Island two and a half weeks before the official opening of the high Arctic season. In this year 270,000 tonnes of lead and zinc concentrates were exported, half of which were carried in the MV *Arctic*. On most of these trips she was unassisted, although icebreakers were in the area.

In 1983 the *Des Groseilliers* made her maiden voyage to the Arctic and eight other Coast Guard ships were active in northern waters.

1984 saw the first transit of the Northwest Passage by a cruise ship, the *Lindblad Explorer*. Conditions were favourable and the ship was the first to achieve the aim of the original explorers: to make a passage from Europe, across the top of North America and arrive in the Orient. Since then cruise ships in the Arctic have become an annual event. The Coast Guard provides icebreaker support when needed. In 1984 the *Labrador* made her final Arctic voyage.

The *Polar Sea's* Transit

In 1985 the USCGC *Polar Sea* made an east to west transit. Apparently, no political statement was intended by the United States: the ship was needed in the Beaufort Sea and the Northwest Passage was the convenient and most economical way to get it there. The question of Canadian sovereignty over the Arctic waters was much in the public view at the time. As the United States does not recognize national jurisdiction over navigable straits anywhere in the world, this otherwise routine trip was seen as an issue by some elements of the press and public. The United States would not request clearance from NORDREG and the ship, although the most effective icebreaker outside of Russia, was not ice classified. The matter had to be treated with some delicacy by the Canadian Coast Guard. The ship's drawings were examined and a classification issued and by an Order in Council, a clearance given whether wanted or not. Two Canadian officials, an ice advisor and a liaison officer, traveled on board the *Polar Sea*. The *John A. Macdonald* was sent to escort her as far as Viscount Melville Sound and Canadian air ice reconnaissance was provided. On the Coast Guard to Coast Guard level, cooperation was close, as has always been the case. In heavy ice the *Polar Sea*, a far more powerful ship, courteously slowed to allow the *Macdonald* to keep up. Nevertheless, private aircraft were chartered to drop messages and Canadian flags on the American icebreaker and the matter received some notoriety at the time. Also in this year, the *Des Groseilliers* escorted the MV *Arctic* to Bent Horn on Cameron Island where she loaded 100,000 barrels of high Arctic oil. The passenger vessel *World Discoverer* was forced by heavy ice to abort plans for a transit.

On the diplomatic front, Canada began to shore up its sovereignty position. In January 1986, Canada declared that the baselines enclosing the Arctic islands as integral to the Arctic land mass and thereby officially setting the base for seaward measures of its extended jurisdiction: the Territorial Sea (twelve miles out from the baselines), the 100 mile limit under the Arctic Waters Pollution Prevention Act and the 200 mile Exclusive Economic Zone (EEZ). This also defined all waters within the archipelago as internal waters.

Beaufort Sea Oil Exploration

The *Manhattan* voyage of 1969 had anticipated oil exploration and production on the north slope of the North American continent—Alaska, the Yukon and the Northwest Territories. Serious exploration in the Canadian Arctic did not really begin until 1972, by which time the Americans had abandoned the idea of tanker transportation through arctic waters and had built the Alaska pipeline to Valdez. In Canada three major oil companies and many minor firms undertook exploration, radiating out from the delta of the Mackenzie River. The main players were Dome Petroleum (a Canadian company), Gulf Canada Resources, and Esso, which were Canadian subsidiaries of the multi-nationals, Gulf Oil and Exxon respectively. The first exploratory wells were on land, then on artificial gravel islands in shallow water. A small company, Panarctic Oils Ltd. pioneered the use of ice islands, only useful when the ice was fast to shore or jammed in inlets. Natural ice sheets were thickened by pumping water on to the surface. This technique was used from 1973 to the late 1980s, especially in the high Arctic. For floating equipment, Dome formed a subsidiary, Canadian Marine Drilling Ltd (Canmar), and Gulf formed Beaudril for the same purpose.

In 1976 Canmar acquired the drill ships *Canmar Explorer I* to *III* (and later the shallow draft *Explorer IV*) and a fleet of ice-strengthened supply tugs. Arctic Transportation Ltd. (ATL) was formed the same year and created a fleet of tugs, barges, dredges and a floating dock. (Canmar also had one). As already mentioned, the CCGS *John A.*

The Drillship *Canmar Explorer* in the Beaufort Sea.
(Fisheries and Oceans Canada FC050202-002)

Macdonald was chartered by Dome in 1977. In time, a method of protecting drillships working in offshore waters was developed. The drill vessel would be supported by a large icebreaker breaking the moving ice sheets before they reached the drillship, backed up by the ice-strengthened supply tugs, working between the large vessels, further breaking the floes into smaller pieces. In 1979 Dome built its own icebreaker, the *Canmar Kigoriak,* in Saint John and another, the *Robert Lemeur,* in Vancouver in 1982. A modified supertanker hull, the Single Steel Drilling Caisson, was also acquired. It was designed to sit on the bottom or on a dredged berm. Gulf's preferred method was to use platforms. The *Kulluk* platform was a floating rig with an icebreaking configuration all round. The *Mollikpaq* was floated into position and then settled on the sea-bed. Gulf (Beaudril) also built four icebreakers, one of which, the *Terry Fox,* was eventually purchased by the Coast Guard. The others were the *Kalvik, Ikaluk* and *Miscaroo* and they were a match for any Coast Guard icebreaker. Canmar and all participants used the caisson method: four sides of the island were floated into place, locked together, sunk and then filled in. Canmar's *Tarsuit* was the first in 1981

Beaufort Sea activity peaked in the years 1981 to 1986. Government grants under the Petroleum Incentive Program encouraged continued activity and made exploration worthwhile; but in 1985 and 1986 many of the original five-year exploration permits were coming up for renewal. The Berger Royal Commission in 1977 had recommended that a Mackenzie Valley pipeline to bring oil south not be built for ten years and that a Yukon branch line not be built at all. Environmental groups were insisting on ever more thorough assessments. Native peoples, while not against development, wanted some control over it. National attention and government support was shifting to the East Coast and the Hibernia project. Between 1987 and 1990, all the companies working in the Beaufort Sea gradually reduced their activity. The docks, tugs, drillships and icebreakers were sold.

While the Coast Guard, apart from chartering the *John A. Macdonald* to Dome, did not participate directly in these activities, it had to maintain navigation aids, help the passage of various vessels and carry out hydrographic surveys. It used one of the floating docks to repair the *Martha L. Black* in 1988. In 1992, the Coast Guard first chartered and then purchased the *Terry Fox*. Until 1997, a small amount of oil continued to be brought out of Bent Horn in the high Arctic but this is now discontinued. Arctic oil and gas is still a national asset and may be considered to be "in reserve" and will be a project for the twenty-first century.

Events in the Arctic from 1986 to 1989

In 1986, the MV *Arctic* arrived at Nanisivik in late May, the earliest ever trip by a commercial vessel. In subsequent years she took several more oil shipments from Bent Horn.

In 1987, the *Sir John Franklin* made an early voyage to assist the MV *Arctic* to Nanisivik. The *Pierre Radisson* escorted supply ships to Thule and the *George R. Pearkes* made her first voyage to the western Arctic.

In the Beaufort sea in 1988, the *Martha L. Black* sustained propeller damage twice. The first time required emergency docking in Tuktoyaktuk. A second incident occurred during her voyage westwards around Point Barrow. The *Pierre Radisson* escorted her east-about to Halifax. She returned to her base via the Panama Canal and on the way took hurricane relief supplies to Kingston, Jamaica. The new icebreaker *Henry Larsen* sailed via the Northwest Passage on her maiden voyage from Victoria to Dartmouth, conducting engine and performance trials during the trip.

In 1988, as a result of the 1986 meeting between Prime Minister Mulroney and President Reagan, a Canada–United States agreement on Arctic cooperation was signed. The U.S. pledged that "all navigation by U.S. icebreakers within waters claimed by Canada to be internal would be undertaken with the consent of the Government of Canada." (This did not imply that the U.S.A accepted Canada's claim.)

In 1989 the *Sir John Franklin* attempted an early Northwest Passage in July but was turned back by severe ice conditions. A later attempt with the USCGC *Polar Star* was successful. This transit did not attract the attention experienced by the previous *Polar Sea* passage.

The Polar 8

Studies of a design for a true polar icebreaker started as early as 1971 when the Standing Committee on Indian and Northern Affairs recommended that the Coast Guard design at least one icebreaker capable of year-round Arctic navigation. This was a reaction to the voyage of the *Manhattan* and the possibility of icebreaking tanker traffic in the near future. In 1973 the Coast Guard requested Canadian and foreign companies with proven expertise to design a Class 7 icebreaker (one capable of continuous progress through uniformly 7-ft. thick ice). By the time the designs were completed in 1975, the world had experienced the first (1974) oil crisis. With escalating costs of fossil fuel, a nuclear powered Polar 10 was now contemplated and the design of such a power plant was subsequently completed, but the Cabinet directed that a less expensive conventionally powered Arctic Class 8 vessel be constructed. With the repercussions of the 1985 USCG *Polar Sea* transit still echoing and the Navy pressing for nuclear powered submarines (with under-ice operation very much in view), Transport Minister the Hon. John Crosbie, announced on 2 March 1987 that a Polar 8 icebreaker would be designed and built at Versatile Pacific Shipyards Inc. in British Columbia to be delivered in 1992, twenty-one years after the initial proposal.

There is no doubt that the sovereignty issue was the main driving force behind the project. The United States' well known policy of recognizing only three mile territorial sea limits could not be effectively challenged but the Arctic Waters Pollution Prevention Act and traffic control regulations (NORDREG) demonstrated Canadian civil jurisdiction over Arctic waters. More year-round commercial and government activity would also show effective control. Another prominent role for the ship was to be scientific research. Yet another was to act as a showcase for Canadian technology, by participating in international studies–possibly in Antarctica, even though that would take her away from other important tasks. It was anticipated that there would be some cost recovery from this employment. The ship was seen as a platform and action centre in case of large scale Arctic emergencies, including oil pollution from blowouts and pipeline failures. Finally, she would provide icebreaker support to the larger and more powerful merchant ships that might start to exploit the Arctic commercially. It was even postulated that she might escort large tankers and bulk carriers between the Atlantic and Pacific, north of Greenland and then through the Bering Strait!

None of this was to be. The program was cancelled in 1990 before the keel was laid. The reason was primarily government cost reductions. Allied to this was the run-down of Beaufort Sea development, making extensive tanker traffic in the Arctic unlikely, together with fading concerns about the American attitudes to the sovereignty issue, exemplified by the "Icebreaker Agreement" of 1988. Although this was "the ship that never was" she was technically extremely interesting and her design and particulars are given in Chapter 5.

Northwest Passages Become More Frequent

Passenger cruise ships made the passage in one direction or the other, in 1988, 1992, 1993(2), 1994(2) 1995(3) 1996(2) and 1997(2). The *Hanseatic*, a fairly regular visitor, ran aground in Simpson Strait on 29 August 1996. CCGS *Nahidik* tried unsuccessfully to tow her off the gravel bar, then provided assistance in taking off the passengers and lightening the *Hanseatic*, after which she was re-floated with the aid of the *Nahidik* and a tug. Five yachts have transited since 1988, some taking several seasons to do so. Numbers of supply vessels and tugs have made the trip. A full Northwest Passage is considered to be between Baffin Bay and the Chukchi Sea, although purists would say between Europe and the Orient. If partial transits, for example Tuktoyaktuk to Resolute, are included there would be many more. Transits by adventurers have also increased. A three-season passage from Tuktoyaktuk to Pond Inlet, was made by Jeff MacInnis, son of researcher Dr Joe MacInnis, and photographer Mike Beedel in 1986 to 1988 this time on a 16-foot sailing catamaran, the only successful passage by a vessel without an engine. As expeditions have been mounted to the North Pole by every possible means of transport: ultra light aircraft, snowmobiles, trail bikes, dog sled, skis, and walking, so also have adventurers tried the Northwest passage in kayaks and inflatable dinghies. A windsurfer passage is only a matter of time!

The *Louis S. St Laurent* and *Polar Sea* to the North Pole

Some of the Polar 8's planned roles have been carried out by existing vessels, despite their more limited capabilities. The 1994 U.S.–Canada Arctic Section expedition is one such. The objective was to conduct a wide variety of scientific studies of the Arctic "as a system." These included: ocean circulation and geochemistry, biology and the carbon cycle, geological observations, chemical contaminants, ice physics, climate studies and the ecology of polar bears and other marine mammals. Hull monitoring as the ships encountered ice added to much data already accumulated.

The *Yamal*, *Louis S. St Laurent* and *Polar
Sea* at the North Pole, August 1994.
(Fisheries and Oceans Canada F100422)

The *Louis S. St Laurent* left Dartmouth on 1 June 1994 and proceeded to San Diego
via Panama. At Victoria on 17 July, she was joined by the USCGC *Polar Sea*, for an
official ceremony inaugurating the expedition. Leaving Nome, Alaska, on 25 July. they
proceeded towards the North Pole, conducting experiments en-route. It was not all
smooth sailing for the scientists from the varied disciplines. Some experiments had to
yield priority to others and heavy ice forced diversion from the planned track. The *Polar
Sea* damaged a propeller. Finally the Pole was reached on 22 August 1994. The next
day, as the two crews and the scientists were still congratulating each other, the large
nuclear powered Russian icebreaker *Yamal* arrived, parting the ice with ease. On coming to a halt, a colourful stage set was disembarked from the Russian ship and erected
on the ice. The purpose of the *Yamal's* visit to the Pole was to film an international television show featuring a large cast of children from countries all around the world. The
Americans and Canadians were more than a little astonished. "We didn't know what
the Pole would be like but we certainly didn't expect this!"

There was entertainment on board all the ships and Captain Phil Grandy of the
Louis, who had been sworn in advance as a Marriage Commissioner under the author-
ity of the Government of the Northwest Territories, performed a marriage ceremony for
Douglas Sieberg and Louise Adamson, both of the Institute of Ocean Sciences in
Sidney, British Columbia. In view of the *Polar Sea's* damaged propeller, it was decided
to accept the *Yamal's* offer to shepherd the American and Canadian ships to the
Atlantic near Spitzbergen (the *Yamal's* route home), instead of returning to Alaska as
planned. The voyage continued to Halifax and Boston via Iceland. This was the first
visit to the North Pole by U.S. and Canadian surface ships, although Russian, German

and Swedish vessels had been there and nuclear submarines of the American, British and, presumably, Soviet and Russian navies had made several visits.

1997 and 1998: The North Water Project

Arctic polynyas are recurring large areas of open water in ice-covered seas. They serve as feeding, mating, spawning and over-wintering grounds for key Arctic species of mammals, birds and fish. They are believed to be the focal points for the production of microalgae and zooplankton that are the basis of the Arctic food chain. There are three main large polynyas. One is in the Bering Sea. Another is in the Greenland Sea and was the destination for scientific expeditions in 1992 and 1993. For the furthering of research in the North Water, which lies between Greenland and Canada from Latitude 72°30' to 78°30' approximately, the Coast Guard provided the *Louis S. St Laurent* in August and September 1997, and the *Pierre Radisson* in April and May and again in August 1998. Among other tasks, deep moored scientific buoys were installed on one expedition and recovered on the next. Leadership of the international expedition was provided by the biology department of Université Laval, Québec. The study of the Northwest Water, off Alaska, will be facilitated by United States Coast Guard ships.

1998: The SHEBA and JOIS Projects

SHEBA stands for Surface Heat Budget of the Arctic and was primarily a U.S. National Research Council scientific program directed from the University of Washington at Seattle, with participation from Canada, Japan and the Netherlands. It was combined with a Canada/U.S. Joint Ocean Ice Studies (JOIS) project. Because of Canada's need to increase its knowledge of Arctic waters and ecology and better under-

The *Des Groseilliers* and the SHEBA ice camp, 1998.

stand the relationship between climate change and biology, the Coast Guard provided the project with its platform, the CCGS *Des Groseilliers*, and supporting vessels, *Louis S. St Laurent* and also the *Sir Wilfrid Laurier* if she was required.

In the summer of 1997 the *Des Groseilliers* and the *Louis S. St Laurent* transited the Northwest Passage to rendezvous with the *Sir Wilfrid Laurier* in Alaskan waters. All ships participated in some aspects of the various scientific programs en route. The *St Laurent* then escorted the *Des Groseilliers* to a drift station in about 75°15' North, 142°30' West, arriving on 2 October 1997, where her main engines were shut down and the ship with a minimum crew and an international team of scientists was left to drift for a year with the ice pack. The *St Laurent* left to return East after fueling and storing the *Des Groseilliers* to maximum capacity. The ship was not entirely isolated. Landing strips were constructed on the ice and fairly frequent trips by Twin Otter aircraft brought equipment and exchanged scientific personnel. The Coast Guard crew of sixteen was changed every six weeks. Communication with the ship went smoothly during the winter of 1997/98 but in the spring, the ice sheets thinned and started to crack. The improvised airfields could no longer be used. To make matters worse, the ship did not drift in the semi-circular pattern that had been predicted but towards Russian waters. Crew changes in late June/early July, mid-August and late September were accomplished by helicopters from the USCGC *Polar Sea* and *Polar Star*. Severe ice conditions, a long transit time and a critically low fuel supply forced the *Polar Sea* to carry out the July transfers with its own helicopters from a position 100 nautical miles from the *Des Groseilliers,* in very foggy conditions. The August and September transfers were completed by the *Polar Star's* helicopters with the ships only a few miles apart, the ice having mostly disappeared by then.

After the *Des Groseilliers* had drifted for a year with the Arctic pack ice, ending in position 80°19' N, 165°46' W, the *Louis S. St Laurent* returned on 9 October 1998 carrying personnel to complete the crew. Exactly on the planned date, 12 October 1998, the two ships proceeded south, then eastward through Amundsen and Coronation Gulfs. Ice conditions were so favourable that both ships proceeded independently, the *Des Groseilliers* returning to Québec on 4 November. The scientific objectives had been met.

Until this project, work of this nature was usually carried out from temporary huts on ice islands, with scientists working in barely livable conditions. With SHEBA / JOIS a new standard for long term Arctic research had been established.

Changing Responsibilities

In the year 2002, responsibility for the Arctic Sealift was devolved to the Government of the Territory of Nunavut, but the Coast Guard's Arctic office continues to plan the annual operations on their behalf, and Coast Guard ships escort the commercial vessels and make deliveries to the more inaccessible destinations, as they have done in the past.

Captain Paul Fournier and officers on the bridge of the *C.D. Howe* in the 1950s. (Fisheries and Oceans Canada P010205)

Captain
Paul Fournier OC

Paul Fournier was born on 11 May 1913 in the beautiful Matapedia valley in the Gaspé.

He first went to sea in 1934 in the *Gaspé County*, a coastal cargo ship belonging to Ellis & Co. By 1941 he was a seaman on the Department of Transport icebreaker CGS *Saurel*, then based at Halifax. He was soon acting as Third Officer, and obtained his Mate's Certificate of Competency in 1946. He had obtained his Master's Certificate by 1948, when he was appointed Chief Officer of the *Saurel*.

In 1950, when the eastern Arctic patrol ship *C.D. Howe* was being completed by Davie Shipbuilding, at Lauzon, he was appointed Chief Officer, seeing the ship through the final stages of construction and fitting out. The *C.D. Howe* was based at Québec. By 1952 he was her commanding officer. In 1959 he was appointed commanding officer of the new *Montcalm*, also based at Québec.

Captain Paul Fournier with Transport Minister Paul Hellyer on the bridge of the CCGS *John A. Macdonald*, Vancouver 1967. (Fisheries and Oceans Canada P020104)

His skill as an icebreaker commander was now well recognized. In 1962, the year the DOT fleet became the Coast Guard, Captain Fournier was offered command of its newest and largest icebreaker, CCGS *John. A. Macdonald,* which was based at Halifax. In 1962, he set a "farthest north" record by reaching the northern tip of Tanquary Fjord. In 1967 a Northwest Passage transit to assist the *Camsell* in the western Arctic was followed by the rescue of USCGC *Northwind,* which had been beset in heavy ice north of Alaska. Transport minister Paul Hellyer met the *John A. Macdonald* on her arrival at Vancouver and congratulated Captain Fournier and the crew. At Seattle, the ship was given a civic reception and Captain Fournier received a citation from the U.S. Coast Guard. The return to Halifax was via the Panama Canal—a circumnavigation of North America.

In 1969, Captain Fournier in the *John A. Macdonald* escorted the tanker *Manhattan* on both westward and eastward transits of the Northwest Passage. This voyage is described in more detail in Chapter 9. Towards the end of the season, the new icebreaker *Louis S. St Laurent* entered service. She was sent to assist the *John A. Macdonald* but certain defects were found in the electric motors. These were corrected by the following year when she escorted the *Manhattan* in a second voyage to carry out a series of specific trials. Captain Fournier was in command but became ill and was relieved by Captain Burdock. For his achievements during the *Manhattan* operation, Captain Fournier was appointed an Officer of the Order of Canada.

Captain Fournier continued in command of the *Louis S. St Laurent* and was the senior icebreaker captain in the Coast Guard until his retirement in 1976. He had spent twenty-six seasons in the Arctic, never had an accident and never failed to complete an assigned mission. He is now (2002) retired and lives in the coastal village of East Petpeswick on the Eastern Shore of Nova Scotia.

Canada is a northern country and and its waters can be dangerous, especially in winter when storms are frequent. Ice fills the Great Lakes and the Gulf of St Lawrence in the winter. In the spring, pack ice and icebergs move down the coasts of Labrador and Newfoundland to their death in the warmer waters near the Gulf Stream. The Arctic in winter is closed to shipping and is usually navigable with caution only in the late summer and fall. No part of the world is more challenging to mariners, but throughout human history sailors have ventured forth, in all seasons to seek their living on the sea and, except in the high Arctic, Canadian and foreign vessels ply our waters year round. The uninformed might think that modern ships and equipment can cope with any conditions that may be encountered but, in recent years, large ships have sometimes sunk so quickly that they have only just had time to send a frantic distress call. Some have not even been able to do that and have disappearedwithout trace. Modern fishing methods and navigation equipment and diminishing resources entice small fishing craft to great distances from the shore and shelter. As mariners have for centuries, we often must utter the ancient prayer: "Oh God, thy sea is so great and my ship is so small!"

Canada is a nation with a vigorous foreign trade and important national shipping interests in the Great Lakes and coastal waters, together with a fishery on which a large part of the coastal population depends. Its airspace is filled with commercial and private aircraft. Accidents are inevitable and Canada has created a Search and Rescue to help ships, aircraft and individuals in distress. Overall responsibility for this lies with the Department of National Defence which operates three Joint Rescue Coordination Centres (JRCC), in Halifax, Trenton, and Victoria. National Defence also provides the air units: fixed-wing aircraft and helicopters, dedicated to the Search and Rescue role. The JRCC personnel include Coast Guard Officers who work closely with their Air Force counterparts. The dedicated sea elements are provided by the Coast Guard and include offshore Search and Rescue cutters, smaller cutters of various sizes, and locally manned lifeboats stationed around the coast. On the waters inside Vancouver Island, air-cushion vehicles (hovercraft) have proved to be

CHAPTER 10

Rescues and Disasters

U.S. Ambassador Adolph Schmidt and Transport Canada Minister Jean Marchand signing the Great Lakes Safety Agreement, 26 February 1973. (Fisheries and Oceans Canada E060101-004)

the most effective vehicles. In addition, when summer brings out thousands of pleasure boaters, an inshore rescue boat program, manned by specially trained students, provides rescue facilities in the most popular boating areas, and fishers and yachters with suitable craft can join a Coast Guard Auxiliary.

The boundary between Canada and the United States extends seaward from the land through the waters that divide our coastal provinces from their next-door American states (Maine from New Brunswick and British Columbia from Washington and Alaska). The boundary passes through the Great Lakes and the upper part of the St Lawrence River. Vessels navigating in all of these areas must often pass from the waters of one country to those of the other, and back again. In these circumstances, the Search and Rescue facilities must respond in the most efficient manner, regardless of where a vessel in distress finds itself. As mentioned in Chapter 2, United States Coast Guard operations in aid of ships in Canadian waters was one of the factors leading to the creation of the Canadian Coast Guard. As our own resources improved, a system of cooperation was developed. As an example of this, the Great Lakes Safety Agreement was signed in 1973. Among its provisions, prime responsibility for SAR in the waters of the

Great Lakes and their connecting rivers was allocated to one nation or the other on a practical, rather than a national basis. The two Coast Guards work closely together on the coasts as well and many joint operations are conducted.

In 1976, as a result of a study on Search and Rescue, some significant improvements were made. Two new Marine Rescue Sub-Centres (MRSC) were formed, one in Québec and one in Newfoundland. These were seen to be necessary because of actual incidents. A number of fishing vessels had got into trouble off the Gaspé coast and language problems arose when Halifax RCC attempted to work with the Gaspé fishermen. A local centre staffed by Laurentian Region personnel was seen as more responsive to the needs of the region. Similarly, another sub-centre was established in Newfoundland. These MRSCs are staffed by Coast Guard but not by Air Force personnel. In another measure, a Coast Guard Rescue auxiliary was formed, composed of owners of suitable fishing vessels and yachts. In any given area, they take turns being on call and are reimbursed for fuel and expenses during training and actual searches. While on a tasking, they are also covered by insurance. The Coast Guard instituted a national program of marine safety education and an interdepartmental committee on Search and Rescue was formed to provide advice to Ministers on SAR policy and prepare a national SAR plan.

The Inshore Rescue boat program was started in the Western Region in 1972, in response to a growing number of incidents related to a rapid increase in the number of pleasure boats in British Columbia waters. Stations were established in the areas of densest use and were in operation during the summer when the greatest number of clients could be expected. At first, 15 to 18-foot (4 to 5-metre) inflatable craft of the Zodiac type were used, a hand-held VHF set provided communications and the crew were summer students with a Coast Guard crewman as coxswain. In 1974, more stations were established and similar programs were started in the Central, Laurentian and Maritime Regions, and in the Newfoundland and Western Regions somewhat later. In the east, the crews were mostly but not exclusively college students, for whom it provided an interesting and sometimes exciting outdoor summer job. Training was provided at Coast Guard establishments in each region. Participants who came back in successive summers would become coxswains or take charge of the station. Equipment was continuously upgraded, and today the craft in use are very capable 19-foot (5.8-metre) and 24-foot (7.4-metre) rigid-hull inflatables fitted with radar, console mounted radios, and GPS navigation systems. The Inshore Rescue boats are the aspect of the Coast Guard that most pleasure boaters come into contact with. They provide 10 to 15 percent of all initial responses to incidents. In the Pacific, where the program was first instituted, the emphasis has now shifted to prevention and many of the assets have been diverted to the Responsible Recreation Boating program. Coast Guard also provides craft with crews for RCMP inspections and police work, whenever necessary. The more numerous inshore fishery patrol stations in combination with the lifeboat stations were considered to provide sufficient coverage. In other regions the IRB program continues as before.

The Canadian Marine Rescue Auxiliary (CMRA) was established in 1978 when a national organization was formed from existing volunteer rescue groups. The federal government signed contracts with each Regional Auxiliary and undertook to provide full insurance coverage while members are on a mission and to pay for out of pocket expenses like fuel. To join, a member must have a seaworthy boat equipped with good navigation and communication equipment. Training is provided in first aid and Search and Rescue techniques. Most auxiliary craft are fishing vessels or yachts. To some, the activities of the Auxiliary are more interesting than ordinary yachting. The first president of the Western Rescue Auxiliary, Mr Phil Matty, happened to live on an island at the entrance to Howe Sound. He found himself responding to most of the incidents in that area, as he was much closer than any Coast Guard unit. On the Bay of Quinte in Lake Ontario, Stu Meeks, the owner of a large, fast steel boat, voluntarily provided a full-time rescue service. This was in the early 1980s: similarly dedicated people do the same today. The Auxiliary usually responds to about 20 percent of all SAR taskings. Many of these incidents are breakdowns in inshore waters, but all could have become serious if no help had been available. In recognition of the valuable services the organization has provided, the name was changed to the Canadian Coast Guard Auxiliary (CCGA) in 1996. Members are permitted to wear a Coast Guard uniform with silver, rather than gold, buttons and insignia. This follows the practice established in the USCG Auxiliary.

In 2001, a series of special awards was instituted for outstanding performance and achievements by CCGA members.

Annual statistics are kept by the Coast Guard and the following typical years may be taken as examples. In 1982 there were a total of 8,562 marine incidents; 1509 lives were

Canadian Forces Labrador SAR helicopter. (Fisheries and Oceans Canada F244502)

saved and 231 lost. In 1990, the corresponding figures were 7,200 incidents, 2,100 lives saved and 214 lost. In 1996, there were 6,706 incidents, 3,048 saved and 187 lives lost. The number of incidents and the lives lost show a steady decline. The number of "lives saved" is perhaps debatable, but when a broken-down fishing vessel, not yet in danger of sinking, is towed in or a lost yacht is found and directed to port, their crews are counted in the total. Although they might not have been in immediate danger at the time, if left while the weather deteriorated they could well have been among those who perished. The number of people assisted each year—including those in no danger but needing some help or information—is usually over 25,000.

Among the regions, the largest number of incidents occur in the Pacific and the majority of those involve pleasure craft. In the Maritimes and Newfoundland regions, fishing vessels, not surprisingly, are the most frequently aided, while large commercial ships are less often in need of assistance, though they have provided some of the more dramatic events recorded in this chapter. As to the reasons for a distress call: medical emergencies and accidents are the most common, especially from fishing vessels whose crews undertake the most hazardous work in any industry. Mechanical breakdown comes next followed by "taking on water," which may be divided into cases where a vessel is saved by pumping, those that founder and those that capsize through loss of stability. Grounding is more common than collision. In 1996, 481 vessels went aground, 57 hit an object such as a log or ice, while only 18 collided with another vessel. Grounding is not always due to navigational errors but might be caused by mechanical breakdown or dragging an anchor. In the same year, fire accounted for 101 incidents.

Armed Forces aircraft and Coast Guard ships, hovercraft, lifeboats, and rescue craft respond to all of these types of distress call. It might be a simple matter of helping with an engine repair or a pump, but sometimes help is delivered in circumstances of extreme danger requiring skilled pilots, the Armed Forces rescue technicians who dangle from helicopters or parachute from fixed wing aircraft, captains who must drive their ships through storm conditions to reach the scene, then lower rescue craft into high seas to recover survivors and bring them back safely. Nor are the rescuers always Coast Guard ships or auxiliaries. By long nautical custom as well as international law, all ships must respond to a distress call. Fishing vessels often are the closest to others in distress and naval vessels, scientific and fishery patrol vessels, and merchant ships all do their share. The Canadian Coast Guard cooperates closely with the United States Coast Guard, especially where their zones of responsibility meet in the Great Lakes, the Pacific Coast and the Atlantic.

Some Notable Search and Rescue Events

The incidents described in this chapter have been selected to illustrate the wide range of challenges faced both by the mariner in Canadian waters and by the dedicated personnel of the Search and Rescue. Several have an unhappy ending: some or all of the crews, and sometimes would-be rescuers, were lost. When the great oil-rig Ocean Ranger sank in 1982, the impact was direct: she was operating off the shores of Newfoundland, the home of most of her crew; but we should also remember those mariners that perished on a foreign shore like the entire Taiwanese crew of the *Lee Wang Zin*, or the crew of the *Marika* swallowed up in mid-Atlantic. These were missions determinedly prosecuted but with no hope of success. In most other cases, a combination of courage, professionalism and modern equipment resulted in a successful outcome. Some of the more dramatic of these are described here. Others have been chosen because they resulted in changes to the SAR or because they were notable for the use of new equipment and technological advances. Times given in this chapter are in the 24-hour notation system as that is how they are recorded in the official incident reports.

The *Douala* (20–22 December 1963)

In the week before Christmas, 1963, the small French motorship *Douala* was located about 30 miles south of Ramea Island on the south coast of Newfoundland. At 1940 on 20 December the *Douala* radioed that she was taking water through a broken hatch and was in danger of foundering. The *Sir Humphrey Gilbert* (Captain Burdock) was in the vicinity, on its way to assist a fishing trawler farther out in the Atlantic. She was diverted to the more urgent case and was in the process of driving to windward against the gale when, at 0600 on 21 December, a barge on the foredeck broke loose, causing damage to the ship, which was also battling icing conditions. Four hours later the barge was secured and the *Sir Humphrey Gilbert* resumed the search. At 0750 the *Douala* sent a distress call but was uncertain of her position. At 1152 she radioed "abandoning ship." Several Canadian and U.S. aircraft searched the area without success. It was not until the afternoon of 22 December at 1500 that a USCG aircraft from Argentia sighted a lifeboat which the *Sir Humphrey Gilbert* was able to pick up half an hour later, and take sixteen survivors on board. At 1800 a second lifeboat was sighted by an RCAF aircraft and the fishing vessel *Rodrique* was directed to it. The total number of crew rescued was nineteen, two of whom died on passage to Newfoundland. Thirteen, including the *Douala's* master were lost. The Coast Guard ship had done its utmost in very difficult conditions and, although there had been loss of life, the combination of communications and air and sea search was considered to be a good example of the new Search and Rescue system that had been one of the reasons for founding the Coast Guard.

The *Aigle d'Ocean* (20 August 1975)

The *Aigle d'Ocean* was a very old ship built in 1919; as the *Ocean Eagle* she had once been a Canadian government vessel, used by several departments between 1927 and 1946. In the summer of 1975, she was on her last voyage delivering cargo to small communities in the Hudson Strait area. At 0800 on the 19 August she sailed from the Inuit village of Koartak at the northwest corner of Ungava Bay. The CCGS *Norman McLeod Rogers* was in the same vicinity on a scientific mission. On receiving a storm warning, the *Rogers* proceeded to Port Burwell, now called Killinek, on the opposite corner of the Bay. To this haven, the *Aigle d'Ocean* also decided to go for shelter. However, on turning across the swells she rolled heavily and a lighter, which was used to unload cargo in remote ports, broke loose in the hold. Inspection revealed a metre of water had entered, exacerbating the list and the rolling. A distress message was sent to the *Norman McLeod Rogers* which was under way in 20 minutes and launched her small helicopter to reconnoitre. At this time the ships were only six miles apart.

On the *Aigle d'Ocean*, Captain Francoeur ordered his crew of nine to abandon ship. The port lifeboat could not be used because of the list and the starboard boat flooded on being launched. Nevertheless, six of the crew jumped into it, hoping that its flotation tanks would suffice, but they were all thrown into the sea. Only four regained the ship. In the meantime, the helicopter had made two flights, one to locate the vessel and drop a liferaft (which drifted away) and a second to maintain contact and drop some lifejackets. By this time the Coast Guard ship was labouring in a heavy sea and the helicopter pilot decided to land ashore. Shortly thereafter radio contact with the helicopter was lost.

In extremely difficult conditions, the *Norman McLeod Rogers* approached the *Aigle d'Ocean,* which was now on her beam ends with the survivors clinging to the hull. A line was successfully passed to the sinking ship and an inflatable liferaft was eased down to it. Three of the desperate survivors, overcome by hypothermia, slipped away into the sea: only one was recovered by the superhuman efforts of a comrade. Finally the master and five others gained the liferaft, cut the line attaching it to the sinking ship, and were pulled back to the *Norman McLeod Rogers*. When the *Rogers* returned to Port Burwell, no sign of the helicopter was found. A Hercules aircraft subsequently located its emergency signal: it had crashed on a hillside in poor visibility, killing both crew members. This affair deeply affected the crew of the *Norman McLeod Rogers*. The helicopter crew had stretched their craft's capability to the limit to try to save lives and had lost the gamble. The seafaring community along the shores of the St Lawrence, the home of the crews of both ships, is in many ways a family. The crews of the two ships knew each other and some were related. On the positive side, five people were rescued in very difficult circumstances. Had a Coast Guard ship not been in the vicinity, all would have perished.

Rescue at Cape Beale, British Columbia (February 1976)

It was a barking dog that first alerted the lighthouse keepers at Cape Beale that the seine boat that they had seen heading for the entrance to Bamfield Inlet had not made it, but had been thrown onto the rocks at the base of the cliffs. They alerted the Bamfield rescue cutter which headed for the scene under Coxswain David Christney. It was dark and visibility was practically zero in driving snow.

The boat on the rocks was the *Bruce I* with four on board. Two managed to get into the inflatable liferaft, which was then torn away from the vessel. It was punctured as it dragged over the rocks and turned over, but reached comparatively calm water and the two occupants, skipper Stanley Beale and his young nephew, managed to hold on. They were spotted by the lifeboat, which sent in its outboard-powered inflatable dinghy and brought them back safely. The nephew was in a state of hypothermia and was taken down to the warm engine room. In the meantime, the lighthouse men on shore could hear cries for help. In fact, the other two men were clinging to separate rocks. The lifeboat was unable to get closer and help was requested from the U.S. Coast Guard. A helicopter was dispatched from Neah Bay, across the strait. In extremely difficult flying conditions in the gusts at the base of the cliffs, the helicopter spotted and rescued one of the men. It searched for the other, but eventually had to leave for Tofino airfield to refuel. As it did so, the engines failed. The helicopter auto-rotated into the water, inside the reefs. It was now the turn of the lifeboat to rescue the rescuers. Under radio direction from Alec Thompson, the lighthouse keeper, Christney felt his way between the rocks; then he sent the inflatable to the helicopter. It was driven into the helicopter's open door and the three crew members and the rescued man jumped in. Once they were in the lifeboat, Christney decided to get them to the Bamfield hospital. Then he went out again. With a Canadian Forces Buffalo aircraft providing illumination, he was able to get inside the reefs to search for the missing crew member. In the most hazardous conditions, one engine failed and debris became wrapped around the other screw. They managed to get back to Bamfield, then went out yet again in the old wooden lifeboat that was still at the station (and is now at the Vancouver Maritime Museum). This search was unsuccessful as the last man was never found. Then the old lifeboat and its tired crew was called to another position, about five miles off the lighthouse, where the Buffalo aircraft had spotted an overturned gill-netter. There were no survivors from that vessel.

Coast Guard Coxswain David Christney and his three crew members all received medals for bravery from Canada and the United States and Alec Thompson, the lighthouse keeper, was commended for his role in the rescue.

The *Lee Wang Zin* (25 December 1979)

The case of the *Lee Wang Zin* is an example of determined efforts by both Canadian and U.S. units in very severe conditions that resulted in the recovery of two bodies, although the other twenty-eight members of the crew were never found. The *Lee Wang Zin* was loaded with an ore concentrate cargo at Tasu, British Columbia. Such cargoes must be treated with care, as concentrates containing more than a certain amount of water can behave like a liquid and flow from side to side, adversely affecting the ship'd stability; but testing of the moisture content in accordance with the regulations had shown that this particular load was within the prescribed limits. Furthemore, the vessel was a purpose-built ore carrier. After leaving Tasu Sound, the ship proceeded outside the Queen Charlotte Islands, then through Dixon Entrance to Triple Island to drop the pilot. She then set out for Japan. It was Christmas Day, 1979 and a there was a southeast gale with winds gusting to 50 knots in an area notorious for steep seas because of the comparatively shallow water. At 0925 local time, Bull Harbour Coast Guard Radio heard a garbled SOS from call-sign 3ESS, which was determined to be the *Lee Wang Zin*. There followed the parallel efforts that typify these cases as search units were tasked while agents, owners, Lloyds, the pilot, diving units and anyone who had useful information or could help were contacted. The rescue coordination centre at Juneau dispatched a U.S. Coast Guard C-130 Hercules and 442 Squadron at Comox sent a Buffalo aircraft, but it was the Coast Guard's helicopter CG122 from Prince Rupert that first sighted the upturned hull of a large vessel. U.S. and Canadian aircraft continued the search for liferafts, survivors and bodies, braving extremely poor weather conditions. On the next day, the tug *Cindy Mozel* and the CCGS *Alexander Mackenzie*, which had been in refit with the crew dispersed, were able to sail from Prince Rupert. They recovered two lightly clad bodies. None of the rest of the Taiwanese crew were ever found. The hull, driven by the gale, drifted into Alaskan waters and grounded there. It was inspected by U.S. naval divers. The hatch covers were gone and the cargo had fallen out. There were no bodies. On 29 December the hull was pulled off the reef but the tow parted and it grounded again. Eventually, a U.S. Coast Guard cutter towed it to sea where it sank in 180 fathoms (330 metres). While the hull was still adrift, aircraft observed damage on both sides of what had been the underwater portion of the bow. It was possible that the *Lee Wang Zin*, off her proper course to the northward, had hit Celestial Reef, almost in the middle of the Dixon Entrance. However, the pilot had pointed out this danger to the ship's master and had noted nothing wrong with the compass. The hole in the hull seemed sharp and unlike damage caused by rocks. Whatever the cause of the damage, the forward holds had flooded and the ship capsized almost immediately. In such circumstances and weather conditions, no survivors could be expected.

The 44-foot self-righting lifeboat *Westfort*. (Fisheries and Oceans Canada F166001)

The Marine Rescue Auxiliary Proves Its Worth (4 September 1980)

On this date, in the first major rescue operation by the newly formed Coast Guard Marine Rescue Auxiliary, sixty-four Portuguese sailors were rescued from their stranded trawler, the *Maria Teixeira Vilharinho*. The ship had lost power and gone aground in Black Tickle, Labrador. Six local long-liners took part in the rescue, two of which belonged to the Marine Rescue Auxiliary. The trawler had gone aground at 0300 but in darkness and 70 knot winds, it could not be safely approached. At daylight, when winds reduced to 50-55 knots (still storm conditions), the coastal tanker *Tana Woodward* pumped some oil on the water to smooth the waves and the long-liners were able to rescue thirty-five people. The operation was directed by David Hann, the skipper and owner of the *Lori and Paul,* one of the Rescue Auxiliary members. The coastal freighter *Kloster* provided the communications link with the Coast Guard radio stations and the Search and Rescue centre in St John's. That afternoon, a Canadian Forces helicopter from Gander took off the remaining twenty-nine of the crew. The survivors were sheltered in the local school at Black Tickle, a small community of 200. The participants in this rescue were commended for their courage and seamanship and the effectiveness of the Auxiliary was amply demonstrated.

Tragedy on the Grand Banks:
The *Ocean Ranger* (15 February 1982)

On 15 February 1982, the Mobile Offshore Drilling Unit (MODU) *Ocean Ranger* capsized and sank during a severe winter storm. All eighty-four crew members perished. The U.S.-owned *Ocean Ranger* was the largest unit of its type in the world. Along with two other MODUs, the *SEDCO 107* (American) and the *Zapata Ugland* (Norwegian), it was engaged in drilling test wells on the Grand Banks and was located about 165 miles east of St John's, Newfoundland. The rig was owned by ODECO International Corporation of New Orleans and was chartered to Mobil Oil, Canada, who employed the drilling crews. The fifteen key personnel were U.S. citizens, experienced in rig operation. The rest were Canadians, mostly Newfoundlanders, and one British citizen.

A semi-submersible MODU floats on two long cylindrical hulls that always remain submerged, unless it is in dry-dock. If it is self-propelled, like the *Ocean Ranger*, there is a propulsion room at the after end of each hull together with a pump room. The remainder of the 400-foot cylinders were, in this case, divided into sixteen tanks, containing fuel, fresh water or ballast. The ballast could be adjusted to increase or decrease the draft or to change the trim of the rig. From these hulls rose a total of eight columns supporting the two decks and the drilling platform. Each of the four corner columns contained a chain locker for two of the eight huge anchors that held the rig in place, while a ballast control room was located in one of the inner columns.

Mobil had made provision for a weather forecasting service especially for the drilling area and the three rigs were prepared for bad weather. As the storm increased, all the rigs ceased drilling and hung off (disconnected) the drill string. There now occurred on the

The offshore drilling unit *Ocean Ranger*, tragically lost on 15 February 1982. (Fisheries and Oceans Canada FC050301)

Ocean Ranger a sequence of events, starting from seemingly insignificant beginnings, that lead to disaster. The *Ocean Ranger*, in fairly continuous communication with Mobil's superintendent in St John's and the other rigs, reported at 1848 local time on 14 February that a 50-foot wave had broken a porthole in the ballast control room and that there was glass and water on the deck. By 2200 one of the other rigs overheard *Ocean Ranger* personnel talking to each other on hand-held VHF sets, reporting that there were electrical shorts in the high powered cables in the control room and that the ballast valves were opening and closing by themselves. The rig started to list, or rather to trim by the head into the swells, which were up to 17 metres in 75-80 knot winds. It will never be known if action to control the ballast manually would have been effective at this stage, or if the personnel on board were capable of doing so. At 0100, the *Ranger* asked its attendant vessel, the *Seaforth Highlander*, which was 7 miles away, to close in and the other two rigs to send their stand-by vessels, the *Boltentor* and *Nordertor* while distress messages were sent and relayed. The *Seaforth Highlander* driving through enormous seas, saw a lifeboat which at first appeared in good shape. It was under power, and managed to manoeuver alongside the port side of the supply vessel. Six survivors emerged through a hatch on the opposite side but every effort to reach them failed. The boat turned over, several more people were thrown into the water, but none were able to get hold of lines, lifejackets or a liferaft deployed by the *Seaforth Highlander*. Then the upturned boat drifted away. Later the *Nordertor* found the boat, which seemed to contain bodies inside, but was unable to recover it. The *Ocean Ranger* itself was last seen by the *Boltentor* at 0230 with a 35-degree list. At that angle, water would have entered the cable lockers. The rig tipped forward and sank inverted to the bottom in 60 metres of water.

In the conditions of a winter storm on the Grand Banks, individual survival in the water is impossible. The aircraft and ships dispatched to the scene, including CCGS *Bartlett* which directed the surface search, could only recover liferafts, debris and 22 bodies. This was the worst tragedy in Canadian waters in the period covered by this book and, at a time of dawning hope for the economy because of the offshore oil development, a severe blow to Newfoundland, the home of the majority of the victims. Doubts had been expressed that lifeboats or life capsules could be launched from rigs in severe conditions, but one 50-person boat seems to have got away successfully and was manoeuvering under power. We do not know for sure if the damage it was later seen to have sustained was caused on launch or in its attempt to come alongside the *Seaforth Highlander*. The supply boats lacked effective means of getting people out of the water in rough weather. This will always be extremely difficult, but Coast Guard vessels are better equipped and practised than supply vessels were at that time and modern immersion suits give a person in the water a far better chance of survival.

Although no Coast Guard vessel was at the scene of the *Ocean Ranger* disaster in time to have rescued any survivors, the 1982 Cross Report and the 1984 Royal Commission Inquiry identified the need for advanced levels of first aid training and the use of hypothermia treatment equipment for Coast Guard personnel involved in marine rescue. In 1985, the Craigmore Report outlined specific requirements for primary Search and Rescue vessels with respect to medical facilities and equipment. These recommendations ultimately led to the Rescue Specialist program. Training began in 1993 and by 1998 these specialists were included in the crews of all primary SAR units (See Chapter 7).

Multiple Missions in the Pacific: Operations "Herring Roe" (1982) and "Hecate Strait" (April 1985)

The herring roe fishery in British Columbian waters is very lucrative and the season is extremely short. The vessels involved are not large, and the temptation for fishers to face rough conditions and to overload their vessels is hard to resist. The Rescue Coordination Centre in Victoria, the Coast Guard, and the Department of Fisheries and Oceans therefore anticipate trouble and station ships and plan air patrols before the season starts. In 1982, Coast Guard dedicated units included the offshore cutter *George E. Darby* and three 95-foot, one 44-foot and one 26-foot cutters, while three hovercraft, three lifeboats and two inshore rescue boats continued their usual readiness. Five Fisheries and Oceans vessels were committed, including hydrographic vessels. Other Coast Guard units, including the large S62N helicopter based at Prince Rupert, continued their normal duties but were briefed to participate if necessary. Military Buffalo aircraft would maintain patrols while Labrador helicopters would be ready, staging to northern fields as the fishery progressed up the coast. Argus and Tracker aircraft from Comox would also be available if necessary. In this year, twenty vessels were assisted, involving seventy-five persons. Unfortunately the first casualty was the loss of the F.V. *Ramsey Isle* with all four of the crew. The search resulting from this incident involved eight military aircraft, the Coast Guard helicopter and six vessels from DFO and the Coast Guard, as well as a shoreline search by the staff of the Estevan Point lighthouse. Other incidents included two other boats that foundered, three groundings, eight vessels broken down, one on fire, four taking in water but surviving and five medical or other emergencies. While this may seem a lot of casualties, it should be remembered that 1500 vessels took part in this fishery during the one-month season. It is described as an example of the regular work of the Search and Rescue units, albeit one that was more eventful than usual. The opening of the lobster season in southern Nova Scotia is another example of an annual event that the RCCs must anticipate.

Three years later in the same area, another group of fishing vessels were hit by a sudden storm. On the morning of 25 April 1985, over 400 vessels were in the Hecate Strait area, returning from the opening of the halibut season and seeking shelter from bad weather in this notorious piece of water between the Queen Charlotte Islands and the coastal islands of British Columbia. Eight of these 12- to 15-metre fishing vessels required assistance. One craft reported taking on water and received the attention of several aircraft and two Coast Guard vessels, but managed to reach sheltered water. A second boat reported it was leaking and again several units were diverted to its aid. The first to arrive was a USCG helicopter, which picked up the four crewmen as they abandoned ship in survival suits. Then a third boat reported she was anchored, with a fouled propeller, just upwind of some rocks. The CCGS *Point Henry* and a Labrador helicopter attempted, in winds of 70 knots, and 10- to 12-metre seas to rescue the crew. After a series of extremely close calls, one of the fishing boat's crew and the Search and Rescue technician from the helicopter, who had been injured by slamming into the fishing boat and then dropping 20 metres into the sea, were recovered by the *Point Henry*, while another fisherman and a crewman from the cutter were pulled from a drifting inflatable dinghy into the helicopter. Both units now had to leave for Prince Rupert, but the fishing boat's anchor held and in the morning her propeller was cleared with the help of the *George E. Darby*. The U.S. Coast Guard helicopters continued to assist and within an hour had rescued the crews of two more foundering boats, taken them to Prince Rupert, and then went back and picked up the crew of a third. Further to the south, two others were not so fortunate. Each vessel had two people on board, but only one survivor was picked up by CCGS *Racer*, which also found two bodies, one person remained missing. Taking part in these searches were three Coast Guard cutters, two Air Force Aurora and three Buffalo aircraft, four Labrador helicopters, one Coast Guard helicopter, a USCG Hercules aircraft and two USCG helicopters. Outstanding competence, dedication and courage were demonstrated by U.S and Canadian Air Force and Coast Guard personnel and particularly by USCG Helicopter R1434. On 3 May 1986, commendations for bravery were awarded by Transport Minister Don Mazankowski to twenty-eight United States and Canadian Search and Rescue personnel for their efforts in the rescue of the nineteen fishermen who were saved.

Death in the Gulf: the *Capitaine Torres* and the *Johanna B* (7–8 December 1989)

No better examples of the extreme conditions in Canada's coastal waters are to be found than those that prevailed in the Gulf of St Lawrence and Cabot Strait on 7 and 8 December, 1989. On that night two ocean-going general cargo ships, the *Capitaine Torres* with a crew of eighteen and the *Johanna B* with sixtenn both sank with everyone on board. The winds were from the WNW at 60 knots, the seas were 10 metres high and the temperature was 10 Celsius, causing freezing spray. Both ships were outbound. The *Capitaine Torres* was fully laden and had wooden crates containing parts of a dismantled factory on deck. At 1944 local time she reported that she had lost three cases of deck cargo overboard and that cargo in the holds had shifted. The engines had to be shut down due to air compressor problems. RCC Halifax tasked CCGS *Sir Wilfred Grenfell* to sail from Port aux Basques, Newfoundland, to assist and a Buffalo aircraft was airborne from Summerside, P.E.I. at 2200. In the meantime the ship's list had increased but no emergency had yet been declared. By 0100 the list was 30 degrees and the master declared an emergency (Mayday) and the crew attempted to abandon ship in a lifeboat and one of the liferafts. The *Sir Wilfred Grenfell* was only 3 miles away at the time but conditions were severe and visibility very limited. One liferaft with persons on board was glimpsed briefly but then lost to sight. On the next day two liferafts were recovered empty. The people in them who had been sighted had been thrown out in the tremendous seas.

When the Buffalo aircraft arrived at the position of the *Capitaine Torres* it was immediately sent to assist the *Johanna B,* which was about 50 miles to the northwest and had reported taking on water. As the aircraft closed and made contact on VHF radio, the ship declared a Mayday. In moments, she had faded from the radar screen and the radio was silent. She had been loaded with a cargo of iron ingots and went down so quickly that no attempt to abandon could have been made, even if it had been possible in the conditions.

For two more days ships, including the CCGS *Earl Grey* from Charlottetown, and aircraft searched the waters of the Cabot Strait but found only capsized lifeboats, empty liferafts, lifejackets and debris. Although this incident occurred during the 1989 ships' crews strike, the officers and crew of several Coast Guard units had immediately responded when called upon to assist their fellow mariners. In the RCCs report, called "SAR Gulf," the following observation was made: in winter storm conditions only closed survival capsules such as were being fitted on oil rigs could be launched successfully and all crew members should have survival suits.

The *Cape Aspy* (30 January 1993)

When the air temperature is below the freezing point of salt water (5°C), and the wind is strong enough to create spray, ships will accumulate ice on their rigging and decks. On the East Coast of Canada in the days of sail, a northwesterly gale in January or February was often a death sentence for crews of ships caught out in it, especially in smaller vessels. The ice both reduces the freeboard and causes the ship to become top

Arun type self-righting lifeboat *Bickerton*. (Fisheries and Oceans Canada F163504)

heavy; then if water enters the holds, the resulting free-surface liquid will inevitably capsize the vessel. In powered vessels with less rigging and the ability to choose a course to minimize spray, the risk becomes manageable, but only if every precaution is taken. The Coast Guard in several publications, for example "Guidelines for Fishing Vessels Likely to Encounter Icing Conditions," explains how to avoid icing. During training courses, and especially in the oral part of the examinations for certificates of competency, this subject is emphasized. Nevertheless, casualties still occur.

The *Cape Aspy* was a steel scallop dragger, 323 tons gross and 35 metres long, with a crew of sixteen including the master. Northwest winds and low temperatures—icing conditions—prevailed when she departed Lunenburg at 0915 on 30 January 1993. She was bound for George's Bank on a southwesterly course which gradually diverged from the coast. As the distance from the shelter of the land increased, the seas became higher and ice began to accumulate. When this happens, the crew must be put to removing it, but this was not done. By 2000 there was a further increase in wind and wave height. By 2300 a starboard list had developed and the ship was down by the head. Analysis later concluded that water must have entered the net store forward and the fish hold through unsecured hatches and air vents. At 2315 the ship rolled heavily to starboard and the list increased to 45 degrees. Water now entered the engine room and stopped the main engine and the generators. The flooding continued until the vessel sank at about 2330.

The following description is from the official report. "Fifteen of the crew members, all but one wearing immersion suits, collected at the port liferaft. Under the directions of the mate, they kicked the ice from the securing device. Difficulties were experienced in launching the liferaft. The painter was cut at its position on the deck and the liferaft started to inflate. As it was inflating, which took a matter of seconds, a wave washed up on deck and swept the crew and the liferaft over the side. Two crew members managed to enter the liferaft and they assisted others to board from the sea. The mate and three crew members could not reach the liferaft and the strong winds caused it to drift away. The master did not manage to leave the wheelhouse."

Several other fishing vessels in the vicinity searched for survivors, and three hours later the liferaft with ten men on board was found. Five hours after the ship sank, the mate, floating alone in his immersion suit, was picked up by another scallop dragger. Three bodies were later recovered; the body of the master and of one crewman who had not donned a suit were never found. Even though there were five fatalities, the value of emergency training and the increased survival chances provided by liferafts and immersion suits were well demonstrated. The well-known dangers of icing were tragically demonstrated as well as the importance of closing all openings through which water can enter a ship while it still can be reached in safety.

The *Marika* (1 January 1994)

It sometimes happens that the only indication that a vessel has sunk is a signal from an Electronic Position Indicating Radio Beacon (EPIRB). Such a signal was picked up

Rigid hull inflatable inshore rescue boat.(Fisheries and Oceans Canada MP450501)

by an aircraft on New Year's Day 1994, relayed to RCC New York and on to RCC Halifax, which took charge of the search. The position was practically in mid-Atlantic and the EPIRB was registered to the *Marika*, an 81,000 GRT oil/ore carrier bound from Sept Iles, Québec to the Netherlands with a full load of iron ore. There followed five days of intensive searching in severe weather. Six Canadian Forces Aurora and Hercules aircraft and a Portuguese Hercules from the Azores participated. The Canadian Hercules flew on to Lajes in the Azores to refuel, rejoining the search on the return trip. Eight ships of various nationalities were diverted from their voyages to participate and they were joined on the second day by CCGS *Sir Wilfred Grenfell*, which assumed control of the search area. The first aircraft on the scene had spotted lights of the type used on liferafts and lifebuoys. As the search progressed, empty liferafts and debris were found but no survivors or bodies. The *Marika* was added to the increasing numbers of ore-carrying bulkers that have sunk suddenly or disappeared at sea without trace.

The *Amphion* (10 January 1996)

The *Amphion* was a Greek-owned vessel of 14,400 GRT bound from Germany to Philadelphia. When 485 miles east-southeast of St John's Newfoundland, her captain reported she was taking water through storm damaged ventilators in two of her four holds. A northwest gale 40–50 knots was blowing with accompanying heavy seas. This message was sent at 1300 UTC on 10 January 1996, using the INMARSAT system. A USCG Hercules aircraft was in the vicinity and was tasked by Halifax RCC to observe and communicate with the vessel. The *Amphion* was seen to be low in the water. In 7

A Coast Guard Auxiliary trawler towing a fishing boat. (Fisheries and Oceans Canada MP450503)

hours, two ships arrived on the scene and stood by but the weather was too rough to take off the crew. At 0700 on 11 January the fisheries patrol vessel, CCGS *Leonard J. Cowley* arrived. She was equipped with two Fast Rescue Craft (FRC) and a crew accustomed to boarding vessels and trained in Search and Rescue missions; capabilities shared with the Coast Guard's Offshore SAR cutters. (With the unification of the Coast Guard and Fisheries and Oceans fleets, all of these vessels are now engaged in combined Fishery and SAR patrols.) The *Amphion* carried only six survival suits, but the relief Canadian Hercules aircraft from Greenwood brought twenty more suits and successfully dropped them on the ship. Although the weather had moderated, more storms were forecast and the Captain elected to seize the opportunity to abandon ship. All the crew, wearing survival suits, were transferred to the *Leonard J. Cowley* by FRC without injury. This rescue was performed well outside the range of Search and Rescue helicopters. The *Amphion* did not sink, but was brought to Halifax by the salvage vessel *Tignish Sea* on 3 February 1996.

Single-Handed Trans-Atlantic Races

One of the main principles of seamanship is to keep a proper look-out at all times. This is impossible when only one person is on board. Nevertheless, single-handed races across the Atlantic have been a regular feature for decades. One of the most eventful was the 1996 race in which 17 of the 58 boats that started had to withdraw or were involved in a distress situation. RCC Halifax was involved with nine of these and had to task Search and Rescue units in the case of six of them. Three of the skippers had to be rescued and the others were assisted to a safe port. All yachts in the race were required to have a certain level of radio and navigational equipment and trimarans (which, unlike monohull yachts, do not right themselves after they capsize) are required to have a hatch in the bottom of each hull through which the occupant can escape. This occurred in one of the cases: the skipper was found sitting safely on the upturned hull. After this, suggestions were made that the organizers should station their own rescue vessels along the route and that arrangements be made for payment for time spent by commercial or even government units. This also raises the question of adventurers of various types, including balloonists who may require assistance. But surely that is what the SAR is for: if not engaged in a real operation, it must practise and, while folly is to be discouraged, the spirit of adventure should not be stifled.

The *Vanessa* (3 October 1997)

The *Vanessa* was a small (4000 GRT) freighter carrying a cargo of fertilizer from Denmark to Colombia. The case is remarkable because it provided a successful test of some new equipment. On 23 October 1997, the MV *Choyang World* reported to RCC Norfolk, Virginia via the International Marine Satellite System (INMARSAT) that she had received a Mayday message on VHF radio from the *Vanessa*. As the position was about 480 miles southeast of St John's Newfoundland, very close to where the *Amphion* had been abandoned, RCC Halifax took charge of the operation. A Canadian Forces

A Labrador helicopter hovers over the grounded tanker *Rio Orinoco*. (Fisheries and Oceans Canada MP459001-001)

Hercules aircraft which was already airborne was tasked to search, and proceeded to St John's to refuel. The *Vanessa* was beyond helicopter range, even using the Hibernia oil platform, but a Labrador helicopter from Gander was positioned at St John's in case a Medevac from returning rescuing vessels was needed. The large container ship *Choyang World* was the first unit on the scene; it spotted a liferaft, but was unable to keep it in sight. Another merchant ship, the *Summer Wind*, arrived and, for a while, was able to maintain communication with the liferaft, learning that the ship had sunk and that nine men had managed to board one of the two liferafts and that another six were thought to be in the water. (The ship carried only three immersion suits.) The Hercules was fortunately carrying a new device: self-locating datum marker buoys (SLDMBs) which were under evaluation. These buoys transmit their position, derived from GPS, and so provide searchers with accurate drift data. The search was into the second day with no results when the relief aircraft spotted a liferaft at the extreme edge of its search pattern and the *Summer Wind* was able to rescue its nine occupants, including the master. At about the same time the SLDMB information was received. It was found that the data these locators transmitted were at variance with the predictions made by the usual drift plot, which takes into account existing weather and predicted currents (the latter being an average of previously observed data). On this evidence, RCC Halifax relocated the search area. A debris field was soon spotted and the fisheries patrol vessel CCGS *Cape Roger*, which had arrived and assumed the duties of on-scene coordinator, recovered four bodies and one survivor, the *Vanessa's* chief officer. His condition was serious, as he was suffering from extreme hypothermia. Two SAR technicians, who are also trained paramedics, now parachuted into the Atlantic from a Canadian Forces C-130 Hercules aircraft, where they were picked up by *Cape Roger's* FRC, and were able to stabilize the patient and gradually re-warm him to a safe temperature. Searching continued for the last missing crewman, and eventually a lifejacket identified as his was found and the search abandoned. The master and radio officer of the *Vanessa* later said that the ship's cargo had suddenly shifted, the ship had listed 50 degrees and they had been unable to get to the radio room to activate the INMARSAT distress call. The handheld EPIRB carried on board had not operated, and it was fortunate that the ship was within VHF range of the *Choyang World*. As a result of this event, the use of SLDMBs will be increased and the time delay in receiving their information reduced.

A Hovercraft Rescue Operation (2 December 1997)

The hovercraft unit based at Sea Island near Vancouver Airport is the busiest Search and Rescue unit in the country, and it can respond to incidents over a much larger area than can a station-based vessel. This is a function of the speed of the hovercraft: up to 55 knots, compared to a lifeboat, say 15 knots. The hovercraft can also traverse mud and sand flats, shallow areas and rocks where no vessel can go. A typical operation was the call to go to the assistance of the *Pacific Charmer*, a fishing vessel which, on the night of 2 December 1997, suddenly capsized in the Pylades Channel in the Gulf Islands of British Columbia. There had been no time to send a radio distress call, but the signal from the vessel's electronic locating transmitter was picked up by the Search and Rescue Satellite System (SARSAT), and at 0200 the stand-by hovercraft *CG 039* departed the Sea Island, Vancouver, base and dashed across the Strait of Georgia, around Saturna Island into Pylades Channel and arrived on scene at 0255. The area was littered with debris—objects that had floated off the boat. After 15 minutes, one survivor was spotted clinging to wreckage. Next, the strobe light of the vessel's EPIRB attracted attention to a second survivor who was holding it. Then a third was rescued from rocks on shore. All were treated for severe hypothermia. At 0333 a USCG heli-

The Canadian Forces' new long-range Cormorant SAR helicopter. (Marcellino Dino F245002)

copter arrived and at 0340 Coast Guard rescue boat *CG 701* with an extra crewman and medical supplies came on scene. The helicopter then spotted another person in the water and directed the *CG 039* to him. At 0352, the hovercraft left to take the four survivors to the town of Ladysmith, leaving the *CG 701* and the helicopter looking for a fifth crew member, known to have been on board. A crewman from the hovercraft accompanied the survivors to the hospital in the ambulance, continuing to treat the worst case for hypothermia, but unfortunately the last person to be rescued succumbed. At 0450 the hovercraft returned to the search area and at 0648 a fishing vessel that had joined the search found the missing man floating face down. At 0740 the hovercraft was back at its base and the body of the victim was handed over to the coroner. The operation had lasted 5 hours and 40 minutes. The total was two lost and three saved.

The *Flare* (16 January 1998)

At 0843 UTC, or 0513 local time, a hurried and incomplete VHF call was received at Stephenville Marine Communications and Traffic Services Centre via the remote VHF site at Ramea, Newfoundland. No name or call-sign was given and communications were immediately lost. Then an INMARSAT distress call that had been received in Norfolk Virginia was relayed to RCC Halifax and on to the MRSC in St John's. This identified the ship as the bulk carrier *Flare*, in ballast, which was proceeding at 3 knots into a 40-50 knot gale with 6-metre seas. Based on an earlier ECAREG traffic management system report, the INMARSAT position did not appear to be correct, but the VHF call had, at least, given a latitude and based on this a position was estimated. Ships and aircraft were despatched to the scene: a merchant ship, the CG lifeboats *W.G. George* and *W. Jackman*, a Labrador helicopter from Gander and a Hercules from Greenwood; but it was a Coast Guard surveillance King Air fisheries and pollution patrol aircraft that spotted the bow section of the ship at 1329 UTC, then four survivors on an upturned lifeboat. At 1423 they were rescued by the Labrador helicopter and taken to St Pierre for treatment. Other units, including HMCS *Montreal* arrived on scene and the search continued. There were no more survivors. Fifteen bodies were found amid heavy oil contamination and recovered with difficulty. Six were not located.

The survivors reported that the ship had suddenly broken in two and the bow section had swung completely around, so that it was initially thought to be another ship with which they had collided. Everybody was on the stern section, which was abandoned in some confusion and soon sank. (The large bow section remained afloat for about 90 hours before eventually sinking.) Six survival suits were carried, but they were not used. The EPIRB, which would have given an immediate exact position, did not operate for unknown reasons, as in the case of the *Vanessa*. It was found that the position error in the INMARSAT call was the result of a software problem in the shore station, but this did not affect the time of arrival of the search units. The *Flare* was added to the list of lost bulk carriers, a class of ship that suffers a disproportionate number of casualties of a type unknown in the days of smaller, more traditionally designed cargo carriers. The

CCGS *Racer* and *Ready* assist the burning Norwegian cruise ship *Meteor* in the Strait of Georgia on 23 May 1971. (Fisheries and Oceans Canada MP457101)

survivors owe their lives to the sharp ears of the Stephenville Coast Guard radio operator and the efficiency of the Canadian Search and Rescue system.

The Coast Guard Auxiliary's Longest Mission: the *Royal Mariner* (21 to 25 August 2001)

At about 1330 UTC on 21 August 2001, the crew of the fishing vessel *Royal Mariner*
advised Iqaluit MCTS station that they were disabled in Baffin Bay due to transmission
failure. Storm force winds were predicted and they required assistance. The JRCC in
Halifax was informed and a General Marine Broadcast message was issued by Iqaluit
MCTS. This was answered by the fishing vessel *Newfoundland Tradition,* a member of
the Coast Guard Auxiliary, which accepted the task of towing the *Royal Mariner* to the
nearest safe haven—Nuuk in Greenland. It was not until the following day that a rendezvous was made. The weather at the scene featured 40 knot winds and 5 metre seas
but the tow commenced at 1640 UTC on 22 August. By 2230, towing speed was
reduced to 5 knots. Conditions worsened and on the 23rd at 1550, the towline parted.
The towline was re-attached after 30 minutes but by 2120 the towing speed was reduced
to 2 knots due to the heavy swell. Conditions scarcely improved until the two ships
entered Nuuk Fiord at 0300 on 25 August. They secured alongside two hours later. The
total duration of this incident was 113 hours and the total compensation paid to the
Newfoundland Tradition was $20,000, the highest ever paid to a CCGA vessel for par-
ticipation in an SAR operation.

The *Kella-Lee* (26 October 2001)

At about midnight on 25 October 2001, Tofino Coast Guard radio received a
Mayday call from the fishing vessel *Kella-Lee.* Her skipper reported that she was sinking in a position 13 miles north of Cape Scott on the west coast of Vancouver Island.
The four-person crew abandoned ship, taking their EPIRP radio beacon with them.
CCGS *John P. Tully* was 70 miles away and imediately proceeded towards the scene but
in the conditions prevailing, a full gale with gusts up to 80 knots, could not reach the
area until 0600. A deep-sea vessel and a Buffalo aircraft joined the search, later assisted by a Labrador helicopter and two fishing boats. At 0615, the lookout on the *John P.
Tully* spotted a light. This turned out to be one of the crewmen, alone but afloat in his
survival suit. He was recovered and brought on board by the ship's rigid hull inflatable
boat. The search continued throughout the day and two more persons in survival suits
were spotted. Unfortunately they had not survived. Then at 1600 a Buffalo aircraft
located the fishing vessel's liferaft, with another survivor waving. He too was picked up
by the *John P. Tully's* RHI.

This event again showed the advantage of survival suits: although two of the crew
had not made it through the ordeal, those who did certainly would not have survived
without them. The efficiency of the the Coast Guard's RHIs that can be launched and
recovered in heavy weather, as well as the skill and bravery of their crews, was also
demonstrated.

Collisions

Collisions in Canadian waters are not as common as other types of casualty, but the consequence of a collision when one vessel is much larger than the other is usually tragic for the crew of the smaller vessel. The Coast Guard itself is not immune to accidents. On 18 March 1991, the CCGS *Griffon* encountered the fishing tug *Captain K* near Port Dover in Lake Erie. After being struck, in fog, by the *Griffon*, the *Captain K* sank with its three crew members, in about 30 seconds. In another case, on 21 July 1993, the tug-barge composite unit *Arctic Taglu / Link 100* collided with the small fishing vessel *Bona Vista* just north of Active Pass, British Columbia. The fishing vessel was rolled over by the impact and all six people on board lost their lives. The *Bona Vista* incident involved several people being trapped in the upturned hull and no one being able to reach them until a diver arrived hours later, which proved to be too late. This, and a similar case in the Fraser River, led to a pilot project for a rescue diver capability at the Sea Island hovercraft base. This is the Coast Guard's public safety diving unit.

Active Pass in British Columbia, which is S-shaped with strong tides, has been the scene of several collisions. It is on the ferry route between Vancouver Island and the mainland. Ferries pass through safely many times a day, year in and year out but on 6 February 1992 two of them, the 9300 ton *Queen of Saanich* and the 580 ton high speed catamaran ferry *Royal Vancouver* collided at the entrance to the pass, with injuries to a number of passengers and crew members.

On 31 July 1982, 9 miles southeast of Lunenburg, Nova Scotia a collision occurred in dense fog between the new trawler *Cape Beaver* and the scallop dragger *Margaret Jane*. The *Margaret Jane* sank and four of her crew were lost. The entire episode was recorded by a Swedish film crew who happened to be on board the *Cape Beaver*. At the formal enquiry it was found that "the collision was caused by lack of knowledge of, or disregard for, the internationally accepted procedures to be followed by all vessels proceeding in fog." This finding resulted in enhanced training requirements for holders of Fishing Certificates. While there have been other collisions with occasional loss of life, we can be thankful that no major disaster of this type has occurred in Canadian waters since the *Empress of Ireland* sank in the St Lawrence in 1914.

Shipboard Fires

The 1959 fire on board the *Ferngulf*, which had a significant influence on the formation of the Coast Guard, has already been described in Chapter 2. In 1971, another tragic event occurred on a Norwegian ship in British Columbia waters. On 22 May the cruise ship *Meteor* was southbound in the Strait of Georgia, returning from a cruise to Alaska. At 1:30 a.m. a fire was discovered in the crew's quarters. Fire-fighting parties, led by the master, Captain Morner, managed to rescue some of the crew and brought out fourteen bodies. Some of the casualties were trapped behind a watertight door they were unable to open. One was jammed in a porthole. As some of the crew continued to contain the fire, the lifeboats were lowered and the sixty-seven passengers were transferred to the Alaskan car ferry *Malaspina* which took them to Vancouver.

All this had occurred before the Coast Guard cutter *Racer*, followed by the *Ready*, arrived on the scene. Captain Clapp of the *Racer* was designated on-scene coordinator. He put a party on the *Meteor* to assist the crew and the two cutters used the jets from their fire monitors to cool the hull. With all the water being pumped into the ship, she began to list, but two tugs on the scene were able to pump some of the water out from holes cut in the hull. In the early evening, the salvage tug *Sudbury II* arrived and was able to put down the fire with foam. Twenty-two hours after the fire had been discovered, the tug *La Garde* left for Vancouver carrying crew members and bodies. A small party remained on board with Captain Morner and with Coast Guard and salvage personnel. Thirty-six hours later, the ship arrived at Vancouver. The coroner's jury found that "the Captain and Crew and all involved had acted in the highest tradition of the sea." However Captain Clapp of the *Racer* had realized that his ship's crew had no formal training and little expertise in fire fighting. He arranged for training for his own crew, and as a result of this incident increased training in all aspects of rescue work was provided to Coast Guard personnel.

Two fires in Canadian merchant ships resulted in changes to regulations and improved fire-fighting training for all mariners. These were the fire that broke out in the crew's quarters on the lake vessel *Cartiercliffe Hall* on 5 June 1979 while it was crossing Lake Superior, and the fire on the coastal tanker *Hudson Transport* which occurred in the lower St Lawrence on 25 December 1981. In each case, seven crew members lost their lives. In the latter case, badly executed abandon ship procedures were chiefly to blame. Recommendations from these inquiries included improved lifeboat and lifesaving equipment standards, revalidation of officers' certificates, tests for physical and mental fitness, leadership training for officers and emergency training for all crew members.

The Coast Guard lost the services of the *Louis S. St Laurent* for nearly a year when the ship suffered a serious fire on the bridge. The following account is taken from Fleet News No. 2 (1982). Just before noon on Saturday, 6 March 1982, CCGS *Louis S. St Laurent* was standing by to assist shipping through ice in the Cabot Strait, about twenty miles from the approaches to Sydney, Nova Scotia. The Officer of the Watch noticed smoke coming from the port main engine control console and sounded the general alarm. Within minutes, the bridge filled with smoke and intense heat and had to be evacuated. Fire-fighting parties arriving on the deck just below the bridge were met with a searing fire-ball travelling at high speed, although no explosion was heard. Several firefighters were injured. For many hours, far into the night, the ship's fire-fighting teams continued their efforts to contain the fire, get it under control and extinguish it. Eventually they succeeded, with the assistance of equipment supplied by CCGS *Wolfe*, which made her way through the ice to the *Louis S. St Laurent* to provide communications with the shore and any other help possible. Captain Tanner of the *Louis S. St Laurent* (who in spite of serious injuries remained in command), manoeuvred the ship by the engines to place the stern upwind. This reduced interference by smoke and allowed the helicopter deck to be used. The helicopters, carried by the two ships were used to transfer injured personnel ashore and Dr Peter Jackson, a physician from Sydney who had volunteered his services, was flown on board. When the fire was out, the *Wolfe* brought the damaged ship into Sydney Harbour. Captain Tanner was awarded a Commissioner's Commendation for his meritorious performance in directing the team effort that controlled the fire.

The Global Maritime Distress and Safety System

Satellites have provided mariners with vastly improved means of ship/shore communication. Before the advent of radio, a ship at sea was utterly cut off from the world until it reached its next port. Then, for most of the twentieth century, the radio operator with his Morse key provided an increasingly reliable method of communication. The *Titanic's* Morse Code "CQD" and the later, internationally adopted "SOS" might bring help in distress and often did. Large ships had radio operators continuously on duty; smaller ships carried only one, but a coded transmission triggered an automatic alarm on the bridge and in the radio opearator's cabin. Very high frequency (VHF) radiotelephone next provided plain language communication over short distances and medium and high frequency signals over longer distances. Like "SOS" in Morse Code, the international voice signal "Mayday" indicates distress. With satellite communication, however, voice, data or facsimile can be sent and received as if one were in an office on shore. The ship's position, derived and updated from the Global Positioning System (GPS) can be constantly monitored ashore. On the same level of technology, the Global Maritime Distress and Safety System (GMDSS) uses Digital Selective Calling and the INMARSAT network. The position of a ship in distress or calling for emergency assistance can be sent by pressing the requisite button, or may be automatically transmitted by the Electronic Position Indicating Radio Beacon (EPIRB). This alerts the shore-based rescue and communication authorities as well as all the vessels in the vicinity and provides improved means of locating survivors. It is mandatory for all ships subject to the International Convention for the Safety of Life at Sea (SOLAS) as of 1 February 1999. As well as having the equipment, ships must carry personnel trained in the system. However there are some problems when it comes to organizing searches: Digital Selective calling is not a substitute for conventional MF or VHF radio, as many vessels, especially pleasure craft, may not be fitted with it. Conscientious shipmasters should, after the implementation, continue to monitor existing distress frequencies. Nevertheless, together with such advances as the self-locating datum marker buoys used in the *Vanessa* case and immersion survival suits, these developments greatly improve chances of survival but there will always be times when no human intervention can save the crew of a ship overwhelmed by the sea.

More detailed accounts of Search and Rescue incidents can be found in the book *Heroic Rescues at Sea—True Stories of the Canadian Coast Guard*, by Carolyn Matthews (Halifax 2002).

No aspect of nautical activity has attracted so much critical public and press attention as the oil spills from large tankers that have occurred during the last four decades. Before the wreck of the *Torrey Canyon* on the Scilly Isles in 1967, oil pollution was hardly considered to be a problem. During the Second World War, thousands of ships, including hundreds of tankers, were sunk in the Atlantic. Off the coast of the United States, tanker losses were particularly heavy in early 1942, characterized by the U-boat commanders as "the happy time," but most ships were sunk in the Gulf Stream which swept the oil away into the Atlantic. All across that ocean, from 1939 to 1945, ships were being sunk, but the coasts of Britain and Europe were fortified against invasion, often mined and forbidden to the public. Oil must have washed ashore, but by the time the barbed wire, tank traps and mines were lifted and the holiday resorts reopened, there was little sign of it. Marine organisms and oil-eating bacteria in the soil will eventually cleanse the water and dispose of the oil, but when a really large spill of heavy oil occurs in a limited area, the results are serious and apparent to the public, and every effort must be made to minimize the impact on the environment and prevent future occurrences.

Canada has been fortunate in never having suffered a really large spill from a supertanker, but a smaller, very significant event—the wreck of the *Arrow* in 1970—initiated regulatory, practical and financial policies that have to date served us well. Major spills abroad, like that from the *Exxon Valdez* in 1989, have served to remind us to continuously update our countermeasures. Both of these events initiated studies that have guided Canadian policy: in the case of *Arrow* the McTaggart-Cowan committee report "Operation Oil" and the Brander-Smith Report which, while not specifically directed at the *Exxon Valdez* event was, in practice, a response to public pressure to prevent similar occurrences. Other minor spills have occurred and quick action has on several occasions prevented pollution. These events do not make headlines. Oil has been pumped from sunken ships and an oil barge, the *Irving Whale*, has been raised after 26 years in the depths. Canada's expertise has been recognized internationally, and the Coast Guard has performed clean-

CHAPTER 11

Oil Spills and Pollution Countermeasures

ups while training local workers in the Middle East and South America, and has been consulted for technical advice by other countries. Canada has also been influential in framing IMO conventions relating to tanker safety.

The *Arrow* (4 February 1970)

On the morning of 4 February 1970 the tanker *Arrow* was approaching the entrance to Chedabucto Bay, a fairly open body of water bounded on the south by the Canso Peninsula and on the north by Ile Madame and leading to the entrance to the narrow Strait of Canso separating Cape Breton from the mainland of Nova Scotia. There was a southeasterly gale blowing and the visibility was moderate. The *Arrow* was loaded with 16,000 tonnes (108,000 barrels) of Venezuelan Bunker C oil consigned to the Nova Scotia Pulp Ltd. pulp and paper mill at Point Tupper. She flew the Liberian flag (a flag-of-convenience registry) and was on charter to Imperial Oil Ltd. who owned the cargo.

The *Arrow* was a single-screw steam turbine tanker built in the United States in 1948. By 1970 she had become, by any measure, a substandard ship. As subsequently revealed during the Department of Transport investigation, she had suffered recent minor structural failures (repaired), and on this voyage from the refinery in Aruba, the radar was unreliable, the echo sounder was not working at all, the gyro compass had errors of up to 3 degrees and the magnetic compass had large deviations. At this date, the Gulf Oil refinery at Point Tupper was under construction. In anticipation of the arrival of very large tankers drawing up to 24.5 metres (80 feet), plans were in preparation to mark a deep water channel with large buoys, institute a traffic separation scheme monitored by radar and have the pilots board at the entrance to the bay. However, in 1970 none of this was in place, nor did it need to be. Chedabucto Bay is about 7 miles wide and has ample water depths for a ship the size of the *Arrow*. The only danger is Cerberus Rock which still left 6 miles of deep water to the south and is marked by a buoy. Normally this is a large lighted buoy, but during the season when ice can be expected this and other similar buoys are replaced by spar buoys, which are less prone to being dragged out of position by drifting floes. This had been done, and a Notice to Shipping to this effect had been promulgated and transmitted to ships at sea by radio, but the *Arrow* had not received it. As the ship entered Chedabucto Bay, her course was altered to the westward and speed reduced, but after an hour, when the master and third mate on the bridge were looking to starboard for the light buoy, the ship went hard aground on Cerberus Rock. The *Arrow*, because of a combination of factors including the error of the gyro, leeway on the westerly course caused by a southeast gale and, probably, a delay in turning, combined with the lack of an echo sounder or any other means of determining depth, was well north of the planned track. Not until after the ship struck was the replacement buoy seen.

The *Arrow* had taken the ground at 0930 but it was not until 3 hours later that the first report was received ashore that the ship was on Cerberus Rock and that it carried a fuel oil cargo but that no assistance was required. The subsequent period was marked

USS *Curb*, *Irving Whale* and *YMT-12* anchored at wreck of *Arrow*, 17 March 1970. (Fisheries and Oceans Canada MP050201-001)

by inaction both on the ship and ashore. At 1537 the *Arrow* reported "Ship leaking oil into the sea." The Canso radio station asked if assistance was required and was told no. Eventually, at 1725, the pilot boat, which had been waiting at the entrance to the Strait of Canso, was asked to standby to disembark the crew if necessary. During all this time, the gale persisted, and at about 1840 at high tide, with the ship lifted somewhat off the rock, she swung through 100 degrees. This movement caused fatal damage. The CCGS *Narwhal* had arrived at the scene and stood by to take off the crew, if necessary. The next morning found the deck level with the sea, the ship listing and still grinding on the rock. Large quantities of oil had escaped. As the weather was still bad, the crew was removed, mostly by the *Narwhal's* barge. On the following day, the master, the chief and second engineers, some divers from the Atlantic Salvage Company and senior Coast Guard officials re-boarded the ship. Over the 6 days various plans for salvage were formulated and abandoned. First it was intended to pump the cargo into the tanker *Imperial Acadia*, then to use explosives to separate the stern and tow it out to sea, but each day the condition of the ship deteriorated. On 8 February the ship broke in two at No.5 tank and by 12 February both parts of the ship had sunk. The wheelhouse and radar mast on the forward part and the top of the funnel on the after part remained visible above water.

As the shorelines around Chedabucto Bay began to be fouled by oil, the press and public became aware that we had a situation in Canada similar to the *Torrey Canyon* disaster off the coast of Cornwall. In March 1967 this Liberian flag tanker had attempted to pass between the Scilly Isles and Land's End and had run aground, spilling 120,000 tons of oil: the worst oil pollution to that date. The efforts to deal with the spill were largely ineffective. The Royal Air Force bombed the wreck with incendiary bombs but while some oil was burned, much more was released into the water. The toxic dispersants used to break up the oil inflicted as much damage to marine flora and fauna as the oil itself. The *Torrey Canyon* affair caused the International Marine Consultative Organization (IMCO) to start work on two conventions relating to the consequences of oil pollution, but in 1970 these were not yet in effect, although a Tanker Owners' Voluntary Organization for Oil Pollution (TOVOLOP) had been formed. Canada was now faced with a similar situation, although much reduced in scale. In the end, it was to result in new legislation and regulations, the institution of financial arrangements and the creation of an emergency measures organization in a more expeditious manner than is possible in the international arena. The lessons learned as a result of the *Arrow* wreck and the subsequent clean-up formed the basis for dealing with similar events to this day.

In Chedabucto Bay, measures to deal with the oil spill continued in a desultory fashion. This was soon to change. On 13 February the Vice-Chief of the Defence Staff authorized the military to assist the Department of Transport. Attempts at beach clean up were made by the Army, using flame-throwers. On 20 February Minister of Transport the Hon. Don Jamieson formed a task force consisting of Dr P.D. McTaggart-Cowan, Executive Director of the Science Council of Canada, Dr H. Sheffer, Vice-Chairman of the Defence Research Board and Navy Captain M.A. Martin. On 21 February they arrived in Port Hawkesbury and from this time on effective measures were taken. The subsequent operations were truly a team effort by personnel from the Navy, the Army, the Coast Guard, chartered vessels, the Department of Energy, Mines and Resources, the Department of Fisheries, the oil industry and local fishermen.

The task force set up a headquarters at a motel in Port Hawkesbury and one of their first acts was to form a Community Relations group that kept the local inhabitants as well as the press informed of progress. It was able to re-establish good relations with a population, largely dependent on fishing, which had become understandably agitated by the confusion of the first 3 weeks. The armed forces provided a communications system and a mobile control tower to assist the air operations: Coast Guard Jet Rangers for oil reconnaissance and utility craft and an army Voyageur to transport troops. A meteorological centre was established. A fleet of army trucks was made available and the armed forces logistic system as well as the Provincial Emergency Measures Organization located and provided whatever equipment was needed. One of the most important measures in the long term was the establishment of a scientific group under Dr W.L. Ford, Director of the Atlantic Oceanographic Laboratory, Bedford Institute

who worked on immediate problems as they arose and gathered data for future examination. The situation at this time was that many beaches and inlets were already fouled
by oil. Some were being protected by land-fast ice; most of Chedabucto Bay was, however, ice free. Large quantities of floating oil were being driven back and forth by the
wind and creating fresh pollution. Some escaped and ended up on Sable Island, 100
miles to the southward. The wreck still contained considerable quantities of oil which
was slowly escaping and adding to the pollution.

On the shore, the first priority was to protect the four fish-packing plants that used
large quantities of water from the bay. Three were provided with fresh-water supplies
and a filter was devised for the other, which worked successfully when a small quantity of oil appeared at the intakes. Two dams were built, one across Lennox Passage
which separates Ile Madame from Cape Breton Island, put into place while ice was still
holding back the oil, and one at Canso Tickle on the southern shore. Several commercial and experimental booms were tried to protect the inlets. None were effective in currents above 1.5 knots, but chain-link fencing with interwoven conifer boughs supported
by empty oil drums proved very effective. The oil attached itself to the spruce needles
and the boom withstood currents of up to 6 knots. Oil that did end up on beaches was
removed, so far as possible, by machinery or manually by local workers. Contaminated
soil, sand and seaweed were dumped in carefully chosen sites, but large areas of coastline had to be left to nature.

On the water, a considerable flotilla was assembled. The Coast Guard ship *Narwhal*
was used as a dormitory for the army personnel. (All available accommodation on Ile
Madame was occupied by various members of the task force.) On 1 April the *Narwhal*
was relieved by the navy repair ship *Cape Scott* which was also able to provide workshops and expert technicians and machinists. The survey ship *Dawson* brought an
oceanographic team to the area on 12 February and this ship and the *Sackville* continued to monitor the water condition from time to time throughout the operation.
Between 23 and 27 February an advanced diving team, operating from the Coast Guard
ships *Sir William Alexander* and *Rally*, surveyed the wreck. On 27 February the navy
diving tender *YMT-12* arrived with a team of divers under Lieutenant Commander D.B.
Hope. Two vessels were chartered: the American salvage tug *Curb* and the oil-barge
Irving Whale, to receive the salvaged oil, while for local work the Coast Guard provided and manned 27-foot (powered) utility (S.P.) barges and 50-foot landing craft. The
latter were chiefly used in boom construction and were not always available for transportation, so local fishing craft were chartered to transfer personnel.

Several very innovative devices were invented or received further development during the clean-up. The Scientific Coordination Staff attached to the operation designed
a net laundry, which was speedily constructed by Ferguson Industries of Pictou. Several
giant purse seines that had been badly contaminated were successfully cleaned. The
operation provided a comprehensive test of the "oilevator," more commonly known as
the slick-licker. Its originator was R.B.H. Sewell of the Pacific Naval laboratory and its

An oil containment boom being deployed. (Fisheries and Oceans Canada MP053001)

original purpose was to clear up oil spills during refueling operations in Esquimalt Harbour. The existing model was quickly obtained and others constructed. There were two types: one mounted between the hulls of a catamaran which was effective in calm, shallow water, and another at the bow of an S.P. barge, which could work in a moderate sea. An endless belt of absorbent material picked up oil which was wrung out into containers at the inboard end.

The major and potentially most dangerous problem facing the Task Force was the recovery of the remaining oil from the wreck. The services of Captain Sven Madsen of Esso International, New York, were obtained through Imperial Oil. He was appointed Salvage Master for the recovery of the oil in the after end of the *Arrow*. (All the oil in the forward section had escaped into the sea.) The *Curb* laid four-point moorings by which means the *Irving Whale* was positioned over the wreck. The Salvage Master had invented the "Madsen valve" for the recovery of oil under water. A valve was positioned on the deck by the Navy divers, holes were made in the tank top by a Cox gun which, if a heavy frame was not encountered, allowed the valve to be bolted to the deck. The valve was then opened to allow a pneumatic or hydraulic tapping machine (both were used) to be lowered through it and a hole was drilled in the deck. The tapping machine was removed, the valve closed, and a 90-degree elbow bolted on, to which a hose was attached. This had to be done twice on each of the nine tanks in the after section that contained oil. Steam from a boiler on the barge was then pumped into the tank and heated the oil enough for it to be pumped out through the other valve. This sounds simple but in fact there were many misadventures and small leaks and adjustments to be made because of the cold temperature. On 13 March oil began to flow from the wreck to the barge. After interruptions due to weather (two moorings parted in a storm on 16 March), pumping was completed on 11 April and 37,000 barrels had been recovered–about 35% of the original cargo. On 15 April the *Curb* departed for Halifax with the *Irving Whale* in tow and the operation began to wind down. The *Cape Scott* left on 22 April and by 10 May the Coast Guard and armed forces involvement for the year 1970 had come to an end. During the summer local workers continued with the restoration of beaches.

Unlike many government-appointed bodies and commissions, the Operation Oil Task Force (as it was called) was admirably prompt in making its report, which contained recommendations that Canada take initiatives in IMCO to prevent oil pollution, including the banning of all pumping out of oil or oily waste in any body of navigable water. Nationally, they recommended that control zones be established to cover the rest of the coasts of Canada, similar to that already instituted for the Arctic, that the polluter should pay the cost of clean-up, that tankers and their crews entering Canadian waters should meet certain standards and that Transport Canada and the Coast Guard should have the responsibility of dealing with major spills. To this end, major ports should keep stock piles of absorbent material, booms, slick-lickers and similar equipment The relationships between the various levels of government was also discussed. Although there were some suggestions that could not be implemented, the importance of the "Operation Oil" report should not be underestimated. The majority of the recommendations by Dr McTaggart-Cowan and his colleagues were incorporated, in one form or another, into new Canadian regulations. In July 1971, the Canada Shipping Act was amended. Pollution Prevention Regulations that had been in force since 1954 were updated. The Non-Canadian Ships Safety Order authorized Classification Society inspectors abroad and Coast Guard surveyors in Canada to issue Compliance Certificates when a ship that was to enter Canadian waters complied with a standard that was, in effect, the same as a Canadian ship. Canada's influence in IMCO (later IMO) resulted in conventions that were subsequently ratified by the member states. In 1993, the Canadian regulations were repealed when the IMO Marine Pollution Convention (MARPOL) was amended to include equivalent provisions. Research into the effects of oil pollution continued and in the Coast Guard an entirely new body, the Marine Emergencies Office was formed to address these problems.

This was not entirely the end of the *Arrow* story. During the summer of 1970, oil adhering to the sides of the tanks warmed up and rose to the tank tops. Oil was also trapped in the hatchways and small leaks had continued. In September 1971, when the water temperature was at its highest point in the year, Lieutenant Commander Hope as Salvage Master returned to the scene with Diving Tender *YMT 11*. The *Sir William*

Alexander laid moorings to enable the small tanker *Imperial Cornwall* to be positioned over the *Arrow*. (After its use as the recovery barge for the *Arrow* the *Irving Whale* had sunk, creating its own pollution story.) By ingenious means a further 6000 barrels of oil and emulsion was recovered, about half of which was Bunker C. Clean-up on shore also continued and after a few years there was little sign of the event. One of the consequences of oil spills is the effect on wild life, especially birds. Well meaning attempts to clean birds are ineffective: in practice an oiled bird is a dead bird. A few seals also perished but fishing, even for lobsters, was little affected. Nature does take care of things in the end, and the *Arrow* was not really a major spill as compared to some others. It was, however, a "wake-up call" for Canada and the Coast Guard and remains, to the date of writing, the largest oil spill in Canadian waters.

The *Kurdistan* (15 March 1979)

For the next 9 years Canada was not subjected to any major tanker accidents but two events abroad served to keep the subject in the public mind. On 4 January 1977, the tanker *Argo Merchant* went aground on Nantucket shoals. She broke up and oil was carried out to the edge of the Gulf Stream. Then on 16 March 1978 the supertanker *Amoco Cadiz* grounded on the coast of Brittany. She had broken down and was drifting, having called for a tug. When the tug arrived, it was not powerful enough to move the giant ship to safety. Large areas of the holiday resorts on the Brittany coast and further up the English Channel were fouled and no oil was recovered. This spill of 230,000 tonnes (twice the size of the *Torrey Canyon's*) was the largest to date.

Fortunately, the next Canadian experience was modest and, in the event, controllable, due in part to the lessons learned from the *Arrow* incident. The British-flag tanker *Kurdistan* was a comparatively new ship, built in Britain in 1975 to Lloyd's specification for Ice Class 1 (fit for navigation in severe ice). She was a single-screw motor tanker of 32,500 tonnes deadweight, capable of 15 knots. She was originally named the *Frank D. Moores* for the then Premier of Newfoundland, having been intended to take oil to the refinery at Come-by-Chance.

On 15 March 1979, the *Kurdistan* left Point Tupper, Nova Scotia, not far from where the *Arrow* had gone down 9 years earlier, with nearly 200,000 barrels of heated Bunker C oil, bound for Sept Iles, Quebec. She was provided with a recommended route issued by the Ice Operations Office in Dartmouth. As she approached the eastern tip of Cape Breton the *Kurdistan* was experiencing heavy weather (gale force winds and heavy swells just abaft the beam). In view of these conditions the master elected to alter course to enter the Cabot Strait shortly after passing Scatari Island, which was somewhat sooner than originally intended. At about 1240 the ship suddenly entered ice, proceeding at full speed. The master went to the bridge and ordered the engine room to prepare for manoeuvers. The ice was close packed and gradually the ship came to a halt. Engine revolutions were reduced to prevent the engine overheating and then, as no progress could be made, the engine was stopped at 1253. At 1313 the ship started to back out of the ice and by 1330 was clear. The ship then started slowly towards the southeast into the swell which had moderated but was still considerable. At 1350 the crew heard a sudden loud noise and felt a shudder. Oil started leaking and vertical cracks were noted on both sides of No. 3 tank. The amount of oil in the tanks was measured and when the ullage ports were opened, there was a marked inrush of air into No. 3 wing tanks, showing that leakage was occurring. Oil was then transferred from No. 3 to No. 4 wing tanks, which were empty. The CCGS *Sir William Alexander* was notified and proposed a rendezvous, but the *Kurdistan* had to alter to the south to reduce the effect of the sea and swell. At 1840 a further shudder was felt, and at 2130 the bow of the ship broke off, the stem rising in the air. The *Kurdistan* stopped and issued a Mayday.

The *Kurdistan* had a complement of forty-one, which included wives and children of crew members. All were in the after section which remained upright with the deck edge at water level. Everyone was mustered at boat stations and two lifeboats were launched, with some difficulty. The *Sir William Alexander*, which was only about 5 miles away when the Mayday was sent, was successful in retrieving all men, women, and children from the boats without injury, for which Captain Claude Green and his crew were later commended at the formal investigation held in the United Kingdom. The chief officer had remained on board the after section, as he had been engaged in lowering the boats. Early the next day, after fitting a stern towing line for later use, he was airlifted to safety by a Search and Rescue helicopter.

The bow of the *Kurdistan* and CCGS *Alert*. (Fisheries and Oceans Canada MP457701-003)

The two parts of the ship were now adrift. The bow section, which was nearly vertical and exhibited no ice damage, was taken in tow by CCGS *Alert* and subsequently by a commercial tug, since it was drifting towards an area of heavy fishing activity. Over the next few days it was taken out to deep water off the Continental Shelf where it was sunk by a few shells from HMCS *Margaree*. It was concluded that in those cold depths the minimal amount of oil left could do little damage. A comparatively small amount of oil washed up on the shores of Cape Breton and was dealt with by methods learned during the *Arrow* clean-up, with some refinements due to more modern equipment and better-trained personnel. The stern was taken in charge by four tugs and, escorted by a procession of Coast Guard ships, was towed to the Strait of Canso. As neither the oil refinery nor any of the other facilities in the area would allow the broken tanker at their docks, a chartered tanker was waiting. The *Kurdistan* was put alongside, her heating boilers flashed up, and her cargo transferred.

Later after cleaning and some strengthening, she was towed to Saint John, New Brunswick, and docked. After considerable investigation, the cause of the accident was determined. The root cause was improper welding at the port bilge keel The ship had been modified to carry heavy oil at a high temperature. The temperature difference between the heated cargo and icy water and the shock of entering the ice initiated a brittle fracture in the hull plating. Starting at a recently welded bilge keel, the crack was transmitted right across the ship. Later, the stern of the *Kurdistan* was towed to Europe, a new bow was fitted. and the ship continued in service under another name.

An Accident Prevented: the *Dodsland* (February 1987)

The *Dodsland* incident is one in which pollution was prevented because of prompt Coast Guard Ship Safety Branch action in light of the experience of the *Kurdistan*. The Panamanian flag tanker reported that it was taking on large quantities of seawater following rough weather in the Atlantic. The ship was diverted to Halifax Harbour for inspection and divers found four large cracks in the ship's hull. With the ship surrounded by floating booms to prevent the spread of any spill, the cargo was carefully offloaded, in a sequence that avoided overstressing the hull, after which repairs were made. Had the ship continued into the ice-filled waters of the Gulf, it would most likely have broken in two like the *Kurdistan*, spilling a large quantity of crude oil. This case is only one example of the type of effective preventative action that does not feature in the headlines but forms an important part of the work of the Ship Safety Branch of the Coast Guard, now the Marine Safety Branch of the Department of Transport.

Remote Shores: the *Nestucca* (January 1989) and the *Rio Orinoco* (16 October 1990)

On the west coast, the oil barge *Nestucca* was damaged off the Columbia River on 23 December 1988 and lost about 6000 barrels of fuel oil. Although this was not a particularly large spill, it was remarkable because of the distance it travelled and the extent of the coastline affected. Two weeks after the spill, oil in varying forms washed ashore all along the outer coast of Vancouver Island. No attempt was made to recover oil from the sea, but the opportunity was taken to experiment with various disposal methods. Napalm and flame throwers to clear oil off rocks and stony beaches were ruled out after tests but burning oiled logs on oiled gravel was successful. Contaminated eel grass was cropped at low tide. The Coast Guard's Environmental Response team and the crews of CCGS *Sir James Douglas* and CCGS *George R. Pearkes* were involved in this effort, along with every available helicopter. Much of the oil was removed using rakes and shovels. Native people in the area were particularly helpful in this task, because of their knowledge of the terrain and their appreciation of the threat to their fishing areas. However, public concern about what was seen as an unsatisfactory, slow and unorganized response, combined with frequent television news footage of oiled birds on the edge of the Pacific Rim National Park, led to considerable criticism of the Coast Guard and the federal government in this case.

The *Rio Orinoco* was a Cayman Islands registered vessel in poor condition that experienced engine trouble while en route to Montreal with a cargo of 8245 tonnes of asphalt. She pulled out of the shipping lane and proceeded to anchor off Port Menier on Anticosti Island to effect repairs. Before they were completed, a gale arose, the anchor dragged, and the ship went ashore on 16 October 1990. All the crew were rescued by Armed Forces Search and Rescue Labrador helicopters in a spectacular aerial ballet, with great waves breaking over the stranded ship.

When the gale subsided, anti-pollution measures were commenced and salvage operations were planned. A large operation was mounted with ships and equipment arriving from the Maritimes to assist the Laurentian Region ships and personnel. Anticosti residents were recruited to clean the beaches, which had been slightly contaminated, particularly the seaweed, which is eaten in winter by the island's large deer population. Asphalt, unless heated, is practically solid so pollution was minimal. Nevertheless, it was necessary to remove the cargo. The 2300 tonnes of asphalt in the side tanks was reheated and salvaged, but winter was approaching. The ship was in a position where it was protected from ice pressure, so it was decided that the remainder of the cargo, which would remain solid in winter temperatures, could be left on board and the empty tanks were filled with water to hold the ship firmly in place. The operation was resumed the following year. The remaining asphalt was heated and salvaged and on a high tide on 8 August 1991, the ship was refloated. This operation, by a contractor under Coast Guard supervision, was considered to be a technical and environmental success.

The Effect of the *Exxon Valdez* Oil Spill in Alaska

On 24 March 1989 the tanker *Exxon Valdez,* 211,000 tons deadweight, grounded in Prince William Sound, Alaska, releasing 240,000 barrels of crude oil. This was to be the most publicized spill ever and the largest in U.S. waters, although far from the largest spill worldwide. The effect of crude oil in such quantities on the pristine coast of Alaska, teeming with wildlife, was dramatic enough to generate intense public inter-

The stern of the *Kurdistan* entering the Strait of Canso. (Fisheries and Oceans Canada MP457701-006)

est and demands for clean-up and prevention, some reasonable and some hysterical. The Canadian Coast Guard was soon involved in the clean-up. A team of experts, mostly from the Newfoundland Region, was dispatched and in the first weeks of the clean-up theirs were among the few measures that were truly effective. The *Exxon Valdez* incident resulted in an emergency debate in Parliament and forced a review of the state of preparedness in Canada in case a similar event occurred here. A Public Review Panel on Tanker Safety and Marine Spills Response was appointed by the Prime Minister on 9 June 1989. It was chaired by David Brander-Smith, QC. In September of the next year the panel published its report. Among its findings were: that the capability to respond effectively to a major spill did not exist in Canada, that more oil entered the water through routine tanker operations than by accidents (and that all such spills were avoidable) and that double-hulled tankers would provide a substantially higher margin of safety in cases of grounding and collision. Chemical spills, which often posed unknown health hazards, were also considered. The panel agreed with the McTaggart-Cowan report that the Coast Guard remain the lead agency for marine spill response and that its capacity for reconnaissance, regulation, enforcement, investigation and prosecution be enhanced. Because of budgetary restrictions, not all of the report's recommendations have been adopted to the extent envisaged by the panel.

The *Tenyo Maru* (22 July 1991)
and the *Irving Whale* (1970–1997)

Two examples of the successful recovery of oil from the ocean depths deserve attention. On 22 July 1991 the Chinese bulk carrier *Tuo Hai* collided with the Japanese fishing factory ship *Tenyo Maru* and the latter sank in 152 metres of water at the entrance to the Strait of Juan de Fuca. There were eighty-five persons on board the *Tenyo Maru* and all but one were rescued. Oil from damaged fuel tanks had risen through the ship and accumulated under the deck at the forward end, which was slightly raised, and then commenced to leak. This was determined by a camera-equipped remotely operated vehicle (ROV) controlled from the CCGS *Martha L. Black.* A more sophisticated ROV with robot arms was then obtained and succeeded in inserting a hose into the flooded area. The oil was then pumped up into a floating inflated tank by a pump on the *Black's* S.P. Barge. It was fortunate that the oil had been trapped in an accessible area of the ship. In very few deep-sea shipwrecks could a robot vehicle reach the source of pollution so easily. Nevertheless, it was an ingenious solution to the problem and the first time that oil had been recovered from such a depth.

The saga of the *Irving Whale,* as recorded in press reports, would fill a book of its own. On 7 September 1970, shortly after its participation in the *Arrow* oil recovery, the *Irving Whale* while under tow sank in a position about 27 miles north of Cavendish Beach, Prince Edward Island. About 400 tonnes of its cargo of 4200 tonnes of Bunker C oil escaped. Divers inspected the wreck immediately after the loss and in the years following and found that the hull was not significantly deteriorating in the cold dark waters of the Gulf. Coast Guard ships frequently visited the site and looked for traces of leakage. It was found that even after efforts were made to block off the tank vents, occasional seepage released perhaps 30 tonnes of heavy oil each year, which might appear on beaches or affect seabirds. As time went by, fishers in P.E.I. and the Isles de la Madeleine began to worry about an eventual breakup of the barge and a sudden release of contaminant oil. In 1990, the Coast Guard began to study the feasibility of raising the barge or pumping out its contents. Eventually plans were formulated and contracts let to raise the *Irving Whale* in the summer of 1995. Some people with fishing interests now changed their mind about the salvage, fearing that the barge would break up when lifted. It was not helpful to the project when it was discovered in June 1995, just as operations were commencing, that the contents of the barge included about 4000 litres of PCB heat-transfer fluid. In 1970, PCBs were considered harmless but by 1995, they were deemed to be a dangerous carcinogen. At this revelation, environmental groups began to protest. On site, two lifting vessels from the United States and a submersible lifting barge from Europe were gathered together with a flotilla of supporting craft and the Coast Guard command ship *Edward Cornwallis.* There were delays because of incomplete preparations and difficult weather. The contracted date for the operation passed and fees began to mount. Then, on 22 August an environmental group persuaded a judge to halt the operation until the PCB danger had been properly assessed. The flotilla dispersed. Eighteen million dollars had been spent, and the *Irving Whale* was still at the bottom of the sea.

That winter technical, legal and environmental experts exhaustively examined the situation. It was concluded that the danger from the PCBs was minimal and worth the risk. In the summer of 1996 the same contractors, McAllister Towing and Salvage of Montreal and Don Jon Marine of New Jersey, resumed the operation. CCGS *Sir William Alexander* was the command ship and the *Earl Grey* prepared to surround the area with a boom, if necessary, while vessels from the Irving companies stood by with additional pollution control equipment in case it was needed. The wreck was in comparatively good condition, as the vessel had sunk gradually, over a 3-hour period, with the stern coming gently to rest at first, followed by the bow slowly settling on the bottom.

Water jets were used to create tunnels under the hull, through which the lifting wires were passed. At 0700 on 30 July the lift commenced. When the *Irving Whale* was a few metres off the bottom, robot cameras were used to inspect the bottom of the hull for penetrations. None were found. At 0845 the barge was on the surface and by 1305 it was positioned on the giant submersible barge, *Boa 10*. The lift had gone off without a hitch and with minimal leakage. The *Irving Whale* was taken to Halifax, where it was transferred to its original owner who undertook the responsibility from that point. The cargo was heated and removed and the PCBs were dealt with separately. In the Gulf, the area where the barge had rested was dredged and 3000 tons of very lightly contaminated spoil was removed. The total cost had been $42 million, part of which was subsequently recovered from the barge's owner. The *Irving Whale* was refurbished by its owners and by mid 2001 was back in service as Barge *ATL 2701*.

The Gulf War: Oil in the Arabian Sea

In 1991 as Iraqi forces withdrew from Kuwait, they fired the Kuwaiti oil wells, creating clouds of black polluting smoke, the fallout from which contaminated land and water for hundreds of miles. Even before this, in another act of ecological sabotage, the Iraqis on 24 and 25 January 1991 had deliberately released an estimated six million barrels of crude oil from refinery tank farms, offshore loading terminals and five loaded tankers. This was actually quite an effective military action as it limited the area in which the coalition ships could operate. When HMCS *Athabaskan*, with her mine-detection sonar, escorted the damaged USS *Princeton* out of the minefields off Kuwait, she had to take care to navigate around the oil slicks. Modern warships can be crippled by large amounts of oil in cooling water intakes. U.S. aircraft, in an attempt to stop some of the flow, made precision attacks on the manifolds at the refinery, which may have reduced the outflow but set the oil there ablaze.

This was a situation in which Canadian expertise could be useful, and on 29 January Minister for External Affairs the Rt. Hon. Joe Clark announced that Canada would respond positively to requests by Bahrain and Qatar for assistance to deal with the Gulf oil spill. On 3 February an assessment team comprising three members from

Environment Canada, two from the Coast Guard, one from Energy, Mines and Resources and a DND liaison officer went to Bahrain and Qatar. They assessed the risks, visited the ecologically sensitive areas and monitored the movement of the spill. These countries and Saudi Arabia had asked the International Maritime Organization (IMO) for assistance and on 7 February Mr W.A. O'Neill, a former Commissioner of the Canadian Coast Guard and now Secretary-General of IMO, formally requested Canada to undertake the task. A German team was also asked to assist. Mr Colin Hendry of the Canadian assessment team was appointed to coordinate IMO efforts in the Gulf States. On 12 February, after completing their inspection, the team briefed IMO officials in London.

In the meantime, equipment from all Coast Guard regions including booms, skimmers, boats and motors, was being assembled at CFB Trenton. This material, together with a four person Coast Guard team, was transported by six Canadian Forces Hercules flights via Lahr, Germany, and Akrotiri, Cyprus, to Bahrain. Before departing, each team member was issued with a Nuclear, Biological and Chemical Warfare kit, including a full suit and gas mask and atropine needles. The team and all the equipment arrived in Bahrain on 16/17 February. After testing, everything was placed in ready storage and a two-day workshop for twenty-seven Bahraini personnel was held on 26/27 February. While the team was engaged in this work, from 21 to 26 February Bahrain was under attack from Iraqi Scud missiles. The Chemical Warfare suits and masks were worn! On the 28th, a ceasefire was declared.

The oil had not travelled down the coast as quickly as had originally been predicted and much of it had been pushed by currents into a bay (enclosed by a long peninsula) in Saudi Arabia and did not reach Bahrain. The Coast Guard team was not called on to actually deploy their booms and skimmers but, having trained local personnel, they left the equipment (overhauled and tested) and departed for Lahr on 5 March. As a sideline to this story, Colin Hendry of the Coast Guard's Marine Environment Response branch found himself assisting the Canadian Ambassador as they followed U.S. troops into Kuwait City and became the first Canadian to re-enter the boarded-up Canadian embassy. This was the first occasion since the founding of the Coast Guard in 1962 that its members had served in a war zone.

The *San Jorge* Spill in Uruguay

The Canadian Coast Guard had become known for its expertise dealing with oil pollution and has been called in on several occasions to provide technical information, advice on procedures and sometimes to provide materials and equipment. An example of this role occurred inUruguay in 1997. On 8 February 1997 the tanker *San Jorge* went aground on an uncharted rock 20 miles SSW of Punta del Este, near Montevideo. Some of the cargo was lightered into another tanker but an uncertain amount, at least 5000 tonnes, of crude oil was spilled. About 20 kilometers of shoreline was seriously impacted and oil washed up on Lobos Island, the world's largest sea lion rookery, on which there were an estimated 280,000 sea lions and seals. Three months previously, Uruguay and Canada had signed a Memorandum of Agreement on environmental matters so, after initially attempting to deal with the situation on their own, the Uruguayan government requested Canadian assistance. Mr Gary Sergy of Environment Canada went to Uruguay as an advisor on 20 February. Technicians from the Coast Guard's Newfoundland Region arrived in Montevideo on 14 March with six containers of bagged, treated peat moss and plastic bags. (It would have been more effective if this material had arrived earlier while the crude oil was in a more liquid state). Portable incinerators had also been requested and were readied principally for the disposal of about 60 tons of carcasses of seal and sea-lion pups, but fortunately a local solution was found for this problem. The cost of the operation was recoverable from the International Oil Pollution Prevention Fund.

The Ship-Source Oil Pollution Fund

The Ship-Source Oil Pollution Fund (SOPF) was established by amendments to the Canada Shipping Act which came into force in 1989. It succeeded and took over the funds of the Maritime Pollution Claims Fund which had come into being as a result of the Arrow Task Force recommendations. From 15 February 1972, a levy of 15 cents per tonne had been imposed on all oil cargo loaded or discharged in Canadian ports (including Canadian oil cargo shipped up the pipeline from Portland, Maine). This fund is designed to meet the costs incurred by individuals, companies, or government as a result of oil spills in Canadian waters. Interest was added to the fund by the Minister of Finance and by 1 September 1976, with no major payouts, the fund had accumulated $34.8 million dollars and the levy was discontinued. On 24 April 1989 Canada became a member of the International Oil Pollution Compensation Fund (IOPC). The SOPF is now used to pay our contributions to that organization and the fund has also made payments to cover part of Coast Guard's spill response costs in cases such as the *Kurdistan* and *Rio Orinoco* described earlier in this chapter.

Preparedness and Response

Very quickly after the *Arrow* incident, the Coast Guard placed stockpiles of material at various ports and locations around the country. Major caches, at Coast Guard bases and locations like the Canso Canal have booms, slick-lickers, dispersants, absorbents and special watercraft. Trailers containing sufficient equipment to respond to a small spill are placed at lifeboat stations (because the crews are trained to use it) and other points where experience has shown that spills are likely. Coast Guard ships can embark similar containers and ships bound for the Arctic invariably do.

The Coast Guard continues to be the agency with the primary responsibility for responding to spills and has developed a system of industry-led oil spill response organizations. In 1993, Parliament approved, through amendments to the Canada Shipping Act, a requirement for all ships to pay a levy to these private sector organizations to ensure they are able to maintain the equipment and personnel required. The Coast

A Coast Guard Twin Otter aircraft on pollution patrol. (Fisheries and Oceans Canada F246001-001)

Guard regulates these organizations, and retains the authority to take charge of an incident if that is deemed to be necessary. With the transfer of the Coast Guard to the Department of Fisheries and Oceans, the regulatory aspects remain with the Marine Safety Branch of Transport Canada. The prevention of pollution continues to be discussed at bi-annual Marine Advisory Council meetings between Government and Industry representatives as well as at Regional meetings.

Legally, however, the responsibility for containing spills rests with the polluter and operations that might be damaged by oil in the water find it in their self-interest to cooperate in preventive measures. During the period of Beaufort Sea exploration, Dome Gulf and Esso jointly managed the Beaufort Sea Cooperative which had a large inventory of oil spill equipment and a dedicated response team on location during drilling operations. The Brander-Smith Report had called for increased response capability and in 1995, after two years of consultation with industry, amendments to the Canada Shipping Act (CSA) established the Oil Spill Preparedness Response Regime to supplement the Coast Guard's capabilities. The organizations have changed since 1995 and now have evolved into two major corporations, one covering the west coast and the other practically all of the rest of Canada south of latitude 60° North, except for two smaller localized areas centred on oil terminals that are supported by the major oil companies.

All potential polluters are required to share the costs through mandatory fees, which vary from region to region, depending on the amount of oil shipped. These fees go toward the capital cost of equipment and the maintenance of the private sector organizations with equipment and trained personnel. Nevertheless, the Coast Guard maintains its equipment and conducts exercises in conjunction with industry and retains primary responsibility for very large spills (10,000 tonnes and over) and areas north of 60 degrees latitude.

Pacific Coast Regulations and Agreements

Special arrangements are in effect on the west coast of Canada and in the waters between British Columbia and the United States. The wide publicity given to the *Exxon Valdez* grounding and the vulnerability of the Pacific shoreline to pollution has resulted in a U.S. initiative to provide a "Tug of Opportunity" to assist vessels in trouble. The service is provided by an independent, not-for-profit organization, and the tugs are regularly employed in other duties but are on stand-by for emergencies. Administrative costs are funded through a transit fee imposed on all vessels over 300 GRT. Although this was an initiative by the USCG under the direction of Congress, the Canadian Coast Guard and Transport Canada Marine Safety had considerable input. Tied to this concept is a Canadian Tanker Exclusion Zone. This is based on average drift rates for a vessel without power, and is tied to the response time of the Tug of Opportunity. It keeps tankers laden with Alaskan oil a certain distance from the coast, gradually converging until they enter the Strait of Juan de Fuca traffic system.

The East Coast

The need for a high state of preparedness is confirmed by the development of oil production, not just exploration, on the Sable and Grand Banks. The Hibernia wells on the Grand Banks of Newfoundland are now in production. Specially built tankers with twin screws and numerous thrusters come to a single point mooring and are held in place by dynamic positioning: in fact, by three different means of precise positioning selected from five possible methods. The Marine Institute of Memorial University in St John's, which simulated the towing out of the massive Hibernia platform before the actual event, provides special training for operators of this system. On the Sable Bank off Nova Scotia, where several drilling and production platforms are located, conditions are somewhat less dangerous than on the Grand Banks but require no less expertise and vigilance. The Marine Industry and the Coast Guard cannot afford to accept anything but the highest standards, and even so must be prepared to cope if another disaster occurs.

The Loss of the Tanker *Prestige*

A serious incident off the northeast coast of Spain in November 2002 illustrated the nature of the dilemma facing emergency response authorities in the event of a casualty to a large tanker. The 26-year-old single hulled *Prestige* ruptured in stormy weather on 13 November and started leaking oil, which soon began to affect the coast of Galicia.

A salvage company asked permission to bring the ship into a sheltered bay where she might have been surrounded by a boom while the cargo was pumped out—but what if a major spill had occurred during this operation? The Spanish authorities would not permit it and the ship was towed further out to sea, still leaking. On 19 November she broke in two, releasing more oil, and the two halves subsequently sank. It was hoped that the remaining oil would solidify in the cold ocean depths but an inspection from a mini-submarine showed steady continuing leakage.

A decision to accept, on one hand, the certainty of minor leakage in a harbour (with some possibility of a disastrous large spill) or, on the other, to opt for the certainty of a large spill out to sea that may or may not affect its own coast and fisheries (depending on where the slick drifts), is one that no national authority wishes to have to make.

In the case of the *Prestige,* the resources of the European Union were enlisted to help with the cleanup, including three large vessels, one each from the Netherlands, Belgium and France, designed for oil recovery from the ocean. Canada's resources are much more limited.

Chemical Spills

The emergency organization also has a limited capability to deal with chemical spills. Dangerous goods are carried in ships under conditions regulated by the International Maritime Dangerous Goods Code (IMDG). One of the most dangerous cargoes carried in bulk is sulphuric acid, which is explosive if mixed with seawater. It is a by-product of the paper industry and is transported in specially built tankers. Liquid natural gas, which may be in future shipped from the Arctic is another cargo requiring specialist care. A spill of two or more substances, each innocuous in themselves, can also result in a dangerous situation. Regulation of dangerous goods was the responsibility of the Ship Safety Branch of the Coast Guard, now the Marine Safety Branch of the Department of Transport. We have been fortunate that no serious chemical pollution has occurred on Canadian waterways, so far.

The weather ship CCGS *Vancouver*, in service from 1966 to 1981. (Fisheries and Oceans Canada F120501-001)

Notwithstanding Samuel Johnson's often quoted opinion that "being in a ship is like being in a jail with the chance of being drowned," even in his day adventurous souls would seek a sea career without being pressed. The conventional reason is "to see the world," but in Europe, North America and other developed countries, opportunities for worldwide seafaring in commercial craft are limited, as such ships are now largely crewed by mariners from third-world countries. Of course, the best formula for seafaring is to become very rich and own your own yacht, but only a few manage to do so. For Canadians with a desire to go to sea, opportunities still exist in coastal and Great Lakes ships, the fishing industry, the Navy and the Coast Guard. It is true Coast Guard ships seldom "go foreign," but opportunities arise from time to time and the varied nature of Coast Guard work provides more interesting and challenging work experiences than is usual in cargo ships and tankers. Crews of Search and Rescue cutters are frequently engaged in hazardous missions and have the satisfaction of completing successful rescues and sometimes the disappointment of being unable to save someone in distress. On navigation aids tenders, seamanship and practical skills are paramount. The crew must perform construction work ashore as well as handling and placing buoys and they frequently use barges and small boats for tasks away from the ship. Icebreaker work is perhaps more routine for the crew, but the bridge team has the challenging job of finding ways through the ice in the Great Lakes, the Gulf and the Arctic while escorting shipping and precision shiphandling when aiding a beset vessel. As they are large ships, they are also the ones likely to be selected for special missions.

In the 1960s and 70s, the Coast Guard had some categories of ships other than the three types mentioned above. These were the weather ships, which occupied a station in the Pacific from 1950 to 1981, the cable ship *John Cabot*, which served from 1965 to 1993, and a number of Arctic service vessels of various types that became redundant when commercial ships took over most Arctic resupply missions. An account of the work of the Coast Guard would not be complete without considering these now discontinued activities and also some of the more unusual

CHAPTER 12

A Variety of Experience

operations that were undertaken from time to time and which added variety to the daily work of our Coast Guard mariners.

The Weather Ships

Weather ships were a post-Second World War development which proved extremely valuable until superseded by weather satellites and unmanned weather buoys. They were provided by several nations and Canada's contribution was to man "Ocean Station Papa" in the Pacific at latitude 50°N, longitude 145°W. The first weather ships were ex-Navy frigates, but they were replaced in 1966 by the purpose-built *Quadra* and *Vancouver*. These were commodious ships with facilities for oceanographic as well as meteorological work. They were fitted with a radio beacon as a navigational aid to the (mostly) propeller-driven aircraft crossing the Pacific. They were in radio contact with the pilots and could confirm their true track, which was very important in the days before GPS and other sophisticated navigational systems. In case of an aircraft or ship distress situation, a plot of surface ships was maintained from the AMVER messages and the weather ships would act as Search and Rescue coordinators in case of need.

Each ship spent 6 weeks on station and 5 weeks in port, with the remaining week taken up by transit time. Oceanographic observations were taken at regular intervals going to and coming from the station. The ship going on duty relieved the other at the edge of the 10 minute square (10 by 6.5 nautical miles) station grid and then switched on the radio beacon, which was coded to indicate which part of the square the ship was in. Bathymetric observations (temperature vs depth) were taken every 4 hours. A staff of meteorologists conducted weather observations including data from weather balloons, which were launched every 6 hours. Phil Irons, who was third officer on the *Vancouver*, gives the following account: "The weather balloons were launched every six hours and these launches were important for station keeping. The ships used to drift downwind at about 2 knots, but when the balloons were launched, the ship had to be turned into the wind, and once the radar was locked on, we set course for the grid centre. This caused no little consternation among the crew, as it interrupted fishing. It was common practice to fish from the windward side and 2 knots is perfect trolling speed and deep-sea salmon tastes great! It should be noted that this was perfectly legal at the time. The Pacific Oceanographic Group, known as POGO used to run a fish derby with prizes for the largest and the most fish. The prizes weren't huge—ten dollars each—but the competition was fierce." Bird and whale watching was also carried out. These various scientific activities lost a valuable platform when weather ships were replaced by satellites.

The *Quadra* made another contribution to our knowledge of weather systems. In 1974 she operated in the Atlantic in support of the Global Atmospheric Research Program (GARP), a worldwide climatic study conducted by the World Meteorological Organization of the United Nations. The part that *Quadra* was involved in was the Global Atmospheric Tropical Experiment (GATE), which was concerned with the origin of hurricanes as well as gathering data for GARP. Approximately twenty-four ships were involved: Russian, American, British, German, French and Danish, and two from South American countries. The base for the experiment was Dakar, Senegal and the ships were stationed on a line across the Atlantic between 10 degrees N and 10 degrees S during the hurricane-forming season, from June to September. The *Quadra,* under her very experienced commanding officer, Captain Randy Dykes of Victoria BC was probably the best equipped ship in GATE because of her high definition radar capable of tracking upper-air balloons. In October she returned to the Pacific and resumed her duties at Ocean Station Papa. Eventually weather satellites and better equipment in the new jet aircraft made weather ships unnecessary. The *Quadra* and *Vancouver* were laid up in 1981 and sold the following year.

The Cable Ship *John Cabot*

Cable work is a highly specialized job requiring technical ability and very accurate navigation. From 1965 to her transfer to a subsidiary of Teleglobe Canada, in 1993, the Coast Guard operated the cable ship CCGS *John Cabot*, based in Newfoundland. She provided cable repair services in waters ranging from the Arctic to the Caribbean and from the coastal waters of Canada and the United States to Northern Europe and the Mediterranean. The ship was also an icebreaker and was employed as such in the winter when not required for cable work; hence she was higher powered than other cable ships.

The *John Cabot* often worked for the U.S. Defense Department and for NATO, maintaining cables that carry information of a military or classified nature. Her first commanding officer was Captain George Burdock and the cable officer was Gordon Warren, who had much experience in commercial cable ships. In the ship's first year of operation she was called upon to repair the cable to Thule in Greenland in the high Arctic. It was November and the winter ice was closing in. The *Cabot* found the broken cable and buoyed it, but the ice tore the buoys loose. It was apparent that help was needed and the icebreakers CCGS *d'Iberville* and USCGC *Westwind* were called on. In a 12-hour period, under the glare of floodlights, with the other two ships keeping the thickening floes away from the *Cabot's* bow, the task was accomplished to the relief of the North American defence authorities. The cable carried information from the Ballistic Missile Early Warning installation at Thule and, apparently, also the "hotline" between Washington and the Kremlin!

As well as being more powerful, the *John Cabot* was more manoeuvrable, as she was equipped with side-thrusters fore and aft. This made the ship especially suitable for her defence-related tasks where cables had to be buried to prevent damage by trawlers (or by potential foes). A cable-burying device was especially developed by the U.S. Navy for the *Cabot*. It was an adaptation of a much smaller instrument used by A.T.&T. on land. Despite the ship's capabilities, tugs sometimes had to be employed to assist in bad weather, for once a cable-laying or -burying operation had started, it had to be continued whatever the conditions.

The *Pisces III* Rescue

Because of her special equipment and the skill of her crew, the *John Cabot* was twice called upon in circumstances of a sensational nature and was able to successfully complete tasks that could not have been accomplished without her unique capabilities. In 1973, under the command of Captain Gordon Warren, the *Cabot* participated in the undersea rescue of the mini-sub *Pisces III*. The Pisces series of mini-submarines were all designed and built by International Hydrodynamics in Vancouver. Off the southwest coast of Ireland, the *Pisces III* was being operated from the British support ship *Vickers Voyager* and was employed burying existing submarine cables to prevent their damage by fishing trawls, a technique different from that used by the *John Cabot* and by the remotely controlled vehicles developed later. Having completed her task, the sub had surfaced and was being attached to the mother ship for recovery on board when in a freak accident the recovery line caught on the hatch lock of the sub's rear buoyancy compartment. The hatch was torn open, a ton of water entered and the sub plunged to the bottom, at a depth of 480 metres. It was 0922 on 29 August 1973.

The two occupants, Roger Mallinson and Roger Chapman, were still in communication with the mother ship. They turned off power and remained as quiet as possible— the more activity, the more oxygen would be used up. Two Pisces subs, *P-II* from the North Sea and *P-V* from Halifax were rushed to Cork by air to be put on board the *Vickers Voyager*. CCGS *John Cabot* had been servicing NATO cables in European waters and was alongside in Swansea, Wales. As soon as help was requested, she disembarked her cable-burying equipment and then proceeded to Cork. There she prepared to embark the *CURV III,* an unmanned recovery vehicle, with a specialist team to operate it, which had been airlifted by the U.S. Navy from San Diego, California. The *John Cabot's* arrival at the search area enabled the *Vickers Voyager* to go into port and pick up the Pisces rescue subs and their crews and return to the site. At 0214 on 31 August, with a gale blowing, *P-II* began to descend from the *Voyager* towards *P-III.* There followed a series of mishaps. The recovery line broke loose, forcing *P-II* to resurface with a damaged manipulator arm. *P-V,* crewed by Canadians, descended next but at first was unable to locate *P-III.* Then, with a repaired gyrocompass, she homed in but could not connect the recovery line to the sub's lifting device; however, a line was attached to a propeller guard and provided a link between surface and sub which aided subsequent attempts. In the intervals between the *Voyager's* attempts, the *Cabot* had used her bottom-profiling sonar to locate the precise position of the lost sub and technicians on the ship had designed and constructed a spring-loaded toggle that could be pushed into the *P-III's* open hatchway and then open like an umbrella. At 0410 on Saturday, there was another unsuccessful attempt by the other Pisces, which did not have a good means of connecting a lifting line. Time was running out for Mallinson and Chapman when the *Cabot* moved in to use the *CURV III.* It landed on the bottom and located *Pisces III* just over 100 metres ahead and closed in, illuminating the craft with its powerful lights. Using the TV cameras, the operators directed the control arm to

The cable ship *John Cabot*, operated by the Coast Guard from 1965 to 1993. (Fisheries and Oceans Canada F110101)

The Scarab ROV used by the *John Cabot* to recover the "black boxes" from the site of the Air India disaster. (Fisheries and Oceans Canada FT200101)

insert the toggle into the hatch. This was successful. The *CURV III* then moved sideways out of the way and was recovered. At 1050 the lift commenced, with Captain Warren controlling the operation from the bow of the *Cabot*. The two occupants of the *P-III* were by now suffering from cold and pounding headaches caused by the increase in carbon dioxide. As the sub was raised she bobbed up and down like a yo-yo and swung like a pendulum while the toggle made a horrible clanging sound and the trapped men feared the line would not hold. Realizing that the pitching of the ship would put stresses on the toggle, Captain Warren used the thrusters to turn the ship sideways to the swells. As the sub broke surface a strong lifting wire was attached to the main lifting eye. (An attempt to do this by divers at 60 ft. from the surface had been unsuccessful because of the motion.) At 1317 on Saturday, 1 September the sub was raised clear of the water and the hatch raised. Mallinson and Chapman had been entombed for 76 hours and had been rescued from a depth from which no one had previously been saved. Captain Warren was subsequently made a Member of the Order of Canada for his part in this operation.

The Air India Investigation

In late June 1985, the *John Cabot* was en route to the Bahamas to repair a section of cable. On board was the Scarab II, a remotely controlled submersible vehicle used to inspect, bury and repair underwater telephone cables (a more sophisticated development of the devices used at the time of the *Pisces* rescue). On 23 June came the news that Air India Flight 182 had crashed off the west coast of Ireland, presumably because of a bomb explosion. As the flight had originated in Canada and most of the passengers were Canadians, the government was eager to do everything possible to determine the cause. The *Cabot* was recalled and after a 24-hour turnaround in St John's, sailed for Cork, Ireland. In the meantime, Captain Gordon Warren and a small staff were dispatched to Cork to set up a command post and to represent the Coast Guard. While the *Cabot* was in transit, Captain Warren's team refined the search datum based on the recovery of floating debris, and under their direction a British survey vessel the *Guardline Locator* and the Irish corvette *Aoife* located the signals from the aircraft's "black boxes." The *Guardline Locator* was released and the French cable ship *Léon Thévenin*, which, like the *Cabot*, was equipped with a Scarab, arrived on scene. Some bleak moments ensued: the "pings" from the black boxes could no longer be heard; then, almost by chance, it was discovered that the problem lay in the frequency of the Scarab's listening device. This was altered and, on 10 and 11 July the cockpit voice and flight recorders were recovered. When the *John Cabot* arrived, the *Léon Thévenin* departed after transferring her extra-long Scarab cable. Detailed investigation commenced. The wreckage on the sea floor, nearly 2000 metres below the surface, had to be surveyed and photographed. Then the pieces crucial to the investigation had to be recovered. This required extremely accurate navigation, using special systems and a computer interface giving an accuracy of 125 metres during the ship's approach. (This was before the availability of the present differential GPS system.) Once the wreckage was located, transponders placed on the bottom enabled the Scarab to be controlled with the greatest accuracy in respect to the pieces of wreckage, but the recovery was time-consuming and laborious. It took repeated dives by *Cabot's* Scarab II to retrieve each piece of wreckage. Lifting bridles had to be attached, using the manipulative arms, and a subsequent dive had to be made to attach a recovery line. Large sections were buoyed off and then retrieved by the chartered Canadian off-shore supply vessel *Kreuzturm*, while small items were recovered by the *John Cabot* herself. Captain Warren and his successors at the command post, Captains McGarvie and Nash, had to exercise not only professional expertise but diplomatic skills, as a number of nations were involved: Canada, India, Ireland, the United Kingdom, and the United States, as well as the Boeing company. The whole operation took nearly six months and the performance of the *John Cabot* and her commanding officers (Captains Chafe and Vanthiel) was outstanding in terms of seamanship and skill. On her return the ship encountered severe weather and suffered storm damage and mechanical problems, but a tired ship and crew arrived home on Christmas Eve after a job well done.

Initially operated directly by the Coast Guard, in her later years the *John Cabot* remained a Coast Guard unit but was under a charter arrangement with a Crown corporation, Teleglobe Canada. She was sold to a Teleglobe Canada subsidiary in 1993. This was a distinct loss to the personnel of the Newfoundland Region as she had provided opportunities for foreign voyages and extremely interesting work. Two years later, she was again sold, to a British company, and in 1998 was operating under the Italian flag.

HMS *Fury's* Anchor

In 1824 Captain William Parry made his third attempt to gain the Northwest Passage. His ships, *Hecla* and *Fury* spent the winter at Port Bowen on the northwest coast of Baffin Island. In the summer of 1825 they worked their way south through Prince Regent Inlet when *Fury* was driven ashore by heavy ice on Somerset Island. The ship was given up as a wreck and her equipment, including a large anchor was stored on the beach. Parry and *Fury's* crew returned to England on board *Hecla,* while *Fury's* stores and boats were to prove useful to subsequent explorers.

The anchor served for many years as a landmark for Arctic navigators. It was brought to Halifax by CCGS *Labrador* in 1961 and displayed at the Maritime Command Museum. In 1972, it was placed at the entrance to the Coast Guard Base in Dartmouth, Nova Scotia, until 1981 when it was moved to the entrance to the new Coast Guard College in Sydney. In 1990, it was mounted on a specially constructed plinth on the occasion of the College's twenty-fifth anniversary. It has become a favourite place for class and other souvenir photographs.

Dr Joe MacInnis and the *Breadalbane*

The *Breadalbane* was a supply ship for Captain Belcher's expedition, which was engaged in one of the many searches for Sir John Franklin's lost expedition. In company with the naval steam sloop HMS *Phoenix,* she arrived at Beechey Island, not far from

Resolute Bay, on 9 August 1853 and began to transfer her cargo to the depot ship *North Star*. On 21 August, with most of her cargo discharged, she was crushed by the ice. The crew of 21 managed to escape as their ship quickly sank. They returned to England in the *Phoenix* along with McClure's men from the *Investigator*, another ship searching for Franklin, who had travelled over the ice from Banks Island.

Dr Joe MacInnis is a medical doctor but is best known as a marine scientist, consultant and filmmaker. In 1974 he became the first person to film and dive beneath the ice at the North Pole. He has dived in the Arctic with HRH Prince Charles and Prime Minister Pierre Trudeau. Dr MacInnis had long been interested in finding the *Breadalbane*, since a wreck in cold Arctic waters was bound to be well preserved. It was known she lay at a depth of about 55 metres, just within reach of divers and remote controlled equipment and too deep to have been damaged by the ice.

The usual ice condition off Beechey Island consists of ridged and constantly moving floes which preclude the setting up of an observation camp on the ice. An icebreaker was needed. In September 1979, Dr MacInnis was at Resolute with a photographer, a technician and equipment. He had been promised a few days on Dome Petroleum's new *Canmar Kigoriak* en route to the Beaufort Sea, but as the ship came by Resolute, they learned that it could not stop at Beechey. In the bay was the CCGS *Pierre Radisson*. Dr MacInnis boarded her and, after many telephone calls, the Coast Guard placed CCGS *Labrador* at his disposal for a few days. The *Kigoriak's* owners agreed to meet the fuel costs. The *Labrador* spent several days in an unsuccessful search, but the Coast Guard became interested in the towed side-scan sonar employed.

In the following year the Coast Guard made the *John A. MacDonald,* under Captain Steven Gomes, available. Financial contributions from several sources paid for her hire and high-tech companies contributed equipment including a super accurate electronic navigation system. This time the ice conditions were favourable. The *Breadalbane* was found; the sonar showing her to be largely intact with two of her three masts still standing. She was buoyed and underwater cameras obtained photographs.

The Coast Guard was pleased by the publicity resulting from these expeditions and in 1981 assigned the *Pierre Radisson* (Captain Pelland) to assist. This time the main tool was a remotely piloted vehicle (RPV), which could beam a colour television picture back to the ship where it was recorded. Close-ups were obtained of many parts of the ship including the hole in the hull which caused her to sink, parts of the interior, the masts and the ship's wheel. This was the end of the Coast Guard's contribution to the project but not the end of the story. In 1983 conditions were exceptionally favourable. The area was covered in smooth, land-fast ice that allowed structures to be set up and aircraft to land. Dr MacInnis was able to set up a camp and a deep-sea diving suit was used in which two divers in turn descended to the wreck. Parks Canada archeologists accompanied the expedition, and a few small material samples and the ship's wheel were recovered and delivered to their charge. The *Breadalbane* continues to lie in her chilly grave, the most northerly known shipwreck.

The German Weather Station in Labrador

Franz Selinger, a retired German engineer with an interest in Second World War naval history, was researching an article on German automatic weather stations in Arctic regions, placed there to assist the U-boats in their Atlantic campaign. Most of these were placed on islands north of Norway: Bear Island, Jan Mayen and Spitzbergen, but one had been established in northern Labrador. Mr Selinger wrote to Dr Alec Douglas, the official historian for the Department of National Defense to see if there was any information on the subject in Canadian military archives. There was none, but the log of *U-537* was found in Germany by Mr Selinger and it gave the exact location—Martin's Bay, just south of Cape Chidley at the northern tip of Labrador—together with an account of the operation and several photographs.

Dr Douglas contacted Director General of Fleet Systems J.Y. Clarke, and it was arranged for the investigative team of Clarke, Douglas and Selinger to sail on the *Louis S. St Laurent* which was departing Dartmouth on 16 July 1981 for survey work in the area. The party landed at Martin Bay by helicopter and the remains of the station were found; but it was obvious that someone had already been at the site. All of the canisters containing batteries and equipment had been opened and their contents scattered, and radio equipment had been deliberately smashed, by whom it is not known.

The remains of the station were taken on board the *Louis* and were eventually deposited at the Museum of Science and Technology in Ottawa. The station had been established by *U-537* on 23 October 1943. It was a sophisticated system, far in advance of anything possessed by the Allies at that time, and indeed until the 1960s. For 2 minutes every 3 hours, it automatically obtained and transmitted the temperature, barometric pressure, and wind force and direction. Weather information is vital to naval operations but, as weather moves from west to east, the Germans were at a disadvantage compared to the Allies. The Labrador weather station was not, however, of much help. It transmitted useful data for 2 weeks, but then *U-537* reported that it was being jammed or interfered with, probably by another German weather station on the same frequency, although it is just possible that we might have detected the transmissions, jammed them and subsequently found and destroyed the station. If so, no records have survived.

Looking for the *Answer*

The Panamanian flag vessel *Atlantean I*, renamed the *Answer,* was a small freighter that had been damaged in Lake Ontario in 1974 and had undergone some repairs there, then at Montreal and later at Québec City. An order for her arrest for non-payment of repair bills was about to be issued when her presumptive owner, Captain Brian Erb, took a crew on board and sailed without authorization. Captain Erb was a well-known character on the Montreal waterfront. In the previous year he had been involved in the occupation of a vessel that had grounded on Ile d'Orleans. It was an attempt at salvage, but, although no one was on board, the ship had not been abandoned by its owners. They asked the RCMP to eject the occupiers and the *J.E. Bernier* (Captain Pat Toomey) was requisitioned to put a heavily armed contingent of Québec Provincial Police and RCMP officers on board. To Captain Toomey's relief, no gun battle resulted. (In piloting the ship in, he was the only person not crouched behind steel bulwarks.) As the *Bernier* manoeuvred alongside at the vessel's stern, the piratical crew (or would-be salvagers, depending on one's point of view) decamped over the bow and departed for the city in waiting taxis.

In the case of the *Answer*, it was February 1975 and the Gulf was filled with heavy ice. Captain William Stewart, Director of Coast Guard operations, was informed of a court order from the Federal Court of Canada instructing the RCMP and the Coast Guard to search for and intercept the *Atlantean I (Answer)* and to return her to the Bailiff at the Port of Québec. Captain Stewart contacted Rear-Admiral Andrew Collier (then head of the Navy's Maritime Command) and asked DND to conduct an air search for the vessel. The *John A. Macdonald* was identified as the Coast Guard vessel in the best position to intercept the *Answer.* The fugitive ship was quickly found by the aircraft and by the evening of 26 February the *John A. Macdonald* was standing by the *Answer.* On the 27th a helicopter brought two lawyers from Sept-Iles to the *Answer* (landing on the ice) and its pilot then asked for and received fuel from the *Macdonald.* Later, four RCMP officers arrived on a DND helicopter. The *Answer* asked the icebreaker to escort her outbound but the *Macdonald* instead offered to escort her to Gaspé, which was refused. Several reporters arrived on the *Answer* by another helicopter which then refueled on the *Macdonald.* On 28 February, as no directive had been received to arrest the vessel, the icebreaker returned to its normal duties, leaving the *Answer* safely stuck in the ice.

On 1 March the whole procedure was resumed. Police were taken on board the *Macdonald* at Gaspé and the next day they boarded the *Answer.* A Coast Guard sailing master and engineer and several RCMP officers were put on board and Captain Erb agreed to go with the *Macdonald* to Sept-Iles. However, as soon as open water was reached, the ship broke escort and headed eastward for the Atlantic. During all this time, legal arguments were being heard as to Canada's right to seize a vessel in the Gulf of St Lawrence, but no decision had been made, so instead of arresting the ship at this

The protest ship *Cleveland Amory*, formerly CCGS *Thomas Carleton*. (Fisheries and Oceans Canada MP200201-002)

The *John A. Macdonald* and the *Sir William Alexander* boarding the *Sea Shepherd*, 1982. (Fisheries and Oceans Canada MP200101-003)

point, all the government officials were taken off and the RCMP officers were again landed at Gaspé.

Finally a legal decision was reached and firm orders were issued. For the third time RCMP and Coast Guard personnel were put on board the *Answer* and this time her captain, crew and five reporters were taken off the ship. She was sailed to Sept-Iles, arriving on 7 March. This was the end of Coast Guard involvement, although the litigation continued. This situation would not arise today as the waters of the Gulf of St Lawrence are now considered to be part of the internal waters of Canada.

Conservation Capers

Paul Watson is a feisty Canadian who has constantly challenged governments in defence of whales, seals, fish and the environment. Formerly a member of Greenpeace, he formed his own group, the Sea Shepherd organization and, in 1978, he acquired a former side-trawler and gave it the same name. In previous years he and his colleagues had tried to disrupt sealing on the ice off Newfoundland. In 1979 Watson brought the *Sea Shepherd*, with media people on board, to the sealing area off Iles de la Madeleine and achieved considerable publicity. In 1982 he again brought the ship to the area. Many Canadians (but not fishers and sealers who feel their livelihood is threatened) sympathize with Mr Watson's aims, but the RCMP and the Coast Guard have to enforce the law. On this occasion, the *Sir William Alexander* and *John A. Macdonald,* with an RCMP team embarked, closed in on the *Sea Shepherd* which was defended by a 3-metre electrified barbed wire fence and possibly water cannon. With the helicopter airborne to give room on the flight deck (and to take photographs), the *Alexander* manoeuvred alongside, swept away the fence with mats suspended from her buoy derrick, put out a gangway and eighteen RCMP officers swarmed on board. There was no resistance. Mr Watson and some of his crew had already walked across the ice to the Cape Breton shore. The remainder were embarked in the *MacDonald* while the *Alexander* took the *Sea Shepherd* to Georgetown, Prince Edward Island.

In 1983, a replacement protest vessel, *Sea Shepherd II*, attempted to blockade St John's harbour preventing sealing ships from leaving. She was captured by the Coast Guard and the crew charged under the Seal Protection Regulations, but the charges were eventually dismissed and the regulations found unconstitutional. The Sea Shepherd organization continued its activities all over the world and did not hesitate to sink poaching vessels and vessels fishing or whaling in defiance of United Nations conservation resolutions. In 1993, the society's *Cleveland Amory* (the former CCGS *Thomas Carleton,* painted an ominous black) was used to chase the Cuban trawler *Rio Las Casas* from the Grand Banks by manoeuvring closely, throwing stink bombs on the working deck and similar tactics. She was in turn chased by the CGS *Cape Roger* and the CCGS *Sir Wilfred Grenfell*, with RCMP officers embarked. At the end, Watson was arrested and the protest ship detained. (Watson sold it to pay the various fines.) The Sea Shepherd organization claimed credit for enforcing Canadian law and preserving our fish, an assertion not wholly supported by Canadian authorities.

The Spanish trawler *Estai*, arrested on 9 March 1995 during the turbot dispute. (Fisheries and Oceans Canada MP200301)

The *Estai* Affair

In June 1994, the Coastal Fisheries Protection Act was amended to give Canada the right to regulate straddling stocks of fish—those that were found on the Continental Shelf both within and outside the 200-mile limit. In practice, this meant two areas: the "nose" and the "tail" of the Grand Banks. This was a unilateral action not recognized by the European Union and in February 1995 a dispute arose over turbot quotas. The Northwest Atlantic Fisheries Organization had awarded Canada 60 percent of the turbot catch and the European Union 12 percent. The European Union set its own quota at 70 percent. There followed some rather dramatic events that culminated in the arrest of the Spanish trawler *Estai* on 9 March. However, the involvement of the Coast Guard and Fisheries ships (working together for the first time following the Coast Guard's transfer to Fisheries and Oceans), had started weeks earlier. A close watch was being kept on nearly forty Spanish and Portuguese trawlers. The *Cape Roger* and *Leonard J. Cowley* from Newfoundland and the *Cygnus* from the Maritimes Region, with the *Sir Wilfred Grenfell*, watched the trawlers at close range. The *J.E. Bernier* was employed ferrying relief personnel and equipment from St John's. The *Sir John Franklin* kept in radar range of the foreign trawlers but just out of sight—an ominously large radar echo. Spanish Navy fishery patrol vessels were present and there was a potential for violence as the patrol vessels on both sides were armed. The Canadian Navy ostensibly kept out of the situation but maintained a frigate at 3 hours' steaming from the scene. On 9 March 1995 authorization was given to arrest a Spanish trawler, which turned out to be the *Estai*. The command ship, *Leonard J. Cowley*, fired machine gun bursts across her bow and she was boarded by DFO and RCMP officers from the *Cape Roger*. The *Sir Wilfred Grenfell's* task was to hold off other trawlers with her water cannon and to cut the *Estai's* net warps, using a device made for the purpose, an action in which the *Grenfell* was successful. (It must be admitted that this is exactly what the *Cleveland Amory* had tried to do to the *Rio Las Casas*.) Fisheries Minister Brian Tobin announced a 60-day moratorium on fishing inside and outside the 200-mile limit for Canadian as well as European Union ships. The EU denounced the action as an act of piracy by Canada. On 12 March the *Estai* was brought into St John's and her captain charged with fishing illegally. The Spanish, German and French ambassadors were in St John's to meet the ship amid protests and turmoil. *Estai's* net was recovered and was found to have an illegal small-mesh liner. (This net was later displayed by Minister Tobin on a barge in front of the United Nations building in New York). On 15 March the *Estai* was released on payment of a bond. The dispute continued with many legal ramifications, but it was now a matter for the negotiators, not the seagoing services. Today, Spanish trawlers are back on the banks and Spanish patrol boats peacefully replenish in St John's harbour. On 4 December 1998, the World Court in the Hague refused to hear the appeal by Spain on Canada's actions in seizing the *Estai,* affirming Canada's right to protect its waters from overfishing.

Drug Ship Interceptions

The Coast Guard not infrequently cooperates with the RCMP in attempts to intercept drugs smuggled into Canada by sea. Usually small utility craft or FRCs are
required or a lifeboat stationed in the area is involved. In all of these cases the RCMP
are in charge; the Coast Guard merely supplies the platform for the operation.
Occasionally larger ships are used when a major seizure is anticipated. In July 1990, a
major "drug bust" was made at Baleine, Cape Breton. Police had become aware that a
19.5-metre Nova Scotian fishing vessel, the *Scotia Maid*, had been purchased by interests in Newfoundland for (it was suspected) a drug run. The Armed Forces and the
Coast Guard were asked to assist. The drugs must have been brought to an offshore
location by another vessel, but aerial surveillance failed to detect the transfer to the
Scotia Maid. However she was tracked by aircraft and shadowed by HMCS *Nipigon* and
CCGS *Mary Hichens*. The *Scotia Maid* lay off the coast just north of Louisbourg and
transferred its cargo to a smaller fishing boat to land at the little village of Baleine. After
allowing one tractor-trailer load past (later intercepted on the road), the police ashore
emerged from hiding and arrested the smugglers. At sea, the *Scotia Maid*, still with
some drugs on board, was boarded by police from the *Mary Hichens.* The Coast Guard
cutter then towed the seized vessel to Sydney where it was berthed alongside the Coast
Guard College boatshed. College personnel later transferred it to North Sydney for
storage ashore. Twenty-seven tons of hashish valued at about $325 million was seized.
Eighteen people were tried and convicted for this operation, but so delayed were the
proceedings due to declaration of mistrials, involving the right to be tried in one's mother tongue, that those who initially pleaded guilty had served their sentences before the
last of the group were convicted 6 years later.

Two years earlier, the *George E. Darby* got involved, to the crew's surprise, in an elaborate police stakeout on the deserted west coast of the Queen Charlotte Islands. The
Darby's FRCs were taking Parks Canada officials through the inlets and bays of this
pristine area. Unknown to them, this caused problems to the RCMP who were lurking
in the woods near a large cache of drugs that had been discovered earlier. It appeared
to them that the Zodiac FRCs were the smugglers coming to retrieve the drugs; yet they
did not approach the cache. Eventually RCMP and Coast Guard authorities became
aware of each other's activities and the ship was told to go to a certain inlet. An FRC
then left the ship and was directed by police radio to a secluded anchorage. Once the
fact that the crew members were Coast Guard personnel was verified, several U.S.
Customs officials appeared from the fishing boat and a large group of camouflaged
RCMP officers from the woods. On the next day, the Coast Guard helicopter from
Prince Rupert started airlifting the product to the *Darby* with the FRCs also assisting.
It consisted of bales of hashish, in nylon bags with straps for easy handling and "Past
Inspection" stamps on each one. It was taken as deck cargo to Victoria and handed
over to the RCMP. The street value of the haul was estimated at about $20 million.

The drug ship *Chiloli* on the beach at Capelin Cove, Nova Scotia. (Ron Barrie, Fisheries and Oceans Canada MP052001)

The *Chiloli* Incident

On 13 September 1995, a liferaft was reported floating off the east coast of Cape Breton Island. On recovery by the CCGS *Louisbourg,* it was found to contain not survivors, but hashish. Later that day a search aircraft spotted a second raft, which proved to be in the same condition. Had a drug smuggling ship sunk? On the next day nothing was found; then on 15 September a Coast Guard helicopter spotted an offshore supply type vessel high and dry at Capelin Cove, a remote beach. The smugglers and their cargo, except for the contents of the liferafts and a number of bags of hashish that washed up on the beach, had long gone.

While the RCMP gathered their evidence, a Coast Guard team assessed the situation. The ship had fuel in unexpected tanks and compartments: obviously she had intended to return for another load but for some reason had been abandoned and had floated ashore on a high tide. To the Coast Guard, this was a potential pollution problem. A team from the Environmental Response Branch started the task of removing the oil from the vessel, using portable fuel tanks and pumps. By 2 October 6,000 gallons had been removed. Surveys had shown that the hull was intact, and the next task was to re-float the vessel. CCGS *Terry Fox* was to be used but was unable to get her towing hawser ashore. In the end, the ship was refloated at high tide on 9 October by the *Louisbourg* pulling on the starboard quarter and a bulldozer pushing at the port bow.

The *Terry Fox* then towed the vessel to the Dartmouth Coast Guard base.

The ship's name painted on the hull was *Chiloli* and it was found that she had for-merly been the *Viking Ruby*, registered in Panama. An action against the ship and its Panamanian owners, who did not come forward, was proceeded with on 8 February 1996 and, after a favourable judgement, the ship was sold on 13 February for $226,000. This sum was applied to the salvage costs incurred by the Coast Guard, which was the first time that proceeds of a seized ship had been applied directly to operating expens-es and was solely due to the expeditious manner in which the proceedings had been conducted. The Ship Source Pollution Fund met the costs of the oil removal.

The Red River Flood of 1997

As the snow melts on the central plains of Canada and the United States, the Red River which runs through Manitoba farmland and the City of Winnipeg is prone to flooding. Every year in March the staff at the Coast Guard Base at Selkirk prepares for flood emergencies. Some years are worse than others. In 1997 there was early indica-tion that the water would reach unprecedented heights, as indeed it did. The first call for help came on 20 April and for 3 weeks Coast Guard crews from the Selkirk base and Fisheries personnel from Winnipeg worked to evacuate residents and rescue stranded people and animals. Boats were operating over vast areas of flooded land, pre-senting a unique navigation problem. This was solved by using hand-held Global Positioning System sets in conjunction with the Federal Prairie Farm Rehabilitation Administration database, which accurately locates farm buildings, silos and other sur-face features.

Other boats and emergency response personnel from the Central and Arctic Region, joined by teams from the Laurentian and Maritimes and members of the Coast Guard Auxiliary took part in the relief effort. In normal and even in exceptional years, Winnipeg can rely on the Floodway, a channel constructed to divert the water around the south and east ends of the city. However, in 1997, it was apparent that flooding would be the worst ever experienced, the Floodway would not be sufficient and water would have poured into the city from the southwest. A new 40-kilometre earth dike called the Brunkild was quickly built, but there was no time for it to stabilize. High waves on the new lakes created by the flood, whipped by winds of up to 70 kph, beat against and eroded the dike. A Manitoba Department of Highways engineer, Bob Kurylco suggested that oil spill containment booms might be used to break the force of the waves. On the morning of 30 April. Manitoba officials contacted CCG Deputy Commissioner Michael Turner and the Marine Emergencies staff went into action. Within 18 hours, material was flown in by chartered jet freighters from Coast Guard bases all across eastern Canada. Military and Coast Guard Auxiliary personnel in shal-low draft boats deployed the boom sections and anchored them. Straw was used between the boom and the bank, and the effect was to prevent the waves breaking directly on the dike.

The Coast Guard's DASH-8 pollution patrol aircraft, normally based in Ottawa, transported a load of pumps to the City of Winnipeg's emergency organization and a Coast Guard Bell 212 was used extensively by the provincial authorities throughout the period. The consequences to Winnipeg had all these efforts not been successful would have been extremely serious. Many government departments, federal and provincial, participated in the 1997 Manitoba flood relief efforts and the Coast Guard's contribution was in accordance with the best traditions of the service.

The Swiss Air Flight 111 Crash (2 September 1998)

In 1998 the Coast Guard was again involved in a massive effort to recover bodies and evidence after the tragic crash of a Swiss Air MD-11 aircraft just off the scenic Nova Scotia resort of Peggy's Cove. Fishing vessels from St Margaret's Bay and the surrounding area were quickly on the scene and members of the Coast Guard Auxiliary took a prominent part in a rescue effort that soon turned into the recovery of body remains and debris. Naval and Coast Guard ships and aircraft took part in the subsequent operation–the Sambro lifeboat was one of the first craft to respond. CCGS *Mary Hichens* and *Earl Grey* received recovered items from the fishing craft, fishery patrol boats and RCMP craft and subsequently transferred the human remains to HMCS *Preserver*, from whence they were taken by helicopter to a morgue established in a hangar at Shearwater. Naval vessels at the scene included the submarine *Okanagan*, which located the signals from the flight recorders. In the subsequent long-term salvage operations, several Coast Guard vessels were involved including the *Matthew*, whose side-scan sonar mapped portions of the wreckage. The salvage vessel USS *Grapple* arrived about a week after the crash and her divers joined with Canadian naval divers in operations that were intense and dangerous. Later, a large crane barge and some scallop draggers were chartered to recover more of the remaining debris from the bottom. Throughout this operation, which did not conclude until early in 1999, Coast Guard and naval ships patrolled the crash area. Eventually, almost all of the aircraft was recovered to assist the Canadian Transportation Safety Board in their investigation, and all bodies were identified. Some of the workers who participated in these tasks subsequently experienced quite severe emotional trauma after the event and some are affected to this day.

Ceremonial Occasions

The Governor-General is Honorary Chief Commissioner of the Coast Guard and Governors General have quite frequently visited Coast Guard ships. The commemoration of the Arctic Islands proclamation on the *J.E. Bernier* in 1980 has already been mentioned. On another occasion, from August 2nd to 6th 1982, CCGS *Pierre Radisson* (Captain Pat Toomey), acted as Canada's vice-regal yacht on the occasion of the 1000th anniversary of the settlement of Greenland by Eric the Red. Governor-General and Mrs. Schreyer were flown to Narssarssuaq by Canadian Forces aircraft where they met Queen Margrethe, Prince Henrik and the Danish royal family together with their guests, King Olav and Crown Princess Sonja of Norway and President Finnbogadottir of Iceland, all of whom were embarked in the Danish royal yacht *Dannebrog*, escorted by the warship *Beskytteren*. The *Dannebrog* had been damaged by ice, so when the celebrations and the royal parties moved 30 miles to Narssaq, it was on the *Pierre Radisson* that all embarked. King Olav, who had been a sailor all his life, was particularly impressed by the *Radisson's* capabilities. At the end of the celebrations at Narssarssuaq, the Governor-General and Mrs. Schreyer gave a reception on board the Coast Guard ship for all the heads of state. Then the royal parties returned to the *Dannebrog* by helicopter while the *Radisson* sailed overnight to Narssarssuaq to disembark the Governor-General and the entire Canadian party, who returned to Ottawa by air. The next visit was to Julianhaab (Quaqortoq in Greenlandic). The ship was opened to visitors and about half the population came aboard and much hospitality was extended to the crew. This was a particularly successful diplomatic mission.

In 1987, the *Pierre Radisson* also served during the Sommet de la Francophonie, held in Québec City that year. The ship was used to take over thirty heads of state and their spouses on a 3-hour tour of the St Lawrence off Québec City.

Coast Guard ships again hosted heads of government during the G7 meeting in Halifax from 15 to 17 July 1995. The *Sir William Alexander* (Captain Harvey Adams) and the *Edward Cornwallis* (Captain Larry Meisner) acted as upscale ferries, bringing the presidents and prime ministers from Shearwater jetty to Historic Properties in Halifax. This was judged to provide better security than using the bridge from Dartmouth and the ships' red and white colours are representative of Canadian identity. Prime Minister Chrétien and Presidents Clinton, Yeltsin and Chirac and Prime Minister Major crossed on the *Sir William Alexander* and Prime Ministers Murayama and Lamberto Dini and President Santer of the European Union on the *Edward Cornwallis*. Security precautions were comprehensive: RCMP divers checked the ships for possible mines every day. The Coast Guard also provided helicopters and watercraft for the security forces.

In 2002, a Governor-General again used a Coast Guard ship to visit remote coastal communities. On 5 July 2002, after a tour of Newfoundland's Great Northern Peninsula, their Excellencies Governor-General Adrienne Clarkson and John Ralston Saul embarked in CCGS *Henry Larsen* at St Anthony Newfoundland for a trip to Labrador, visiting Red Bay, Cartwright, Rigolet, Hopedale, Nain and Goose Bay. On 3 July Governor-General Clarkson had been invested as Honorary Chief Commissioner of the Coast Guard, as had all her predecessors since 1976, and the *Henry Larsen* wore her standard during the voyage, which was in the tradition of many such vice-regal expeditions since 1867.

These are a few of the tasks and experiences outside the realms of the usual icebreaking, navigation safety and emergency response situations that can be encountered by Coast Guard ships and personnel and which help to make a Coast Guard career more interesting and challenging.

Captain Gordon
Warren, CM.
(Fisheries and
Oceans Canada
P020201)

Captain Gordon H. Warren, CM

Gordon H. Warren was born on 27 September 1922 in New Perlican, Trinity Bay, on the southeast coast of Newfoundland. His father was an ironworker in a nearby mine. He was the only child of six who chose to work on the ocean.

In 1941, eighteen-year-old Gordon Warren went straight from school into the Royal Navy. (Newfoundland was not, at that time, part of Canada.) After basic training in England, he crossed the Atlantic in a transport ship and the United States by train to Seattle to join the battleship HMS *Warspite*, which was refitting there after war damage. *Warspite* then joined the Eastern Fleet, based first at Colombo and then Mombasa. In 1943, Warren transferred to the battleship HMS *Resolution* which returned to the UK. After a leave at home in

Newfoundland, the first in two and a half years, he was posted to the escort aircraft-carrier HMS *Queen*. He was discharged in 1946.

Upon returning home to Newfoundland, Gordon Warren attended the nautical school at Memorial University and obtained his certificate of competency as Second Mate, Foreign-going. He joined the Federal Commerce Company, eventually gaining his Foreign-going Master's Certificate in 1951. By 1950, however, he had moved to Halifax, where he worked for Western Union as a cable ship officer. Western Union had two ships, the *Cyrus Field* and the *Lord Kelvin*. The company had a "shoelace" promotion system, whereby one vessel is the junior ship and one is the senior ship. So Captain Warren went from a position on the junior ship to the same position on the senior ship, back and forth, until he reached the top.

In 1965, Western Union decided to get out of the business of maintaining cables. At the same time, the Canadian Coast Guard's cable ship, CCGS *John Cabot*, was being commissioned. Cable ship work requires special expertise and at that time few people in the government fleet had any experience in the field. The Coast Guard got in touch with several Western Union officers, including Gordon Warren, who was offered a position back at home in St John's. His first appointment was as first officer on the *John Cabot*. By 1968, he was the *Cabot's* commanding officer.

During his time on the *John Cabot*, and subsequently, Captain Warren was involved in some notable events, two of which are described in detail in Chapter 12: the rescue, in 1973, of the mini-submarine *Pisces III* and its crew, and the recovery of the "black boxes" and other evidence after the Air India disaster in 1985. Both events took place off the west coast of Ireland and the success of these missions was due to the *John Cabot's* special capabilities and Gordon Warren's experience and skill. In the *Pisces III* operation, he was in command of the *John Cabot*, while in the Air India operation he directed a large international effort from a headquarters and command post at Cork. In recognition of his services during the *Pisces III* operation, Captain Warren was appointed Member of the Order of Canada on 14 January 1976 and was invested on 7 April 1976.

In 1974, Captain Warren came ashore and took over the position of Director of the Canadian Coast Guard in Newfoundland. He remained on shore until 1988, when he retired. He now lives at home with his wife in St John's. They have two grown children, Lorne and Linda. Although he did not inherit his love of the sea from his own father, he maintains his nautical associations through his son Lorne, who now works for the Canadian Coast Guard.

Marine Legislation

Among the responsibilities of the Department of Marine and Fisheries as constituted by the act of 1868 were: "Classification of Vessels and examination and granting of Certificates of Masters and Mates and others in the Merchant service; Inspection of Steamboats and Boards of Steamship Inspection and Enquiries into causes of ship-wrecks." At the time of Confederation, vessels operating in the inland waters of Canada were regulated under an act passed by the Legislative Assembly of the Province of Canada in 1859 (An Act Respecting the Registration of Inland Vessels). Measurement for tonnage of inland vessels was still in accordance with an earlier act of 1845. However, in 1854, the Imperial Parliament had passed the Merchant Shipping Act, and ships in salt water were registered and measured for tonnage under its rules. It was not until 1873 that the Parliament of Canada rationalized the rules for both ocean-going and inland vessels (An Act Relating to Shipping and for the Registration and Classification Thereof). This brought the rules in line with the British Act of 1854.

The next major advance was in 1906 when the Canada Shipping Act was passed. A new version was made law in 1936 (the same year as the creation of the Department of Transport). This act, although updated to meet changing conditions over the years, still has many antiquated provisions which would not be acceptable in law today. Its replacement, the Canada Shipping Act of 2001, was passed by Parliament; however, it will not come into force until all its regulations are ready, which is expected to be in the fall of 2005.

The Canada Shipping Act is the principal piece of legislation governing personal safety and environmental protection in the marine sector. Its objectives are to:

1. protect the health and well-being of individuals, including the crews of vessels, who participate in marine transportation;

2. promote safety in marine transportation;

3. protect the marine environment from damage due to navigation and shipping activities;

CHAPTER 13

Marine Safety

4. develop a regulatory scheme that encourages viable, effective and economical marine transportation and commerce;

5. promote an efficient marine transportation system;

6. develop a regulatory scheme that encourages the viable, effective and economical use of Canadian waters by recreational boaters;

7. ensure that Canada can meet its international obligations under bilateral and multilateral agreements with respect to navigation and shipping;

8. encourage the harmonization of marine practices; and

9. establish an effective inspection and enforcement program.

In short, it is the instrument of government that is designed to ensure that Canadian ships and foreign vessels that enter Canadian waters are built, crewed and sailed in a safe and legal manner. The reponsibility for enforcing the Canada Shipping Act lies both with the Minister of Transport and the Minister of Fisheries and Oceans.

Under the Canada Shipping Act and other laws, such as the Arctic Waters Pollution Prevention Act of 1970, there are numerous regulations. The body responsible for enforcing these regulations is the Marine Safety Branch, formerly the Ship Safety Branch, of the Department of Transport. Until 1995, the marine surveyors or inspectors of the Ship Safety Branch were part of the staff of each Coast Guard region, but their district offices were distinct from the Coast Guard bases and were located in busy ports and shipbuilding centres. When the Coast Guard was transferred to the Department of Fisheries and Ocean on 1 April 1995, the Marine Safety Branch remained with Transport Canada, working alongside its air and surface transportation counterparts. Its work and responsibilities have been expanded to include oversight of Marine Pilotage.

The rules that regulate how ships should be built were developed in the nineteenth century, principally for the benefit of insurers. As Britain had the largest merchant marine at that time, the pioneer classification society was Lloyd's Register of Shipping, but all the principal maritime nations soon had their own. The societies provided an essential service to everyone connected with the shipping industry. Passengers and shippers of cargo wanted assurances that they or their goods were embarked in a vessel that was as safe as possible. Governments welcomed the higher standards required because they benefitted and promoted the national merchant marine. The Plimsoll mark (named for the British Member of Parliament who introduced the legislation), or load-line, was introduced in 1875. This revealed if a ship was being overloaded. Examinations for Certificates of Competency were required from about the same date. The first international agreements were drafted, notably the Rules for the Prevention of Collisions at Sea.

The classification societies function internationally, responding to the requirements of owners and shipbuilders, rather than governments. In Canada, most ships have been built under the rules of one of the three oldest societies, whose mark may be seen on the ship's hull: Lloyd's Register (LR), the American Bureau of Shipping (AB) or the Bureau Veritas (BV). Transport Canada approves plans and inspects ships under construction, but in some instances accepts also the rules and the inspections of the recognized classification societies. However, the Canada Shipping Act regulations are comprehensive enough that ships can be built under the aegis of Transport Canada without recourse to a classification society, in which case the distinctive letters (CM) on either side of the load-line disc stand for the Canadian Marine Administration.

Canadian Ships

Before a commercial ship or fishing vessel is built, its plans must be approved by the Department of Transport. After construction has commenced, it is subject to frequent surveys by government inspectors and the surveyors of the classification society. Surveys are not confined to structural matters: the machinery and every item of equipment must be approved by the inspectors, who are naval architects, marine engineers, electrical engineers and navigation specialists. When the ship is completed, the load-lines for different seasons and geographical areas are assigned and a Load-line Certificate is issued (not to fishing vessels, which do not have load-lines). The ship is measured for tonnage and the official number and net registered tonnage are engraved on the main cross-member at the deck amidships. When the ship is complete, it receives a Certificate of Registry which attests to the ownership of the vessel and authorizes it to fly the Canadian flag. With all safety and fire-fighting equipment on board and a qualified crew, the Safety Certificate is issued. This must be renewed annually in the case of vessels over 150 gross registered tons and every 4 years for vessels under that size. Since the 1970s, however, a computerized program of continuous inspection has been found to save time for both shipowners and surveyors.

International Conventions

All maritime nations are members of the International Maritime Organization (IMO). Canada has been influential within this body. The Secretary General of IMO since 1990 has been Mr William A. O'Neill, who had previously served as Commissioner of the Canadian Coast Guard (from 1975 to 1980) and, subsequently, as head of the St Lawrence Seaway Authority.

Canada is a signatory to many IMO conventions. Among the most important are:

1. The International Convention on Load Lines (LL); (adopted 1966, entry in force 1968)

2. The International Convention for the Safety of Life at Sea, 1974 (SOLAS; adopted 1980)

3. The International Convention for the Prevention of Pollution from Ships, 1973 as modified by the Protocol of 1978 relating thereto (MARPOL 73/78; entry into force 1975)

Mr William A. O'Neill, Commissioner of the Canadian Coast Guard 1975-1980 and Secretary General of the International Marine Organization since 1990. (Fisheries and Oceans Canada P060801-001)

4. The Convention on the International Regulations for Preventing Collisions at Sea, 1972 (COLREG; adopted 1977, but in Canada issued, with Canadian amendments, as a regulation under the Canada Shipping Act, effective in 1978)

5. The International Convention on Standards of Training, Certification and Watchkeeping for Seafarers, 1978 (STCW; entry into force 1984). At a time of the registration of the majority of the world's ships under flags of convenience and the introduction of new technology at an increasing pace, it was found necessary to update this Convention at least twice. A major amendment was made in 1991 (entry into force 1992), and a complete revision in 1995 (entry into force 1 February 2002).

Many of these conventions superseded earlier ones, and all are subject to updating from time to time. Committees meet at regular intervals and make recommendations to the parent body, IMO. With so many administrations involved, it is often several years between the passing of a convention or an amendment and its adoption, which only occurs after a sufficient number of nations have ratified it. Marine Safety and Coast Guard representatives attend all of these meetings, and Canada has played a prominent part in drafting and implementing conventions which promote safety at sea.

Inspection of Foreign Ships: Port State Control

In 1970, the wreck of the tanker *Arrow* in Chedabucto Bay, Nova Scotia, raised concerns about sub-standard ships. New regulations were issued requiring foreign ships arriving in Canadian waters to carry efficient navigation equipment and prescribed navigation publications and charts. Inspections were carried out and if a ship did not meet the standard, it was required to do so before proceeding. Other nations enforced their own regulations, but there was no coordination until a group of northern European countries signed a Memorandum of Understanding known as the Paris MOU. This provides for the inspection of ships of all flags to assure that they comply with the important IMO conventions listed above. The interval between inspections is 6 months and may be done by any member country. The results are entered into a database which was established in France, at St Malo, that can be accessed by any signatory country. Canada became an associate member of the Paris MOU in April 1988 and a full member in May 1994, the first non-European member to be so accepted.

Canada was a driving force in creating a similar program in the Asia-Pacific region (Tokyo MOU) and has been a member from its inception in 1993. We are also the custodian of the Tokyo MOU database. Canada, being a member of both Paris and Tokyo MOUs, held the first Joint Ministerial Conference on Port State Control. The conference was convened in Vancouver in March 1998. There are two other regional MOUs: South America (Vina del Mar MOU) and Caribbean (Caribbean MOU), Indian Ocean, Mediterranean and North Africa MOUs are planned. It is probable that Port State Control (PSC) will become a global organization.

Hazardous Cargoes

Certain types of cargo are inherently dangerous, either because of their inflammable nature, toxic properties, extreme density or propensity to shift and destroy a ship's stability. Inspectors enforce regulations applicable to explosives, dangerous goods, timber, grain and ore concentrates. In the past this was done by Port Wardens, who were not members of the Branch but employees of a port authority or specially appointed. By 1998, Marine Safety inspectors had taken over all of these duties except in one major port, Québec City. The suitability of a ship to carry a particular type of cargo and the distribution of weights within the ship is critical. In the last two decades, a series of accidents and losses of large bulk carriers loaded with heavy ores has drawn particular attention to this type of ship and the way such cargoes are loaded.

A Transport Canada Inspector examines repairs done on this hull. (Fisheries and Oceans Canada TM900101-001)

Examinations for Certificates of Competency

The Ship Safety/Marine Safety Branch is responsible for examining candidates and issuing Certificates of Competency. Engineering certificates are in four classes: the First Class Certificate entitles the holder to be chief engineer of the largest and most powerful ships and the others, down to Fourth Class, are graduated as to position and engine power. Validity may be for steam, motor or both. These qualifications have remained the same throughout the period, apart from the updating of the technical content of the exams.

The master's and mate's examinations and certificates were originally similar to those issued by other Commonwealth countries. They were valid for foreign-going, home trade or inland waters voyages, the last named principally for the Great Lakes. Commencing in 1975, new Canadian examinations were introduced in which a modular system of examination papers allowed a candidate to obtain credits towards the requirements for one or more certificates of competency. The certificates issued were classed as CN or ON, which probably were intended, originally, to designate coastal or ocean navigation but, in practice, did not retain those specific connotations. The possessor of an ON I

Ships loading ore concentrate. (Fisheries and Oceans Canada FC010003)

Certificate, for instance, could be master of a home trade ship or first mate on a foreign-going ship. The highest certificate was Master Mariner (MM), which qualifies the holder to be master of a foreign-going vessel. Fishing certificates on the same principle came into force at the same time. In 1978, they were modified as Fishing Master Certificates, levels one to four. Although they are valid only on fishing vessels, many of the "building blocks" (the examinations for different subjects) are common to what is known as the "general stream." On 30 July 1997, new examination regulations came into force and certificates were classified as "local trade" or "intermediate trade," with Master Mariner remaining the highest qualification. Local trade is a relative term: the holder of a Master, Local Trade Certificate is entitled to command a large vessel on a voyage from Lake Superior to ports on the north shore of the Gulf of St Lawrence, a distance of well over 1000 miles. As in the case of the CN and ON certificates, the new qualifications have validity for lower positions on foreign-going vessels.

Special Qualifications

Marine Emergency Duties (MED) courses are a prerequisite for all Certificates of Competency and masters and mates must attend prescribed Simulated Electronic Navigation (SEN) courses, all of which are conducted at provincial nautical schools.

The schools have also been granted authority to qualify people in Tanker Safety and other safety courses: for example, the Global Maritime Distress and Safety System (GMDSS). In the establishments that also have cadet programs, when a course of studies as a whole has been preapproved by the Department, certain credits towards certificates of competency are granted when the course is completed.

International Obligations

Canadian certification, training and crewing standards must now conform to the International Safety Management Code (ISM) as agreed to by member nations of IMO. This code originated as IMO guidelines, drafted in 1989 and issued in 1993. It became mandatory in 1998.

Marine Surveyors

The Canada Shipping Act gives the Marine Safety Branch surveyors powers in their own right (and not simply delegated from their superior). This includes the authority to stop a ship from sailing if it is deemed by the inspector to be unsafe. The head of the branch has powers derived directly from the Canada Shipping Act and holds the historic title "Chairman of the Board of Steamship Inspection," which differentiates this post from other directors general on the same administrative level. For this reason, the names of those who have held the post during the existence of the Coast Guard are given here:

Allen Cumyn	1953-1965
H.O. Buchanan	1965-1968
G.W.R. Graves	1973-1976
Donald L. Findlay	1978-1980
James Hornsby	1981-1988
Michael J. Hubbard	1988-1996
Bud Streeter	1997-2002

The Polar Code

In 1998, Canada took an important initiative in the development of an International Code of Safety for Ships in Polar Waters. This initiative brings together the expertise of the world's icebreaker builders and operators in an effort to have agreed standards for high ice class ships, which will then be able to operate in Arctic and Antarctic waters with assurance of international safety approval. The Polar Code criteria would include personnel requirements as well as construction features. Canada's many years of experience in Arctic ship design, operation and experimentation are being freely contributed to the harmonization of international standards. This work has been going on for many years and the results are now on the IMO agenda for final review. This is only one example of international cooperation in the shipping field to which Canada has taken a leading role.

Pilotage

For as long as commercial shipping has existed, shipmasters have engaged the services of pilots to guide them in unfamiliar waters. With the growth of trade in recent centuries, states and local governments have made pilotage mandatory in the ports, rivers and canals under their control. In almost all areas, Pilotage Authorities have been set up and granted the sole right to provide these services. Generally, they are self-regulating and admit new pilots after long apprenticeships or by adding experienced mariners to their ranks. The role of government is usually to oversee and ensure that the needed services are provided at a cost that does not discourage trade.

This is the situation that prevails in Canada. Four Regional Pilotage Authorities (replacing a greater number of local authorities) were set up as Crown corporations under the Pilotage Act of 1972, while Transport Canada provides general surveillance of pilotage administration and operation. Initially, any losses sustained by the authorities were covered by annual government appropriations in order to keep the cost of pilotage within reasonable bounds. However, since the passing of the Canada Marine Act on 10 June 1998, the corporations are on their own and are self-supporting. (The Canada Marine Act of 1998 is the law that governs the operation of ports and harbours, the Seaway and other canals.)

Pilot boat approaching merchant ship. (Fisheries and Oceans Canada F229003)

The four Regional Authorities are: Atlantic, Laurentian, Great Lakes, and Pacific. They all operate in somewhat different ways. Atlantic and Great Lakes pilots are employees of the Authority, Laurentian pilots are entrepreneurs, working within two cooperatives, one for the lower and one for the upper part of the St Lawrence River and Gulf. These cooperatives are then contracted by the Authority to provide pilotage services. The Pacific Pilotage Authority uses a combination of the two methods.

Besides having up-to-date knowledge of local conditions, pilots are experts at handling ships in confined waters. As tankers, container ships and passenger ships have become larger, their expertise has had to be upgraded. Pilotage simulators have been developed that exactly reproduce the effect of currents, winds and ship characteristics as well as the geography of the port. Nevertheless, actual experience is the best teacher, and Canadian pilots are second to none in their abilities.

Ports and Harbours

One of the responsibilities of the Department of Marine and Fisheries under the 1868 Marine and Fisheries Act was the administration of government harbours, ports and wharves. When the Department of Transport was formed in 1936, eight of the principal deep-water harbours—Halifax, Saint John, Chicoutimi, Québec, Trois Rivières, Montreal, Churchill and Vancouver—were placed under a newly created National Harbours Board. The Board was responsible to the Minister of Transport and had secretarial, legal, traffic and engineering branches. It was responsible for such matters as grain storage and loading facilities, cold storage warehouses, heavy lift cranes, and power and water supply systems, as well as for administration and management. Capital expenditures, fees, and charges and by-laws proposed by the board had to be approved by the Governor-in-Council after recommendation by the minister. In 1983, the Canada Port Authorities Act replaced the National Harbours Board Act and other related legislation. Since 1995, matters relating to harbours, other than navigation aids and pollution prevention, are no longer a Coast Guard responsibility.

The evolution of the Department of Fisheries and Oceans and the present location of the Coast Guard within that department merits a short review. There had been many organizational changes throughout the twentieth century as the government of Canada evolved to meet new demands. New departments were created to serve new needs, a variety of programs demanded expanded or new civilian fleets to support their activities, and numerous studies were initiated to assess how federal activities (especially the fleets) could be operated more efficiently. These studies are described in Chapter 15.

It has already been indicated in Chapter 1 that the Department of Fisheries had parted company from Marine and become a separate department in 1930. In 1936, the activities associated with the Marine fleet were taken over by the new Department of Transport. Simultaneously, responsibility for charts and surveys and the Hydrographic Service were assumed by the Department of Mines and Resources. Responsibility for fisheries activities remained with the Department of Fisheries. This meant that principal functions of the old Marine and Fisheries were now divided between three departments.

The Second World War

At the outbreak of war in 1939, the four offshore fisheries patrol vessels: *Arleux, Arras, Givenchy* and *Malaspina*, were taken over by the Navy. So were the hydrographic survey ships *Cartier* and *Acadia*, but not the *Wm. J. Stewart*, which continued its work on the British Columbia coast. The hydrographers were, nevertheless, busier than ever, producing confidential charts for defence purposes. In June 1941 a group of surveyors were sent to southern Newfoundland to re-chart prospective sites for the rendezvous of the RN and USN warships (HMS *Prince of Wales* and USS *Augusta*) that brought Prime Minister Churchill and President Roosevelt to their historic conference in Placentia Bay later that year.

The Postwar Expansion of the Fisheries Protection Service

By 1945, the elderly prewar vessels that had been taken over by the Navy were worn out and the first postwar ships

CHAPTER 14

The Evolution of the Department of Fisheries and Oceans

were a converted minesweeper on the East Coast (the first *Cygnus*) and a pair of former RCMP patrol vessels in the Pacific (*Laurier* and *Howay*). Small craft with local crews continued fisheries enforcement in inshore waters.

On 16 July 1964, Canada expanded its territorial sea from 3 to 12 miles from the coast, and on 1 January 1977 a 200-mile economic zone was declared. Foreign vessels could fish within this zone, but only with permission and for certain species within specified quotas. To patrol this large area, military and civilian patrol aircraft were used for surveillance. New specially built offshore vessels were added to an expanded fleet and naval ships also occasionally performed patrols with fisheries officers on board. A type of fishery patrol vessel was developed and evolved from the second *Cygnus* of 1956 through the somewhat larger *Cape Freels, Chebucto* and *Tanu*, to the very capable *Cape Roger* and the third *Cygnus*, which were fitted to operate helicopters when required. Smaller coastal aluminum craft did not prove so satisfactory, but the *Leonard J. Cowley*, a design shared with the hydrographic ship *John P. Tulley*, was a successful ship and, at 2243 tons, the largest to date. A large fleet of inshore patrol craft with crews of five, later reduced to three, were based on fishing vessel designs and regulated the coastal fishery on both coasts and the Great Lakes.

The Hydrographic Service

At the end of the Second World War, the RCN returned the survey ship *Acadia* to the hydrographers. (The *Cartier*, renamed *Chambly*, was fit only for scrap.) Also available on the west coast was the *Wm. J. Stewart*. In 1944, she had struck the notorious Ripple Rock in Seymour Narrows and had subsequently sunk in shallow water, but by the summer of 1945 she was repaired and ready for service. (In 1958, Ripple Rock was removed as a navigational hazard by driving a tunnel from the shore and destroying it with explosives.) There was a large backlog of surveying to do and more vessels were needed. This was met by former naval ships: one ex-American minesweeper (the *Marabell)* and three Canadian (the second *Cartier* and the *Fort Frances* and *Kapuskasing,* the last two on loan from the Navy) and two ex-patrol craft. Another resource was the Newfoundland sealing fleet, whose vessels with crews experienced in northern navigation could be chartered during the summer and fall.

Starting in the mid 1950s, an effective fleet of modern ships was built up. The two large ice-strengthened ships *Baffin* and *Hudson* of over 3500 gross tons were capable of work in the Arctic. Two medium-sized ships, *Dawson* and *Parizeau,* two smaller vessels, *Maxwell* and *Vector* and two ships for research in the Great Lakes, *Limnos* and *Bayfield,* formed an effective fleet. All these ships were equipped for oceanographic research as well as hydrographic survey. The *Baffin* and *Hudson* carried out important work in the Arctic. The *Baffin* transited the Northwest Passage in 1970. In 1969 and 1970, the *Hudson* undertook a voyage in which she circumnavigated both the American continents. In 1985 the *John P. Tulley* joined the fleet. In 1990, two coastal vessels, the *R.B. Young* and *Matthew* were added. The twin-hulled *F.C.G. Smith* with transducers on sus-

Top: Bedford Institute of Oceanography, Bedford Nova Scotia. (Fisheries and Oceans Canada F200303)

Bottom: The small fisheries protection vessel *Bajo Reef*. (Fisheries and Oceans Canada F182501)

Top: Fisheries protection vessel *Cape Roger*. (Fisheries and Oceans Canada F180808)

Bottom: Hydrographic survey boat *Shark*. (Fisheries and Oceans Canada F203201)

pended booms can check the depth over a wide swath of water, and another twin-hulled craft, the *Frederick G. Creed*, has side-scan sonar and positioning systems of such accuracy that she is called upon for dynamic wave studies and bottom profiling in circumstances such as the Swissair crash off Nova Scotia in 1998.

Fisheries and Oceanographic Research

Oceanography is the study of the oceans, not only the body of water but the nature of the bottom, while marine geology refers to the structure of the seabed and what lies under it. Research in these areas is relevant to the fisheries, to resource development, to the study of climate change and to defence. Canadian research in this broad envelope was initially carried out by the government departments responsible for fisheries and hydrological research and by the Department of National Defence, which is particularly interested in sound propagation and submarine detection.

In 1937, the Fisheries Research Board was established to conduct research into practical and economic problems connected with marine and freshwater fisheries. Physical and chemical studies were conducted by Atlantic and Pacific research groups, under the aegis of the board, until the late 1950s. By 1957, the board was finding it difficult to fund oceanographic research in addition to its ongoing fisheries research programs. At the same time, the Department of Mines and Technical Surveys, which operated the hydrographic survey ships, wanted to add oceanography to its other resource programs, especially in the Arctic. In 1961, after two years of discussions, it was agreed to consolidate technical surveys in hydrography and oceanography, under the Marine Sciences Branch of the Department of Mines and Technical Surveys. In 1962, the Bedford Institute of Oceanography was formally opened. Specific fisheries research remained with the Fisheries Research Board.

In 1969, the Department of Fisheries and Forestry was created, but the two branches operated independently and this change did not substantially affect the activities being discussed here. However, under the Government Organization Act of 1970 a new Department of the Environment (DOE) was created, which incorporated the fisheries protection activities along with oceanography and hydrography. In 1973 the ships and research establishments of the Fisheries Research Board were also assigned to the Fishery and Marine Services of DOE. In 1976 the department was renamed the Department of Fisheries and Environment. The centre for research activities in the Atlantic was the Bedford Institute. In the Pacific, it was the Institute of Ocean Sciences, first at Victoria and then at Sidney, British Columbia. In the Great Lakes, the Canada Centre for Inland Waters at Burlington, Ontario, was opened officially in 1971.

In 1979, the Department of Fisheries and the Environment was split in two: the Department of Fisheries and Oceans (DFO) and Environment Canada. The latter department retained responsibility for limnological research—limnology is the study of fresh water lakes as opposed to oceans—using vessels that were part of the DFO fleet until 1986, when all marine and aquatic research was integrated into the Science Sector

Top: The large hydrographic and oceanographic research ship *Hudson*. (Fisheries and Oceans Canada F200408)

Bottom: Great Lakes research vessel *Limnos*. (Fisheries and Oceans Canada F201507)

Opposite: Fisheries Research vessel *W.E. Ricker*. (Mike Mitchell, Fisheries and Oceans Canada F190605)

within the Marine Sciences Branch of DFO. This arrangement continued through the transfer of the Coast Guard from Transport Canada in 1995. Hydrographers and scientists had used Coast Guard ships in the past for special programs or when their own ships were not available. From 1 April 1995, all ships would be in one fleet and their use in the DFO's varied programs would only be limited by their capability.

Table 14.1 Summary of Departmental Name Changes and Responsibilities

Abbreviations

FSH	Fisheries	FRB	Fisheries Research Board
F&F	Fisheries and Forestry	MAR	Marine
ENV	Environment	M&R	Mines and Resources
F&E	Fisheries and Environment	M&TS	Mines and Technical Surveys
F&O	Fisheries and Oceans	EM&R	Energy, Mines and Resources

Date	Fisheries Protection	Fisheries Research	Oceanography	Hydrography
1930	FSH	FSH	-	MAR
1936	FSH	FSH	-	M&R
1937	FSH	FRB	FRB	M&R
1949	FSH	FRB	FRB	M&TS
1961	FSH	FRB	M&TS	M&TS
1969	F&F	FRB	EM&R	EM&R
1970	ENV	FRB	ENV	ENV
1973	ENV	ENV	ENV	ENV
1976	F&E	F&E	F&E	F&E
1979	F&O	F&O	F&O	F&O

The icebreaker *Henry Larsen*. (Fisheries and Oceans Canada F100907)

Studies and Reports Related to the Operation of the Federal Marine Fleets

The transfer of the Coast Guard to the Department of Fisheries and Oceans in 1995 was the final action taken after a long series of government studies and reports which started almost immediately after the Coast Guard was formed from the Marine Services fleet of the Department of Transport. Since then, six major studies have examined the operation of the federal fleets and recommended various forms of rationalization or consolidation.

In 1962, the Glassco Royal Commission on Government Organizations found that thirteen separate departments and agencies operated watercraft of various sizes and types. The commission concluded that transferring all vessel operations to a single agency would be impractical, but it recommended the progressive consolidation of all civilian patrol and law enforcement activities to the Canadian Coast Guard (Department of Transport). It further recommended that the Coast Guard own and manage all large civilian vessels and provide technical and personnel support services.

In 1969-70, the Audette Interdepartmental Task Force was established by the Cabinet Committee on Priorities and Planning to investigate the advantages of consolidating all civilian vessels under the Department of National Defence; that is, under naval control. The task force recommended that a single agency, within DND, should be formed to operate all civilian government vessels, which would provide vessel services to other departments on a cost recovery basis. However, there was no interdepartmental agreement on these recommendations and no action was taken.

A subcommittee of the Standing Committee on External Affairs and National Defence also addressed the subject in 1970. It recommended that the government consider consolidating all vessels engaged in transport, fisheries protection and law enforcement at sea in an enlarged Canadian Coast Guard. At the same time, a new autonomous agency would be formed to integrate all marine research, both military and civilian. In effect, this would mean the transfer of the fishery enforcement vessels to the Coast Guard while the fishery research and the hydrographic and oceanographic ships would have joined the naval research vessels in the new agency.

CHAPTER 15

Organizational Changes

The light icebreaker and navigation aids vessel *Sir William Alexander*. (Fisheries and Oceans Canada F131603

The recommendations of the subcommittee were not accepted, but by 1973 some consolidation did occur. The enforcement vessels formerly operated by the Department of Fisheries, the research vessels of the Fishery Research Board, and the hydrographic and oceanographic ships of the Department of Mines and Technical Surveys were formed into one fleet under the new Department of the Environment (renamed Fisheries and the Environment in 1976). The Coast Guard remained as it was.

The civilian fleets continued to be closely scrutinized. In August 1977, the Task Force on the Integration of Government Vessels and Aircraft submitted a report. It concluded that there had been considerable consolidation of the government fleets since the Glassco Report and stated that the department having the mandate to carry out a program should have control of the vessels and aircraft needed to carry out that mandate; but that if new approaches and marine policies were developed that cut across existing departmental lines, a consolidation of those resources might be desirable. In the meantime, it was recommended that multi-tasking be encouraged with appropriate cost recovery between departments.

In 1986-87, another study was conducted by External Affairs and Transport Canada regarding an expanded role for the Coast Guard in coastal patrol and protection. It concluded that some future integration of Fisheries and Oceans patrol vessels into the

Coast Guard warranted future study, but that the Coast Guard should not become a paramilitary organization and should remain in Transport Canada.

Looking at all these reports and their recommendations, it is apparent that successive governments kept appointing committees that they hoped would recommend the unification of the civilian fleets, but each committee in turn, after looking at the facts and the presentations of the various departments, did not do so. However, a final effort to rationalize the fleets was successful. The 1990 study and report entitled "All the Ships that Sail: A Study of Canada's Fleets," by Gordon F. Osbaldeston, PC, was a thorough study of the utilization of all the Canadian government fleets: National Defence, Transport Canada, and Fisheries and Oceans. The purpose of this investigation was:

1. to examine the current management of the federal fleets, including their practices and operations,

2. to assess the alternatives to the current management and delivery of these services and,

3. where findings warranted, to identify options for fleet consolidation.

Findings *did* warrant consolidation of some type and the options discussed in the conclusion were:

1. total consolidation under one department which, given the inclusion of the Navy's warships, would have to be the Department of National Defence,

2. total consolidation of the civilian elements under one of the fleet operators or a new agency,

3. the preservation of the status quo; that is, three operating departments, or

4. a rationalization of duties and tasks without total reorganization.

In the end, the last choice was the recommended option. Here matters rested until the 1994 government budget, which emphasized the efficiency of government services in general. This was followed by program reviews in all departments. A joint CCG/DFO working group considered several options including creating a special operating agency for marine (fleet) operations and a Crown corporation. The ability to recover costs was examined and the following comment was made: "it may be difficult to implement increased cost recovery for operations because of political pressures." This has proved to be true.

On 1 April 1995, the Canadian Coast Guard was transferred from the Department of Transport to the Department of Fisheries and Oceans, thus returning to the original arrangement of 1868. DFO's hydrographic, oceanographic and fisheries research ships and fisheries patrol vessels were integrated into the Coast Guard fleet. The mission statement of the new expanded organization was "to manage Canada's oceans and major waterways so that they are clean, safe, productive and accessible; to ensure sustainable use of fisheries resources and to facilitate trade and commerce."

Even after the merger, studies continued to examine the most efficient ways to deliver programs. Buoy placement and maintenance has been privatized in some areas and cooperation with industry in a number of fields, including pollution cleanup, continues. Like all large organizations and particularly government departments, management methods are continually being scrutinized and changes, some of them beneficial, are being introduced. The main purpose of the Coast Guard, however, remains substantially unchanged. The latest mission statement is: "Ensure the safe and environmentally responsible use of Canada's waterways, to support understanding and management of ocean resources, to facilitate the use of our waters for shipping, recreation and fishing, and to provide marine expertise in support of Canada's domestic and international interests." This is substantially the same as that defined in the Osbaldeston Report of 1990.

The Effect of Amalgamation

Periodic reorganization is essential for any large administrative entity, such as government departments, so that they can adjust to changing national policies. Reorganization "cuts the fat" and some real improvements and useful changes often result. The transfer of the Coast Guard from Transport Canada to Fisheries and Oceans and later internal reforms at Coast Guard Headquarters are examples of government reorganization introduced with the main objective of curbing growth and reducing spending. Coincidentally, at the same time as the fleet was being integrated, the Coast Guard had to cope with a budget reduction of 30% arising out of a program review affecting all departments. The size of the fleet had to be reduced, and a number of good ships were declared redundant, but one obviously beneficial effect was the rationalization of patrol vessels: the fisheries patrol craft and the SAR vessels were reclassified as "multi-tasked cutters." For the crews, integration was complicated by the need to reconcile two different fleet management and operating cultures. (The differences were subtle but real.) This was done over a couple of years by cross-appointing personnel to ships that used to be in the "other" fleet. Eventually, people adjusted to unfamiliar styles of management, uniforms were standardized, and the remaining ships were all painted the same: Coast Guard red.

The integration of management, both at headquarters in Ottawa and in the regions, also caused some inevitable soul searching. Those elements of the Coast Guard that are shore based including rescue, safety and environmental response, marine navigation services, marine communications and traffic services and the icebreaking program, had to adjust to the new reality, which proved to be more than simply changing their offices from one Ottawa high-rise to another. However, by 2002, the Coast Guard was firmly within the Fisheries and Oceans family.

Marine Services Fees

One of the first challenges the Coast Guard faced after its transfer to DFO was the question of marine services fees. Throughout its history, the Coast Guard had been in a dilemma regarding the question of imposing fees directly on the recipients of its services. Faced with the budgetary restrictions that came with the amalgamation, cost recovery seemed a desirable measure to administrators, at least if the receipts could be used to defray the cost of services or to improve them, rather than being paid into the government's general revenue. However, there is a general public perception that, if there is a service that the government should deliver, such as navigation aids and ice-breaking, it should be provided without billing the recipients who need it because they are engaged in a business that could not be carried out without such measures, which also is of benefit to all Canadians.

Similarly, the provision of Search and Rescue resources—a prime reason for the existence of the Coast Guard—is the duty of any society that can afford it. In 1950, as mentioned in Chapter 2, the head of a large tug company had been concerned that a Coast Guard would undertake salvage operations in addition to performing rescues. In practice, this has never been a problem. The line between a rescue and a tow is usually easy to determine and the recipients who are the borderline cases are generally small vessels—fishing boats and yachts. When larger vessels are in trouble, the Coast Guard will hand over the operation to private tug or salvage operators once the danger to life is over, but normally will continue to monitor the situation to guard against pollution.

Nevertheless, the question of marine services fees is periodically revived, and has been under intense review since the transfer of the Coast Guard from Transport to Fisheries and Oceans. Opposition to such a proposal was expected and did indeed materialize.

The offshore patrol vessel *Leonard J. Cowley*. (Fisheries and Oceans Canada F181303)

The coastal research and survey vessel *Matthew*. (Fisheries and Oceans Canada F200902)

The Coast Guard recognized that, if fees were to be imposed, the industry had a right to expect a well-costed and rational basis for the charges. The Coast Guard and the Marine Advisory Board (a council comprising commercial shipping interests providing advice to the Commissioner) began to examine options for developing a fair and equitable user fee structure for marine navigation services. In May 1995, the House of Commons Standing Committee on Transport examined the issue further, making recommendations of its own on CCG cost recovery, excluding Search and Rescue activities.

More than a year's efforts between the Coast Guard and the marine industry resulted in the definition in June 1996 (modified in 1997) of Marine Navigation Services Fees (MNSF). Industry had accepted the primary objective of recovering some of the cost of providing aids to navigation, including fixed and floating aids and electronic systems. Separate fee structures were established for the West Coast, the Great Lakes, the St Lawrence and the Atlantic area, the rather complex details of which need not be examined here. Ships fitted with GPS and ECDIS, and therefore capable of more precise navigation, would benefit from a discount.

An Icebreaking Service Fee (ISF) was to have been introduced in 1996, but this was deferred one year, and then again in 1997 until 1998. The fee would cover routing and ice forecasting services and would have applied to ships operating in Great Lakes, the St Lawrence River and Gulf and Cabot Strait during a defined ice season. Ships built to the highest ice class would receive a discount. Not all ships would be subject to these fees. Vessels operating to ports in remote areas, or north of latitude 60° and all fishing vessels and pleasure craft would be exempt.

In 1998/99, the MNSF was set to recover 30.8% (or $26.7 million) of the estimated cost of providing services to commercial shipping, and the Icebreaking Services fee rate was calculated to generate $6.65 million (or approximately 8%) of the cost of providing a package of icebreaking services. However, in 1998 the government imposed a three-year freeze on both the navigation services fee and the icebreaking fee, while Coast Guard and industry consultations continued and Treasury Board undertook an impact study. It was intended to have a long-term arrangement in place by the fall of 2002. However, all this, in fact, is still a plan. This is an issue that is still not resolved.

The Oceans Act

In Canada, marine issues have been addressed by a wide range of Acts of Parliament, several of which have already been cited in previous chapters. Among these are the Canada Shipping Act, the Canada Marine Act, the Canada Transportation Act, the Navigable Waters Protection Act, the Pilotage Act and several others. The most recent of these is the Oceans Act, which defines the limits of Canadian sovereignty and is also the act under which the Coast Guard operates.

The Oceans Act was first passed on 18 December 1996 and came into force on 31 January 1997. The Act establishes Canada's maritime boundaries and zones. Where these zones are adjacent to the territorial sea of another state or areas over which another state has sovereign rights, they terminate at the boundary between Canadian waters and those of the other state. The following boundaries and zones are defined.

1. the baselines (straight lines joining consecutive geographical coordinates of designated points at the low-water line along the coast)

2. the internal waters (which lie inside the baselines),

3. the territorial sea (which extends to 12 nautical miles from the baselines),

4. the contiguous zone (which extends from 12 to 24 nautical miles from the baselines),

5. the exclusive economic zone (which extends to 200 nautical miles from the baselines),

6. the Continental Shelf (being the submerged prolongation of the land mass of Canada including the slope at its outer limit, but not the deep ocean floor).

The Minister of Fisheries and Oceans has the principal duty to administer the Oceans Act, although other ministers, boards and agencies of the federal government, provincial and territorial governments, aboriginal organizations and coastal communities must be consulted when they are affected.

1. In the internal waters and the territorial sea, all the laws of Canada, including those of provinces, apply.

2. In the contiguous zone, ships and persons who have committed

offences in Canada can be arrested, and this action can also be taken if there is reason to believe that they may do so; but the Attorney General must consent to the boarding of non-Canadian ships.

3. In the exclusive economic zone (EEZ), Canada has sovereign rights for the purpose of exploring, exploiting, conserving and managing natural resources, both living and non-living (gas, oil and minerals).

4. On the portion of the Continental Shelf that lies outside the EEZ, Canada claims sovereign rights over mineral and other non-living resources and over living species that stay on the seabed (e.g., crabs and shellfish) but not pelagic fish. Canada also asserts jurisdiction over installations and structures attached to the Continental Shelf (i.e., oil exploitation platforms or rigs).

The main purpose of the act is to create an oceans management strategy based on the principles of sustainable development and integrated management of activities in Canadian waters. A precautionary approach, erring on the side of caution, is adopted. Marine protected areas may be established and activities within them regulated. The powers of enforcement officers are defined in the act. Its application has gradually evolved as the Department of Fisheries and Oceans developed the organizational structure to give effect to this new mandate. At its introduction, there was concern for duplication between DFO and Environment Canada in the approach to environmental issues. However, it was argued that the added complexity of "oceans" developmental issues did seem to justify this new approach.

The Oceans Act gave full definition and legal authority to the previously executed integration of the Canadian Coast Guard with the Department of Fisheries and Oceans. Section 41 of the Oceans Act authorizes the minister to provide specified services through the CCG Fleet. In Section 41 of the act they are defined as all matters not assigned by law to any other department, board or agency of the government of Canada, relating to:

- services for the safe, economical and efficient movement of ships in Canadian waters through the provision of aids to navigation systems and services; marine communications and traffic management services; icebreaking and ice management services; channel maintenance;

- the marine component of the federal Search and Rescue program;

- pleasure craft safety, including the regulation of the construction, inspection equipment and operation of pleasure craft;

- the support of departments, boards and agencies of the government of Canada through the provision of ships, aircraft and other marine services.

Many of these services were previously unfounded in formal authorities and existed solely through historical precedence and political will.

The DFO Management Model

As has already been discussed, the government policies behind the transfer of the Coast Guard to DFO and its management since 1995 were those arising out of the budget reduction exercises associated with the government's program reviews of the early 1990s. The key goal was the integration and rationalization of the civilian fleet but, at the same time, all government departments were being asked to structure their activities in such a manner as to be more inclusive, transparent and fair. The challenge facing the Department of Fisheries and Oceans was to introduce new policies and procedures to assure sound management and accountability, enhanced consultative processes, and a service delivery system which more closely reflected client needs. It was also necessary to restore confidence in the department which, in the perception of the public, had been seriously damaged by the decline of the fisheries on both coasts.

One challenge in bringing government closer to the people is moving decision-making closer to those who are chiefly affected by those decisions. Federal programs are intended to provide benefits on a national scale but regional variations need to be considered. One way to achieve this end is to move authority for the quality of program delivery into the regions. This is consistent with major federal policies oriented to transparency, inclusiveness and fairness. Within the DFO, a decentralized process has evolved whereby regional directors general are provided with the budget to achieve the stated national program objectives and are assigned responsibility for the delivery of programs for each of the major sectors in their respective regions. However, they have the authority to move funds between sectors to meet local demands.

Under this management model, introduced in 2000, DFO headquarters is responsible for the development of program budgets and the implementation of appropriate national-scale performance measurement systems. In the case of the Coast Guard, headquarters functions would be limited to policy, program development and evaluation. A project team was established to flesh out the new organization and, by 3 April 2002 a new Concept of Operations was formally introduced. This strategic plan identified both the challenges and opportunities facing the department with the ultimate objective of making the Coast Guard more adaptable to change. The project team hoped to create a framework for CCG HQ structure, planning and decision-making that would be effective in the twenty-first century. The department, as with other government departments, wants to put its faith in a number of "enabling" tools, including improved planning systems, improved performance measurement systems, and (eventually) a move to fully integrated business performance management.

Every system has its drawbacks and regional flexibility naturally introduces regional diversity which, over time, tends to give the impression of lack of coordination. In 2002, just as DFO was congratulating itself on the effectiveness of its new flexible management methods, an Auditor General's report levelled criticism at what was perceived as lack of central control. It is only fair to say, however, that all this has been done before—in fact, the authors of every reorganization hope for improved efficiency, which they usually claim to have achieved, but only because the front-line personnel have adapted to whatever new measuring and reporting methods have been introduced while continuing to perform the same essential services that they have always provided.

The Future

It is always difficult to take one moment in history and forecast long-term implications. Still, there is little doubt that the terrorist attacks of September 11th 2001 in New York and Washington have changed the priorities of the world in favour of safety and security issues. In Canada, cooperation with the United States, questions of coastal surveillance, a common border protocol and port security are sure to be driving issues for many years. In response to the events of September 11th the federal government established the Ad Hoc Committee for Public Security, known as the Manley Committee: $60 million was allocated for marine security over the next 5 years, with $15 million over 3 years going to the DFO to increase on-the-water presence and aerial surveillance. It was also decided to continue the Loran-C navigation system beyond its planned phase-out (in case the United States decided to degrade or scramble the GPS system). An interdepartmental group on Marine Security includes membership from Transport Canada, the Coast Guard, security forces and federal central agencies.

The fisheries research vessel *Teleost*. (Fisheries and Oceans Canada F191002)

In addition to security issues, the marine community will continue to develop more consolidated and integrated communication and information processes. In the area of navigation, DGPS, ECDIS and AIS systems are expected to reduce the need for government-provided infrastructure like navigation systems and aids. The impact of improved communications and the Internet will be profound. The "marine electronic highway" offers a significant improvement in both safety and effectiveness for mariners.

In the area of Search and Rescue, significant changes are also imminent. Although the number of lifeboat stations will be increased during the next few years, the "Search" element has already, to a great extent, been taken out of Search and Rescue, chiefly due to the extensive use of compact self-contained GPS receivers, which provide an exact position at sea or on land. In the future, based on new satellite constellations, any person travelling on the surface of the ocean (commercial, fishing or recreational) could carry an inexpensive and effective transponder. All this will usually allow units to concentrate on "Rescue" rather than "Search." (But this is not always the case: when diving vessel *Lacuna* caught fire off Halifax on 24 October 2002, there was no time for the crew to get into the wheelhouse and read off the GPS position and they owed their rescue to the fact that a Sea King helicopter in the vicinity spotted the plume of smoke from their burning vessel.)

In close coastal areas, cellular phones are now often used when previously a radio call would have been made and the use of the Internet for the improved availability of environmental data will also improve safety. To the maximum extent possible, enhanced training and crew certification will be stressed as an effective means of taking human error out of SAR incidents.

Finally, in the new century, an important Canadian technical advance promises to provide the ability to track ships, low flying aircraft and icebergs out to about 200 nautical miles—in fact to the limit of the exclusive economic zone. HF long-range surface wave radar uses land based fixed-array antennae that transmit high frequency (HF) vertically polarized radio pulses that follow the earth's curvature. It will operate only over the ocean, as the seawater and particularly its salt content is essential to its function. The value of such an installation in the fields of security and defence, sovereignty, fisheries protection, Search and Rescue and iceberg tracking is obvious. Although not capable of detecting very small craft at long range, it is an enormous advance over previous surveillance systems such as normal radar, which has a range of just over line-of-sight, and aircraft and ship patrols which can only be sporadic. When combined with information from satellites, AIS, AMVER, and traffic control measures such as ECAREG, enhanced surveillance of our seaward approaches by DND and DFO can be maintained. At the time of writing only two stations have been installed, at Cape Race and Cape Bonavista in Newfoundland, but they cover almost all of the Grand Banks. This will be a real contribution to North American security enforcement that has become so important since September 2001.

The new station-based lifeboat *Cape Sutil*.
(Frank Jess, Fisheries and Oceans Canada
F164603)

Conclusion

It should be noted that the first major task of Gordon W. Stead when he assumed responsibility for the DOT fleet in 1958 was the reform of the headquarters structure and this is again the focus of Coast Guard senior management at the present time. The changes instituted in the year 1995 and still in progress mark an important turning point in the history of the Canadian Coast Guard, which, in 2002, is still undergoing major adjustments. The new strategies are in accord with recent Treasury Board directives on the use of business planning processes. Some of the measures are experimental and the results are yet to be seen, but the Coast Guard service has undergone many management system changes and undoubtedly will continue to serve the Canadian maritime community as it has in the past, doing its best to ensure the safety of all who use the seas.

Saluti Primum, Auxilio Semper

APPENDIX I

Ministers, Deputy Ministers, Senior Officials and Honorees

Ministers of Marine and Fisheries, 1867-1930

Peter Mitchell	1867-1873		James Sutherland	1902
Sir Albert Smith	1873-1878		J.F.R. Préfontaine	1902-1905
James C. Pope	1878-1882		L.P. Brodeur	1906-1911
A.W. McLelan	1882-1885		Rodolphe Lemieux	1911
Sir George Foster	1885-1888		Sir John D. Hazen	1911-1917
Sir Charles Tupper	1888-1894		C.C. Ballantyne	1917-1921
John Costigan	1894-1896		Ernest Lapointe	1921-1924
Sir Louis H. Davies	1896-1901		P.J.A. Cardin	1924-1930

Ministers of Marine 1930-1936

A. Duranleau	1930-1935		C.D. Howe	1935-1936

Ministers of Transport 1936-1995

C.D. Howe	1936-1940		Otto Lang	1975-1979
P.J.A. Cardin	1940-1942		Don Mazankowski	1979-1980
J. E. Michaud	1942-1945		Jean-Luc Pepin	1980-1983
Lionel Chevrier	1945-1954		Lloyd Axworthy	1983-1984
Leon Balcer	1960-1963		Don Mazankowski	1984-1986
G.J. McIlraith	1963-1964		John C. Crosbie	1986-1988
J.W. Pickersgill	1964-1967		Benoît Bouchard	1988-1990
Paul Hellyer	1967-1969		Douglas Lewis	1990-1991
Don Jamieson	1969-1972		Jean Corbeil	1991-1993
Jean Marchand	1972-1975		Douglas Young	1993-1996

Ministers of Fisheries 1930-1979

Cyrus MacMillan	1930		James Sinclair	1952-1957
Edgar N. Rhodes	1930-1932		John Angus Maclean	1957-1963
A. Duraneau (acting)	1932-1934		Hédard Robichaud	1963-1968
Grote Stirling (acting)	1934-1935		Jack Davies	1968-1974
William G. Ernst	1935		Jeanne Sauvé	1974-1975
Joseph-Enoil Michaud	1935-1942		(Minister of the Environment)	
E. Bertrand (acting)	1942-1945		Roméo LeBlanc	1974-1975
H.F.G. Bridges	1945-1947		(Minister of State, Fisheries)	
E. Bertrand (acting)	1947		Jean Marchand	1974-1975
Milton F. Gregg	1947-1948		(Minister of the Environment)	
James A. MacKinnon	1948		Roméo LeBlanc	1976-1979
Robert W. Mayhew	1948-1952			

Ministers of Fisheries and Oceans 1979-2002

James A. McGrath	1979-1980	Bernard Valcourt	1990-1991
Roméo LeBlanc	1980-1982	John Crosbie	1991-1993
Pierre de Bané	1982-1984	Brian Tobin	1993-1996
Herb Breau	1984	Fred Mifflin	1996-1997
John Allen Fraser	1984-1985	David Anderson	1997-1999
Eric Nielsen (acting)	1985	Herb Dhaliwal	1999-2002
Thomas E. Siddon	1985-1990	Robert Thibault	2002-

Deputy Ministers of Marine and Fisheries 1868-1930

William Smith	1868-1884	George J. Desbarats	1909-1910
Col. John Tilton	1884-1892	Alexander Johnson	1911-1914
William Smith	1892-1896	George J. Desbarats	1914-1920
John Hardie (acting)	1896	Alexander Johnson	1920-1928
LCol. F.F. Gourdeau	1896-1909	William A. Found	1928-1930

Deputy Ministers of Marine 1930-1936

Alexander Johnson	1930-1933	R.K. Smith	1936
(Office vacant)	1933-1936		

Deputy Ministers of Transport 1936-1995

V. Irving Smart	1936-1940	Arthur Kroeger	1979-1983
C.P. Edwards	1941-1948	Ramsey Withers	1983-1988
J.C. Lessard	1948-1954	Glen Shortliffe	1988-1990
C.W. West	1954	Huguette Labelle	1990-1993
J.R. Baldwin	1954-1968	Jocelyne Bourgon	1993-1994
O.G. Stoner	1968-1975	Nick Mulder	1994-1997
Sylvain Cloutier	1975-1979		

Deputy Ministers of Fisheries 1930-1979

William A. Found	1930-1938	George R. Clark	1954-1963
John J. Cowie	1939-1940	Alfred W. Needler	1963-1971
Donovan Bartley Finn	1940-1946	Robert F. Shaw	1971-1974
Stewart Bates	1947-1954	J. Blair Seaborn	1974-1979

Deputy Ministers of Fisheries and Oceans, 1979-2002

Donald D. Tansley	1979-1982	Bruce Rawson	1990-1994
Arthur W. May	1882-1986	William Rowat	1994-1997
Peter Meyboom	1986-1990	Wayne G. Wouters	1997-

Director General Marine Services and Assistant Deputy Minister, Marine

Gordon W. Stead	1958-1970

Administrators, Marine Services and Assistant Deputy Ministers, Marine

Pierre Camu	1970-1973	A.W.Allan	1982-1983
Roy Illing	1973-1977	John Allan	1984-1985
G.M. Sinclair	1977-1982		

Note : From 1970 to 1985, the Administrator, Marine Services was also the Assistant Deputy Minister, Marine. In 1985, the Commissioner of the Coast Guard assumed this title. From 1990 to 1993, Mr R.A. Quail was the Associate Deputy Minister of Transport, as well as Commissioner.

Commissioners of the Coast Guard

William A. O'Neil	1975-1980	John F. Thomas	1993-1996
Andrew L. Collier	1980-1983	David B. Watters	1997-1998
Ranald A. Quail	1984-1993	John Adams	1998-

Honorary Chief Commissioner

On July 5th 1976, the Rt. Hon. Jules Leger, Governor-General of Canada, agreed to become Honorary Chief Commissioner of the Canadian Coast Guard, and all subsequent Governors- General have held this title.

Honorary Commodores of the Coast Guard

(and the dates of their appointment)

Charles A. Caron	1962	J.R. Baldwin	1970
Eric S. Brand	1963	Anthony H.G. Storrs	1973
Gordon W. Stead	1970	William A. O'Neil	1981

APPENDIX II

Fleet Lists

Table 1   The Department of Transport Marine Fleet in 1942

Agency	Name	GRT	Built	Remarks
Icebreakers (4 +1)				
Halifax	*Montcalm*	1432	1904	Preparing for delivery to USSR
Québec	*Lady Grey*	733	1906	
Québec	*Saurel*	1176	1929	
Québec	*N.B. McLean*	3254	1930	
Québec	*Ernest Lapointe*	1179	1941	
Lighthouse Supply Vessels and Buoy Tenders (14)				
Québec	*Druid*	503	1902	
Halifax	*Lady Laurier*	1051	1902	
Victoria	*Estevan*	1161	1912	
Saint John	*Dollard*	835	1913	
Prescott	*Grenville*	497	1915	
Montreal	*Argenteuil*	165	1917	
Saint John	*Laurentian*	355	1902	Transferred from RCN 1919
Charlottetown	*Brant*	285	1928	
Montreal	*Safeguarder*	665	1914	Purchased 1929
Halifax	*Bernier*	317	1930	
Parry Sound	*St Heliers*	930	1919	Purchased 1930
Prince Rupert	*Alberni*	502	1927	Formerly a powered coal barge, converted 1936
Prescott	*Franklin*	613	1919	Transferred from Dept. of Interior 1939
Québec	*Chesterfield*	734	1928	Converted 1943
Small Buoytenders (2)				
Victoria	*Berens*	73	1921	
Prince Rupert	*Birnie*	73	1921	

Agency	Name	GRT	Built	Remarks
Survey & Sounding Vessels (5)				
Québec	*Bellechasse*	417	1912	
Québec	*Detector*	584	1915	
Sorel	*Berthier*	368	1916	
Québec	*Lanoraie II*	177	1928	
Sorel	*Frontenac*	248	1930	
Tugs (4)				
Québec	*Jalobert*	278	1923	
Montreal	*Vercheres*	104	1901	Purchased 1929
Rimouski	*Citadelle*	431	1932	Pilot vessel & fire-tug
Halifax	*Ocean Eagle*	420	1919	Transferred from NHB 1938

Table 2   The Coast Guard Fleet in 1962

Base	Name	GRT	Built	Remarks
Icebreakers (6)				
Charlottetown	*Saurel*	1176	1929	
Québec	*N.B. McLean*	3254	1930	
Montreal	*Ernest Lapointe*	1179	1941	
Québec	*d'Iberville*	5678	1952	
Dartmouth	*Labrador*	3823	1953	Transferred from RCN 1958
Dartmouth	*John A. Macdonald*	6186	1960	
Eastern Arctic Patrol (1)				
Québec	*C.D. Howe*	3628	150	
Weather Ships (3)				
Victoria	*Stone Town*	1883	1944	Transferred from RCN 1950
Victoria	*St. Catharines*	1895	1943	Transferred from RCN 1950
Victoria	*St. Stephen*	1895	1944	Transferred from RCN 1955

Base	Name	GRT	Built	Remarks
Navigation Aids Vessels / Light Icebreakers (6)				
Québec	*Montcalm*	2017	1957	
Charlottetown	*Wolfe*	2017	1959	
St.John's	*Sir Humphrey Gilbert*	2053	1959	
Victoria	*Camsell*	2022	1959	
Dartmouth	*Sir William Alexander*	2154	1959	
Parry Sound	*Alexander Henry*	1674	1959	
Navigation Aids Vessels, Ice-strengthened (6)				
Dartmouth	*Edward Cornwallis*	1965	1949	
Saint John	*Walter E. Foster*	1672	1954	
Québec	*Montmorency*	751	1957	
Charlottetown	*Tupper*	1353	1959	
Victoria	*Simon Fraser*	1353	1960	
Saint John	*Thomas Carleton*	1217	1960	
Navigation Aids Vessels (9)				
Victoria	*Estevan*	1161	1912	
Prescott	*Grenville*	497	1915	
Sorel	*Safeguarder*	665	1914	Purchased 1929
Québec	*Chesterfield*	734	1928	Converted 1943
Dartmouth	*Brant*	285	1928	
Parry Sound	*C. P. Edwards*	338	1946	
Prince Rupert	*Alexander Mackenzie*	576	1950	
Victoria	*Sir James Douglas*	564	1956	
Sorel	*Verendrye*	297	1957	
Small Navigation Aids Vessels (3)				
St. John's	*Sea Beacon*			
Goose Bay	*Prima Vista*	64	1956	
Thunder Bay	*Nokomis*	64	1956	

Base	Name	GRT	Built	Remarks
River Navigation Aids Vessels (3)				
Lake Athabaska	*Miskanaw*	104	1958	
Hay River	*Dumit*	104	1958	
Hay River	*Eckaloo*	133	1961	
Northern Supply Vessels: (9)				
Dartmouth	*Mink*	543	1944	Purchased from RN 1958
Québec	*Marmot*	543	1944	Purchased from RN 1958
Dartmouth	*Auk*	1089	1944	Purchased from RN 1958
Dartmouth	*Gannet*	1089	1944	Purchased from RN 1958
Dartmouth	*Skua*	1089	1944	Purchased from RN 1960
Québec	*Raven*	1089	1944	Purchased from RN 1959
Québec	*Puffin*	1089	1944	Purchased from RN 1960
Québec	*Eider*	1089	1944	Purchased from RN 1961
Dartmouth	*Nanook*	1155	1946	Purchased from RN 1960
Survey & Sounding Vessels (6)				
Québec	*Detector*	584	1915	
Sorel	*Frontenac*	248	1930	
Montreal	*Glenada*	101	1943	
Hamilton	*Porte Dauphine*	347	1952	On loan from RCN 1960
Montreal	*Ville Marie*	390	1960	
Québec	*Beauport*	813	1960	
Station Lifeboats (3)				
Bayview, NS, Bamfield and Tofino, BC				

Table 3 The Coast Guard Fleet in 1982

Region	Name	GRT	Built	Remarks
Icebreakers (7+1)				
Laurentian	d'Iberville	5678	1952	Retired –for sale
Maritimes	Labrador	3823	1953	Transferred from RCN 1958
Maritimes	John A. Macdonald	6186	1960	
Maritimes	Louis S. St Laurent	10908	1969	
Laurentian	Norman McL.Rogers	4179	1969	
Laurentian	Pierre Radisson	5910	1978	
Newfoundland	Sir John Franklin	5910	1979	
Laurentian	Des Groseilliers	5910	1982	
Cable Ship (1)				
Newfoundland	John Cabot	5234	1965	
Weather Ships (0+2)				
Western	Quadra	5537	1966	Not required - for sale
Western	Vancouver	5537	1966	Not required - for sale
Navigation Aids Vessels / Light Icebreakers (8)				
Laurentian	Montcalm	2017	1957	
Western	Wolfe	2017	1959	
Newfoundland	Sir Humphrey Gilbert	2053	1959	
Western	Camsell	2022	1959	
Maritimes	Sir William Alexander	2154	1959	
Central	Alexander Henry	1674	1959	
Laurentian	J.E. Bernier	2475	1967	
Central	Griffon	2212	1970	

Region	Name	GRT	Built	Remarks
Navigation Aids Vessels, Ice-strengthened (11)				
Maritimes	*Edward Cornwallis*	1965	1949	
Maritimes	*Walter E. Foster*	1672	1954	
Central	*Montmorency*	751	1957	
Maritimes	*Tupper*	1353	1959	
Laurentian	*Simon Fraser*	1353	1960	
Maritimes	*Thomas Carleton*	1217	1960	
Central	*Simcoe*	962	1962	
Maritimes	*Narwhal*	2064	1963	
Laurentian	*Tracy*	962	1967	
Newfoundland	*Bartlett*	1317	1969	
Maritimes	*Provo Wallis*	1317	1969	
Navigation Aids Vessels (7)				
Western	*Alexander Mackenzie*	576	1950	
Western	*Sir James Douglas*	564	1956	
Central	*Verendrye*	297	1957	
Laurentian	*Montmagny*	328	1963	
Central	*Kenoki*	310	1964	
Newfoundland	*Skidegate*	238	1964	Enlarged 1978
Maritimes	*Robert Foulis*	258	1969	
Small Navigation Aids Vessels (3)				
Central	*Nokomis*	64	1956	
Central	*Cove Isle*	80	1980	
Central	*Gull Isle*	80	1980	
River and Lake Navigation Aids Vessels (6)				
Western	*Miskanaw*	104	1958	Lake Athabaska
Western	*Dumit*	104	1958	Mackenzie River
Western	*Eckaloo*	133	1961	Mackenzie River
Western	*Tembah*	189	1963	Mackenzie River
Western	*Nahidik*	856	1974	Mackenzie River
Central	*Namao*	218	1975	Lake Winnipeg

Region	Name	GRT	Built	Remarks
Survey & Sounding Vessels (6				
Laurentian	*Ville Marie*	390	1960	
Laurentian	*Beauport*	813	1960	
Laurentian	*Nicolet*	887	1966	
Laurentian	*Jean Bourdon*	81	1968	
Laurentian	*GC 03*	57	1973	
Laurentian	*GC 06*	57	1973	
Training Ship (1)				
CG College	*Mikula*	526	1959	Converted 1972
Offshore SAR Cutters (5)				
Maritimes	*Alert*	1752	1969	
Maritimes	*Daring*	657	1958	Trans. from RCMP 1971
Western	*George E. Darby*	942	1972	Purchased 1977
Newfoundland	*Grenfell*	877	1972	Purchased 1978
Newfoundland	*Jackman*	877	1972	Purchased 1979
SAR Cutters (6+5)				
Maritimes	*Rally*	140	1963	For transfer to the RCN
Maritimes	*Rapid*	140	1963	For transfer to the RCN
Central	*Relay*	140	1963	For sale
Western	*Racer*	140	1963	
Western	*Ready*	140	1963	
Western	*Rider*	140	1963	Transferred from Fisheries 1969
Central	*Spindrift*	56	1964	
Central	*Spray*	56	1964	
Central	*Spume*	56	1964	
Laurentian	*Ile Rouge*	57	1982	Completing
Central	*Point Henry*	57	1982	Completing

Region	Self-righting Lifeboats	Other Small Craft	Hovercraft
Western	5	5	3
Central	6		
Laurentian	1	1	1
Maritimes	9		
Newfoundland	2		

Table 4   The Fisheries and Oceans Fleet in 1982

Region	Name	GRT	Built	Remarks
Offshore Hydrographic/Oceanographic Ships (4)				
Atlantic	*Baffin*	3567	1956	Ice-strengthened
Atlantic	*Hudson*	3740	1963	Ice-strengthened
Maritimes	*Parizeau*	1360	1967	
Atlantic	*Dawson*	1360	1968	
Coastal & Lake Hydrographic & Science Ships (4)				
Atlantic	*Maxwell*	244	1961	
Pacific	*Vector*	516	1967	
Great Lakes	*Limnos*	460	1968	
Great Lakes	*Bayfield*	178	1960	Purchased 1974
Offshore Fisheries Research Ships (4+3)				
Atlantic	*A.T. Cameron*	753	1958	Retired - for sale
Pacific	*G.B. Read*	768	1962	
Atlantic	*E.E. Prince*	406	1966	
Atlantic	*Wilfred Templeman*	925	1981	
Atlantic	*Alfred Needler*	959	1982	Completing
Atlantic	*Gadus Atlantica*	2350	1967	Chartered from 1977
Atlantic	*Lady Hammond*	897	1972	Chartered from 1978
Inshore Fisheries Research Ships (4)				
Atlantic	*Navicula*	80	1968	
Atlantic	*J.L. Hart*	89	1974	
Atlantic	*Shamook*	117	1975	
Atlantic	*Marinus*	117	1977	

Region	Name	GRT	Built	Remarks
Offshore Fisheries Patrol Vessels (4+1)				
Maritimes	*Lamna ex Cygnus*	524	1959	Retired – for sale
Maritimes	*Chebucto*	750	1966	
Pacific	*Tanu*	754	1968	
Newfoundland	*Cape Roger*	1255	1977	
Maritimes	*Cygnus*	1210	1982	Completing
Coastal Fisheries Patrol Vessels (3+1)				
Pacific	*Howay*	201	1936	Acquired 1946 For Sale
Pacific	*Laurier*	201	1936	Acquired 1946
Newfoundland	*Cape Harrison*	295	1976	
Maritimes	*Louisbourg*	295	1977	
Small Inshore Fishery Patrol Vessels (44)				
Newfoundland (8) Scotia-Fundy (6) Québec (1) Mackenzie River (1) Pacific (28)				

Table 5   The Coast Guard Fleet in 2002

Region	Name	GRT	Built	Remarks
Icebreakers (5+1)				
Maritimes	*Louis S. St Laurent*	11441	1969	Modernised 1988-1993
Québec	*Pierre Radisson*	5910	1978	
Québec	*Sir John Franklin*	5910	1979	Under conversion
Québec	*Des Groseilliers*	5910	1982	
Newfoundland	*Henry Larsen*	6166	1987	
Maritimes	*Terry Fox*	4234	1983	Chartered 1991 Purchased 1993

Region	Name	GRT	Built	Remarks
Navigation Aids Vessels / Light Icebreakers (10+1)				
Newfoundland	*Sir Humphrey Gilbert*	2153	1959	For sale
Newfoundland	*J.E. Bernier*	2475	1967	
Central	*Griffon*	2212	1970	
Central	*Samuel Risley*	1967	1985	
Maritimes	*Earl Grey*	1988	1986	
Québec	*George R. Pearkes*	3809	1986	
Québec	*Martha L. Black*	3816	1986	
Pacific	*Sir Wilfrid Laurier*	3812	1986	
Maritimes	*Edward Cornwallis*	3727	1986	
Maritimes	*Sir William Alexander*	3727	1987	
Newfoundland	*Ann Harvey*	3853	1987	
Navigation Aids Vessels, Ice-strengthened (4+1)				
Maritimes	*Simon Fraser*	1353	1960	For sale
Central	*Simcoe*	962	1962	Modernised 1988
Québec	*Tracy*	962	1967	Modernised 1986
Pacific	*Bartlett*	1317	1969	Modernised 1988
Maritimes	*Provo Wallis*	1462	1969	Modernised 1990
Small Navigation Aids Tenders (7)				
Central	*Cove Isle*	80	1980	
Central	*Gull Isle*	80	1980	
Central	*Caribou Isle*	92	1985	
Maritimes	*Partridge Island*	92	1985	
Maritimes	*Ile des Barques*	92	1985	
Québec	*Ile des Saint-Ours*	92	1986	
Pacific	*Tsekoa II*	161	1984	From DPW 1995
River and Lake Navigation Aids Vessels (6)				
Central & Arctic	*Tembah*	189	1963	In reserve
Central & Arctic	*Nahidik*	856	1974	
Central & Arctic	*Namao*	218	1975	Lake Winnipeg
Central & Arctic	*Dumit*	569	1979	
Central & Arctic	*Eckaloo*	661	1988	
Central & Arctic	*Traverse*	71	1998	Lake of the Woods

Region	Name	GRT	Built	Remarks
Offshore Research and Survey Vessels (3)				
Maritimes	Hudson	3740	1963	Modernised 1990
Maritimes	Parizeau	1360	1967	
Pacific	John P. Tully	2021	1985	
Coastal Research, Survey and Sounding Vessels (8)				
Pacific	Vector	515	1967	Modernised 1995
Central	Limnos	460	1968	Modernised 1981
Québec	GC 03	57	1973	Twin hulls
Newfoundland	Louis M. Lauzier	322	1976	On charter to MUN
Québec	F.C.G. Smith	438	1985	Twin hulls
Maritimes	Matthew	857	1990	
Pacific	R.B. Young	300	1990	
Québec	Frederick G. Creed	151	1988	Twin hulls. Purchased 1994
Offshore Fisheries Research Vessels (4)				
Newfoundland	Wilfred Templeman	925	1981	
Maritimes	Alfred Needler	959	1982	
Pacific	W.E. Ricker	1105	1978	Purchased 1986
Newfoundland	Teleost	2405	1988	Purchased 1993
Inshore Fisheries Research Vessels (8)				
Pacific	Caligus	41	1967	
Maritimes	Navicula	80	1968	
Central	Shark	30	1971	
Maritimes	J.L. Hart	89	1974	
Newfoundland	Shamook	117	1975	
Maritimes	Pandalus III	28	1986	
Maritimes	Opilio	74	1989	
Québec	Calanus II	160	1991	
Offshore Patrol Cutters (4)				
Newfoundland	Cape Roger	1255	1977	Modernised 1996
Maritimes	Cygnus	1210	1982	Modernised 1998
Newfoundland	Leonard J. Cowley	2243	1984	
Newfoundland	Sir Wilfred Grenfell	2404	1987	

Region	Name	GRT	Built	Remarks
Coastal Patrol Cutters (7)				
Pacific	*Tanu*	754	1968	Modernised 1987
Québec	*Louisbourg*	295	1977	
Québec	*E.P. Le Québécois*	186	1968	Purchased 1987
Newfoundland	*Harp*	180	1986	
Newfoundland	*Hood*	180	1986	
Pacific	*Gordon Reid*	880	1990	
Pacific	*Arrow Post*	228	1991	
Small Multi-tasked Cutters (10)				
Central	*Advent*	72	1972	
Pacific	*Sooke Post*	59	1973	
Pacific	*Kitimat II*	57	1974	
Pacific	*Atlin Post*	57	1975	
Pacific	*Comox Post*	57	1975	
Central	*Cape Hurd*	55	1982	
Pacific	*Point Race*	55	1982	
Pacific	*Point Henry*	57	1982	
Laurentian	*Isle Rouge*	57	1982	
Maritimes	*Cumella*	80	1983	
Air Cushion Vehicles (4)				
Pacific	*CG 045*		1969	SRN-6
Québec	*Waban-Aki*		1987	
Québec	*Sipu-Muin*		1998	
Pacific	*Siyäy*		1998	

Vessel	Nfld.	Mar. Québec	Central	Pacific
Self-righting Lifeboats (25)				
Cape Type	3	3		
Arun type	2	7	1	
44-foot Type	3	2	3	
RHI type		1		
Other Small Craft (23)				
Inshore patrol craft	8	1	1	1
Inshore fisheries research	1	1		
Utility craft	1	1.4	4	

FCIP Vessel Type Definitions

Type No. **Vessel Type and Work Programs**

1500*   Polar Icebreaker. Year-round operations–all Arctic waters.

1400*   Sub-Polar Icebreaker. Year-round operations–all Arctic waters except Ice Zone One. Extended season operations throughout remaining areas.

1300   Heavy Gulf Icebreaker. Large vessel escort in most severe Atlantic and Gulf operations. Extended season operation through areas of Arctic ice zone six and less severe conditions.

1200   Medium Gulf/River Icebreaker. Large vessel escort–all areas of southern Canada plus summer Arctic operations.

1100   Major Navaids Tender/Light Icebreaker. Buoy handling and heavy cargo. Small to large vessel escort–all areas of southern Canada and sub-Arctic.

1050   Medium Navaids Tender/ Light Icebreaker. Buoy handling; restricted to mainly deck cargo. Small and medium vessel escort in more restricted waters.

1000   Medium Navaids Tender (ice-strengthened). Buoy handling and medium capacity cargo. Small and medium vessel escort in more restricted and shallow waters.

900   Small Navaids Tender (ice-strengthened). Buoy handling in sheltered waters. Small vessel escort in light ice conditions in more restricted and shallow waters.

800   Small Navaids Tender. Checking and servicing aids in restricted, shallow waters. Capable of lifting small floating aids.

700   Special River Navaids Shallow Tender. Light draft and high endurance with the capability to carry out Mackenzie River System tasks.

600   Large SAR Cutter. High endurance, offshore all weather patrol operations.

500   Intermediate SAR Cutter. Medium endurance, moderate weather patrol close offshore and all weather patrol in semi-sheltered waters.

400   Small SAR Cutter. Good range, moderate speed , all weather patrol in semi-sheltered waters. Station mode.

310*   SAR Ocean Lifeboat. Long-range lifeboat; all weather, exposed waters. Station mode.

300A   SAR High Endurance Lifeboat. High endurance self-righting lifeboat, exposed coastal waters. Station mode.

300	SAR Lifeboat. Medium endurance self-righting lifeboat, exposed coastal waters. Station mode.
200	Small SAR Cutter. Small ice-strengthened vessel capable of SAR operations in ice-infested waters. Station mode.
100	Small SAR Utility Craft. Moderate to fast rescue craft; all weather operation in sheltered waters. Station mode.

(* None in fleet)

Coast Guard Ship Naming Policy

Originally there was no set policy for naming Coast Guard ships, although the names of explorers, pioneers, colonial administrators, governors-general, prime ministers and ministers of the department were frequent choices. Traditional and descriptive names (Alert, Racer, Spindrift,) and the names of birds and other fauna were used.

With the introduction of the Fleet Capital Investment Plan in 1979 a naming policy was developed and formally promulgated in 1984. Names of new ships should fall into the following categories.

- Icebreakers (Type 1200). Explorers of the Canadian Arctic and northern coastlines.

- Light icebreakers/Navaids tenders (Type 1100): Former members of government, including but not restricted to prime ministers, provincial premiers and ministers.

- Medium Navaids Tenders/ Light Icebreakers (Type 1050). Former senior officials of the public service.

- Navaids Tenders (Types 1000 and 900). Not allocated and none constructed since 1979.

- Small Navaids Tenders (Type 800). The names of islands in the area of initial deployment.

- Special River Navaids Tenders (Type 700). Appropriate Indian or Inuit words.

- Offshore and Intermediate SAR Cutters (Type 600 and 500)): Mariners and others who are recognized as having made major contributions to assist the maritime community

- Small SAR Cutters (Type 400). Geographical features found in the region in which the vessel is stationed such as capes, bays etc.

- SAR Lifeboats (Type 300). Until 1994, the name of the location where the vessel is stationed. More recently, the same criteria as for Type 600, 500 and 400 vessels have been used.

- Ice-strengthened SAR cutters (Type 200). Names of species of seal.

- Small SAR utility craft (Type 100). Names of seabirds.

- The names assigned, even to ships built under the FCIP, have often varied from these rules. The name Ann Harvey, for instance, *should* have been assigned to a Type 600 ship, not to one of Type 1100.

Naming Policy for Former DFO Ships

- Research and Survey vessels have been named for explorers (Hudson and Baffin) and for hydrographers and oceanographers.

- Large Fishery Research ships are named for biologists

- Some small research ships have scientific names associated with fish.

- Offshore patrol vessels have had traditional names (e.g. Cygnus), prominent past officials and, sometimes, geographical features.

- Inshore patrol boats have geographical names or those of former local officials.

- Descriptive names are sometimes used (Vector, Limnos).

- As in the case of ships built for the Coast Guard, the names chosen have frequently been inconsistent.

APPENDIX IV

Coast Guard Helicopters and Hovercraft

Table 1 Specifications of Helicopters

Manufacturer and Model	Range (NM)	No. of Engines	Cruise Spd (kts)	Max Gross wt lbs (kgs)	Useful load lbs (kgs)	Seats	Capability
Alouette III	200	1 turbine	90	4630 (2105)	1650 (750)	2-6	Day, VFR
Bell 47G/J	215	1 piston	60	2450 (1114)	480 (215)	2-3	Day, VFR
Bell 206A/B	230	1 turbine	110	3200 (1455)	840 (380)	2-4	Day, VFR
Bell 206 L/L-1	260	1 turbine	115	4040 (1840)	950 (430)	2-5	Day, VFR
Bell 212	285	2 turbines	100	11200 (5090)	3320 (1510)	2-11	Day/Night, VFR
MBB BO 105	215	2 turbines	120	5500 (2500)	1600 (727)	2-5	Day/Night, VFR
Sikorsky S62N	480	2 turbines	120	20460 (9300)	4035 (1834)	2-30	IFR and VFR

Table 2 Helicopter Inventory at Selected Dates

Helicopter Type	1958	1963	1968	1974	1979	1988	1998
Alouette III			3	3	3		
Bell 47G/J	9	17	17	13			
Bell 206A/B			4	17	21	13	
Bell 206L/L-1					7	6	6
Bell 212				3	5	5	5
MBB BO-105						12	16
Sikorsky S51		1					
Sikorsky S62N			1	1	1	1	1
Totals	9	18	25	37	37	37	28

Table 3   Helicopter Distribution by Region in 1979 and 1999

Region	Base	Helicopter type	1979	1999
Headquarters	Uplands airport	Bell 206	4	
Total Ottawa			**4**	
Newfoundland	Torbay airport	Bell 206	1	
		Bell 206L	2	
		Bell 212	1	1
		MBB BO 105		2
	Stephenville	MBB BO 105		1
Total Newfoundland			**4**	**4**
Maritimes	Halifax airport	Bell 206	6	
		then Bell 206L	1	
	Shearwater	Bell 212	1	1
		MBB BO 105		3
	Charlottetown	Bell 206L	1	
		MBB BO 105		1
	Saint John	Bell 206L		1
	Yarmouth	MBB BO 105		1
Total Maritimes			**9**	**7**
Laurentian	Québec City	Bell 206	6	
		Bell 206L	2	3
		Bell 212	1	1
		MBB BO 105		4
	Sorel	Bell 206L	1	
Total Laurentian			**10**	**8**
Central	Prescott	Bell 206	2	
		Bell 206L-1		1
	Parry Sound	Bell 206	1	
		Bell 206L-1		1
		Bell 212	1	1
Total Central			**4**	**3**
Pacific/Western	Victoria	Alouette III	3	
		Bell 206	1	
		Bell 212	1	1
		MBB BO 105		3
	Prince Rupert	Sikorsky S62N	1	1
		MBB BO 105		1
Total Pacific/Western			**6**	**6**
Total inventory			**37**	**28**

Table 4 Specifications of Hovercraft

Name/Type	When and Where Built	Wt. (tons)	Engines & Power	Speed (kts)	Dimensions ft (m)	Remarks
CG 021 (SRN 05)	1968 British Hovercraft, Cowes, IOW, England	8	1 gas turbine, 1 propeller 1100 kW	55	38 x 22.7 (11.8 x 7)	Retired 1984
CG 039 (SRN 06)	1977 British Hovercraft, Cowes, IOW, England	8.5	1 gas turbine, 1 propeller 1100 kW	55	47.5 x 22.7 (14.7 x 7)	Retired 1998
CG 045 (SRN 06)	1969 British Hovercraft, Cowes, IOW, England. Purchased 1981, entered service 1982	8.5	1 gas turbine, 1 propeller 1100 kW	55	47.5 x 22.7 (14.7 x 7)	In service 2002
CG 086 (SRN 06)	1969 British Hovercraft, Cowes, IOW, England. Purchased 1981, rebuilt 1986	8.5	1 gas turbine, 1 propeller 1100 kW	55	47.5 x 22.7 (14.7 x 7)	Retired 1993
Voyageur	1972 Bell Aerospace Canada Ltd. Grand Bend, ON	46.8	2 gas turbines, 2 propellers 1940 kW	50	73.5 x 36 (19.75 x 11.2)	Retired 1987
Waban-aki (AP188-200)	1987 British Hovercraft, Cowes, IOW, England	27.6	4 diesels, 2 propellers 1760 kW	50	79.4 x 36 (24.5 x 11.2)	In service 2002
Sipu Muin (AP188-400)	1998 Designed by GNK Westland Aerospace. Built by Hike Metal Products, Wheatley, ON	35	4 diesels, 2 propellers 2818 kW	50	92.3 x 39 (28.5 x 12)	In service 2002
Siyäy (AP188-400)	1998 Designed by GNK Westland Aerospace. Built by Hike Metal Products, Wheatley, ON	35	4 diesels, 2 propellers 2818 kW	50	92.3 x 39 (28.5 x 12)	In service 2002

APPENDIX V

Who Were They?

The following are brief notes about individuals for whom ships were named. Some ships were named for towns or geographical features which had themselves been named for founders or explorers, but if the connection is clear, a note about those individuals is included.

Sir William Alexander, later Earl of Stirling (c1577-1640). Scottish poet and courtier. In 1621 he received from King James I a grant of land of the whole of Nova Scotia. He gave the province his name but his attempt to settle Scottish colonists there was unsuccessful.

Baffin   William Baffin (c1584-1622). English Arctic explorer who sailed with Robert Bylot on two expeditions, in 1615 and 1616, searching for a Northwest Passage. Baffin himself came to the conclusion that a Northwest Passage did not exist and this discouraged exploration for a considerable time.

Bartlett   Captain Robert Bartlett (1875-1946). Newfoundland seaman and Arctic mariner. He participated in the Peary and Stefanson expeditions and when his ship, the *Karluk*, was crushed in ice in the Bering Sea, he walked with an Inuk companion from Wrangell Island to Siberia and eventually succeeded in rescuing his crew. He continued to make Arctic voyages in his own vessel for two decades.

J.E. Bernier   Captain Joseph-Elzéar Bernier (1852-1934). Between 1904 to 1911, and 1922 to 1925 he led expeditions in the CGS *Arctic* that consolidated Canada's claim to the northern archipelago. He is considered to be Canada's pre- eminent Arctic mariner.

Martha L. Black   (1866-1957) Born Martha Louise Munger in Chicago. In 1896 she was a Yukon pioneer and was always well known in public life in the Yukon, where her husband was Commissioner of the Yukon Territory 1912-1918 and later Member of Parliament. She was herself elected to Parliament in 1935, the second woman member.

Jean Bourdon   (c1601-1668) A surveyor and engineer who came to New France in 1634 and carried out the first hydrographic studies of the St Lawrence River.

John Cabot   Giovanni Caboto (c1449-1498). Italian mariner in the service of the English King Henry VII. He sailed from Bristol in the *Matthew* in 1497 and landed, probably, in Newfoundland. He was lost on his second voyage in the following year.

A.T. Cameron   Professor A.T.Cameron (1882-1947), a biochemist, was chairman of the Biological Board of Canada 1934-37 and continued as chairman of its successor, the Fisheries Research Board, until his death in 1947.

Camsell   Charles Camsell (1876-1958). Mining engineer. Deputy Minister of Mines 1920-1946.

Thomas Carleton   (1735-1817) British army officer and the first Lieutenant Governor of New Brunswick, from 1794 to 1803 (and nominally until 1817).

Cartier   Jacques Cartier (1491-1557). French navigator and first explorer of the Gulf of St Lawrence. He made three voyages to the region, the first two in 1534 and 1535-36 and the third in 1541-42 when he wintered at Hochelaga, the present site of Montreal, and observed the Lachine Rapids and the Ottawa River.

Edward Cornwallis (1712-1776) Soldier and administrator. The founder of Halifax and the first governor of Nova Scotia, 1749-1752. (The first *Edward Cornwallis* was completed in 1949 and named to commemorate the 200th anniversary of the city).

Leonard J. Cowley (1925-1982) Biologist. Director General Newfoundland Region 1974. First Director General, Gulf Region 1981. He became Assistant Deputy Minister, Atlantic Fisheries Service, in 1982 and died while holding office.

Frederick G. Creed (1891-1957) Nova Scotian inventor, considered the originator of the Small Waterplane Area, Twin Hull (SWATH) concept. He died before he had a chance to see his ideas realized in this ship.

George E. Darby   Dr George Elias Darby (1889-1962). A medical missionary at Bella Bella for over thirty-five years, he piloted missionary vessels serving remote settlements and the native peoples of the British Columbia coast.

Dawson   Dr W. Bell Dawson. Founder of the Canadian Tide and Current Survey which was established in 1893 and was an independent organization until 1924 when it was transferred to the Canadian Hydrographic Service.

Sir James Douglas (1804-1877) Hudson's Bay Company officer, known as the "Father of British Columbia." He was appointed Governor of the colony of Vancouver Island in 1851 and of British Columbia from 1858 to 1864.

C.P. Edwards   Charles P. Edwards (1885-1960). He came to Canada in 1904 to supervise the building of radio stations by the Marconi Company. In 1909 he became Superintendent of Wireless Stations for the Department of Marine and Fisheries. After holding other posts, he served as Deputy Minister of Transport, 1941-1948.

Walter E. Foster (1873-1947) Premier of New Brunswick 1917-1923. Senator 1928- 1940.

Robert Foulis (1796-1866) Engineer. Inventor of the steam fog whistle used at lighthouses before compressed air and electric horns became standard.

Terry Fox (1958-1981). A young athlete who developed bone cancer, losing a leg; yet he undertook to run across Canada to raise money for cancer research. He developed lung cancer and died before completing the run. Terry Fox runs are now held annually.

Sir John Franklin (1786-1847) Naval Officer and Arctic explorer. He led a disastrous overland expedition in 1821 to map the Arctic coast, but in 1825-1827 he successfully charted the coast from Prudhoe Bay to Coppermine. In 1845, with two vessels, *Erebus* and *Terror*, he attempted to find a Northwest Passage, but he and his crews disappeared. A logbook was later found recording his death. The many expeditions that searched for Franklin explored vast areas of the Arctic.

Simon Fraser (1776-1862) Fur trader and explorer. Between 1805 and 1808 he explored unknown territory west of the Rocky Mountains, reaching the Pacific coast by the Fraser River (later named after him).

Sir Humphrey Gilbert   (c1537-1583) Elizabethan mariner. Arrived at St. John's in August, 1583 and formally took possession of Newfoundland, England's oldest colony. His ship was lost on the way back to England.

Grenfell/Sir Wilfred Grenfell (1865-1940) Medical missionary who opened a hospital at Battle Harbour, Labrador, in 1893 and later established the Grenfell Mission, based at St Anthony, Newfoundland, which provided services to fishermen, settlers and Inuit in Labrador and northern Newfoundland.

Earl Grey   Albert Henry George Grey (1851-1917), 4th Earl Grey. Governor-General of Canada 1904-1911. He worked to forge strong Imperial ties and to foster Canadian-American relations. Donated the Grey Cup for football.

Des Groseilliers   Medard Chouart des Groseilliers (1618-c1696). Close associate of Pierre Radisson in explorations west of the Great Lakes and the founding of the English Hudson's Bay Company in 1670-1675.

J.L. Hart   John Lawson Hart (1904-1973). Marine biologist and director of the Nanaimo and St Andrews biological stations, 1950-1967.

Ann Harvey   (c1811-1860) The daughter of a fisherman, born at Ile aux Morts, Newfoundland. With her father she participated in 1828 and 1838 in two heroic rescues of the crews of wrecked vessels, which were successful largely through her efforts. Her exploits were recognized and she and her father received awards from the British Government.

Alexander Henry   (1739-1824) Fur trader and explorer in the Lake Superior region and the west. His memoirs, published in 1809, are considered a classic of early Canadian travel literature.

Mary Hichens   Born about 1808, the daughter of a clergyman at Barrington Passage, Nova Scotia, she married a sea captain who had been shipwrecked, and persuaded her husband and her parents to move to isolated Seal Island to set up a lifesaving station. In 1827, the government built a lighthouse there. The Hichens lived on Seal Island for twenty-seven years, during which time some thirty crews were rescued from wrecks.

C.D. Howe   Clarence Decatur Howe (1886-1960). Engineer, businessman and politician. He was Minister of Transport 1936-1940, Minister of Munitions and Supply 1940-44 and held various portfolios to 1957.

Hudson   Henry Hudson, English or Dutch mariner who searched for the Northeast and Northwest Passages to China. In 1610 he explored Hudson Bay and wintered there, but a mutinous crew set him adrift in a small craft with his son and others and he perished in 1611.

d'Iberville   Pierre le Moyne d'Iberville et d'Ardillières (1661-1706). Canadian born French soldier, sailor and trader. He participated in many fierce and successful battles against the English, from Hudson Bay and Newfoundland to Louisiana and the West Indies. He died of yellow fever in Cuba.

Jackman/W. Jackman   William Jackman (1837-1877). Newfoundland sealing captain. In 1867 in Labrador he performed one of the most daring rescues ever accomplished in saving all 27 of the crew of a wrecked vessel, swimming repeatedly through icy water between the wreck and the shore.

John Jacobson (1923-1986) A native of Ahousat on the west coast of Vancouver Island, he was a mariner and boat builder, but his greatest claim to fame was as a native historian. In the 1970s he took up carving and painting and became an accomplished artist and teacher.

Ernest Lapointe (1876-1941) Politician, Minister of Marine and Fisheries 1921-1924 and various portfolios to 1941. He chaired the Canadian delegation in the discussions that led to the Statute of Westminster in 1931.

Henry Larsen Henry Asbjorn Larsen (1899-1964). Born in Norway, he commanded the RCMP patrol vessel *St Roch* from 1929 to 1948. In 1940-1942 he accomplished the first west to east transit of the Northwest Passage. In 1944 he took the *St Roch* back to Vancouver by a more northerly route, the first to make the transit in both directions.

Sir Wilfrid Laurier (1841-1919) Lawyer, journalist and politician. Member of Parliament 1874-1919 and Prime Minister of Canada 1896-1911.

Louis M. Lauzier Dr Louis M. Lauzier (1917-1981). Oceanographer. He led oceanographic research in the Gulf of St. Lawrence for 21 years and was an internationally recognized expert on ocean circulation in the western Atlantic.

John A. Macdonald Sir John A. Macdonald (1815-1891). Lawyer and politician. Member of the legislative assembly of the Province of Canada 1844. Canada's first Prime Minister 1867-1873 and again from 1878 to 1891.

Alexander Mackenzie (1822-1892) Newspaper editor and politician. Member of the legislative assembly of the Province of Canada 1861. Second Prime Minister of Canada 1873-1878.

Maxwell William F. Maxwell, Navigating Lieutenant and later Staff Commander, Royal Navy, was in charge of the Newfoundland Survey from 1872 to 1891.

N.B. McLean Nathan B. McLean (1871-1939). An official of the Department of Marine and Fisheries. In 1927 he led a three-department expedition to Hudson Bay which resulted in the change of the destination of the rail link from Port Nelson to Churchill. From 1930 to 1937 he was chief engineer, St Lawrence ship channel.

Montcalm Louis-Joseph, Marquis de Montcalm (1712-1759). Commanded the French forces in New France from 1756. He lost to Wolfe in the battle of the Plains of Abraham in 1759, both commanders dying of their wounds.

Montmagny Charles Huault de Montmagny (c1583-1653). The first Lieutenant-General of New France, 1636-1648. He defended the colony against the Iroquois who were supported by the Dutch. Montreal was founded during his administration.

Alfred Needler Marine biologist (b.1906). Director of the Fisheries Research Board's biological station at Nanaimo British Columbia 1954-1963. Deputy Minister of Fisheries 1963-1971.

Nicollet Jean Nicollet de Belleborne (c1598-1642). Interpreter and explorer: the first European to travel to Lake Michigan and the Illinois River.

Parizeau   Henri Delpé Parizeau (1877-1954). Distinguished hydrographer. Regional Hydrographer, Pacific, 1920-1946.

George R. Pearkes   (1888-1984) Major-General, Canadian Army (won the Victoria Cross in the First World War). Member of Parliament 1945-1960. Minister of National Defence 1957-1960. Lieutenant Governor of British Columbia 1960-1968.

E.E. Prince   Edward Ernest Prince (1858-1942). Canada's first Commissioner of Fisheries (1893). Instrumental in establishing the first biological research station. Chairman of the Fisheries Research Board until 1921.

Quadra   Juan Francisco de la Bodega y Quadra (1743-1794). Spanish naval officer and explorer. In 1775 and 1779 he explored the Pacific coast as far as Alaska. In 1789 he was put in charge of Spanish activities in the region and in 1792 he negotiated with Vancouver at Nootka Sound.

Pierre Radisson   (c1636-1710) Explorer and fur trader. He was born in Paris and came to Canada in 1651. With Des Groseilliers he explored west to the Mississippi. He worked on behalf of the Hudson's Bay Company 1670-1676 and after 1684. Died in England, 1710.

G.B. Reed   Dr Guilford Bevel Reed (1887-1955). Marine biologist. Chairman of the Fisheries Research Board 1947-1953.

Gordon Reid   (1895-1994) A native of Bella Bella, British Columbia, he commanded fishing vessels, ferries and other craft and his services were much in demand because of his knowledge of the British Columbia coast. He held both Masters and Engineering certificates. He was an accomplished musician and historian. A founder of the Native Brotherhood of British Columbia and a promoter of native culture in his community.

W.E. Ricker   Marine biologist (b.1908). Chief scientist at the Fisheries Research Board 1966-1973.

Samuel Risley   Engineer (b.1821). Appointed as a Steamboat Inspector in 1851, he became Chairman of the Board of Steamship Inspection in 1858. He may be regarded as the founder of the Ship Safety, now Marine Safety Branch of the Department of Transport.

Norman McLeod   Norman McLeod Rogers (1894-1940) Scholar and politician. Elected to Parliament 1935. Minister of National Defence 1939. He died in a plane crash the following year.

Saurel   Pierre de Saurel (1628-1682). Soldier, fur trader and seigneur. His seigneury is now called Sorel.

Simcoe   John Graves Simcoe (1752-1806). Soldier and the first Lieutenant Governor of Upper Canada, 1791-1796. He founded York (now Toronto) and began the policy of granting land to loyalist American settlers.

James Sinclair   (1908-1984) Member of Parliament, first elected 1945. Minister of Fisheries 1952-1957.

F.C.G. Smith   Frank Clifford Goulding Smith (1890-1983). Joined the Hydrographic Service in 1920 after surveying service in the First World War. In charge of the Hudson Strait survey 1931-1935. Superintendent of Charts 1937. Directed the post Second World War surveys of the Arctic. Dominion Hydrographer 1952-1957.

Louis S. St Laurent (1882-1973) Lawyer and politician. Minister of Justice 1941-1946. Secretary of State for External Affairs 1946-1948. Prime Minister of Canada 1948-1957.

Wilfred Templeman (1908-1980) Newfoundland marine biologist and educator. Director of the Fisheries Research Board's biological station at St John's Newfoundland 1949-1972.

Tracy Alexandre de Prouville, Chevalier de Tracy (c1600-1670). Distinguished soldier. Lieutenant-General of the Americas and special envoy of King Louis XIV 1663-1667. He waged war against the Dutch and the Iroquois, constructed forts at Sorel and Chambly and was responsible for improvements in the administration of the colony.

John P. Tully (1906-1987) Oceanographer in charge of the Pacific Oceanographic Group at Nanaimo, British Columbia 1946-1965. He influenced the entire growth of West Coast oceanographic studies and was the recipient of many national and international honours and awards.

Tupper Sir Charles H. Tupper (1821-1915). Politician and diplomat. Premier of Nova Scotia 1846-1867. Member of Parliament from 1867, he held many different portfolios including that of Minister of Marine and Fisheries 1888-1894. He was, briefly, Prime Minister of Canada in 1896.

Vancouver George Vancouver (1757-1798). Naval officer, explorer and cartographer. He served with James Cook on his expeditions to the South Seas (1772-1775) and to the northwest coast of America (1776-1780). He led another expedition there in 1792 and negotiated with Bodega y Quadra at Nootka Sound. After three years exploring the coast of British Columbia, he returned to England in 1795.

Verendrye Jean-Baptiste Gaultier de la Verendrye (1713-1736) and his father, Pierre Gaultier de la Verendrye, explored and set up trading posts in the west and are considered to be the founders of the present Province of Manitoba.

Provo Wallis Sir Provo William Parry Wallace (1791-1892). Naval Officer. A native of Dartmouth, Nova Scotia. He was 2nd Lieutenant of the *Shannon* and the senior officer left standing after the action with the *Chesapeake* in 1813 and he brought both ships back to Halifax. He was Flag Officer, South American station in the 1850s, his last seagoing post; but he progressed through the ranks until he was made Admiral of the Fleet in 1877 and enjoyed the full privileges and pay of that rank until his death at the age of 101.

Wolfe Major-General James Wolfe (1727-1759). He distinguished himself at the capture of Louisbourg in 1758 and commanded the expedition against Québec in 1759, where he defeated Montcalm at the battle of the Plains of Abraham, both commanders dying of their wounds.

R.B. Young Robert Bruce Young (1907-1985). He joined the Hydrographic Service in 1929 and conducted surveys in all areas of the British Columbia coast. He was Regional Hydrographer, Pacific, 1953-1968 and during this time he supervised the pre- and post-demolition surveys of Ripple Rock in Seymour Narrows.

Glossary of Abbreviations and Acronyms

ACV	Air Cushion Vehicle
ADF	Automatic Direction Finder
ADM	Assistant Deputy Minister
AIS	Automatic Identification System
AMVER	Automated Mutual-assistance Vessel Rescue System
ATL	Arctic Transportation Ltd.
CANSARP	Canadian Search and Rescue Planning Program
CCG	Canadian Coast Guard
CCGA	Canadian Coast Guard Auxiliary
CCGC	Canadian Coast Guard College
CCGS	Canadian Coast Guard Ship
CGS	Canadian Government Ship
CGSS	Canadian Government Survey Ship
CIDA	Canadian International Development Agency
CLC	Convention on Civil Liability for Oil Pollution Damage
CM	Member of the Order of Canada
CMRA	Canadian Marine Rescue Auxiliary
CMS	Canadian Marine Service Ship
CMTA	Canadian Marine Transport Administration
CNS	Canadian National Steamships
COLREG	International Regulations for preventing collisions at sea
CQD	The original morse international signal of distress
CSA	Canada Shipping Act
CVTS	Co-operative Vessel Traffic Service
DED 1-7	Deck Department personnel classifications
DEW Line	Distant Early Warning line of radar stations
DFO	Department of Fisheries and Oceans
DGPS	Differential Global Positioning System
DM	Deputy Minister
DMB	Datum Marker Buoy
DME	Distance Measuring Equipment (aircraft navigation device)
DND	Department of National Defence
DOE	Department of the Environment
DSC	The Distinguished Service Cross
ECAREG	Eastern Canada Traffic Zone
ECDIS	Electronic Chart Display
EEZ	Exclusive Economic Zone
EQO 1-7	Equipment Operator personnel classifications
ERD 1-7	Engineering Department personnel classifications
FPV	Fisheries Patrol Vessel
FRC	Fast Rescue Craft
GARP	Global Atmospheric Research Program

GATE	Global Atmospheric Tropical Experiment
GMDSS	Global Maritime Distress and Safety System
GMT	Greenwich Mean time
GPS	Global Positioning System
GRT	Gross Registered Tons/Tonnes
HF	High Frequency
HMCS	His or Her Majesty's Canadian Ship
HMS	His or Her Majesty's Ship
IALA	International Association of Lighthouse Authorities
IFR	Instrument Flight Rules
IHP	Indicated Horsepower
IMCO	Inter-Governmental Maritime Consultative Organization
IMDG	International Maritime Dangerous Goods Code
IMO	International Maritime Organization
INMARSAT	International Maritime Satellite
IOPC	International Oil Pollution Compensation Fund
ISF	Icebreaking Services Fee
ISM	International Safety Management Code
JOIS	Canada/U.S. Joint Ocean Ice Study
JRCC	Joint Rescue Coordination Centre
KHz	Kilohertz
LORAN	Long Range Navigation (electronic navigation system)
LCT	Landing Craft (Tank)
MAO 1-13	Marine Operator (ships' officer) classifications
MARPOL	International Convention for the Prevention of Pollution from Ships
Mayday	The International voice signal of distress
MCTS	Marine Communication and Traffic Services
MED	Marine Emergency Duties
Medevac	Medical Evacuation (usually by helicopter)
MNSF	Marine Navigation Services Fee
MODU	Mobile Drilling Unit
MOU	Memorandum of Understanding
MRCC	Marine Rescue Coordination Centre
MRSC	Marine Rescue Sub-Centre
MTC	Maritime Training Centre (at TCTI, Cornwall)
MTR	Marine Traffic Regulator
MUN	Memorial University of Newfoundland
MV	Motor Vessel
NAVLINK	A ship/aircraft/helicopter navigation device
NORDREG	Arctic Canada Traffic Zone
OBE	Order of the British Empire
OC	Officer of the Order of Canada
ODECO	Ocean Drilling and Exploration Company
OMEGA	A low frequency electronic navigation system

PCBs	Polychloralbiphenyl compounds
PSAC	Public Service Alliance of Canada
RCAF	Royal Canadian Air Force
RCC	Rescue coordination centre
RCN	Royal Canadian navy
RCNR	Royal Canadian Navy Reserve
RCNVR	Royal Canadian Navy Volunteer Reserve
RHI	Rigid Hull Inflatable craft
RMS	Royal Mail Ship
RN	Royal Navy
ROV	Remote Operated Vehicle
SAR	Search and Rescue
Sartech	Air Force Search and Rescue Technician
SATNAV	Satellite Navigation (Transit) system
SEN	Simulated Electronic Navigation
SHEBA	Surface Heat Budget of the Arctic
SHP	Shaft Horsepower
SLDMB	Self-locating Datum Marker Buoy
SOLAS	International Convention for the Safety of Life at Sea
SOPF	Ship-source Oil Pollution Fund
SOS	The international signal of distress
S.P. Barge	A Coast Guard utility craft.
S.S.	Steam Ship
STCW	International Convention for Standards of Training, Certification and Watchkeeping for Seafarers
STD 1-7	Logistic Department personnel classifications
SWATH	Small waterplane area, twin hulls (type of catamaran vessel)
TC	Transport Canada (Department of Transport)
TCTI	Transport Canada Training Institute
TOVALOP	Tanker Owners Voluntary Agreement for Ocean Pollution
UAE	United Arab Emirates
USCG	United States Coast Guard
USCGC	United States Coast Guard Cutter
USS	United States Ship (Navy)
UTC	Universal time – formerly GMT
VFR	Visual Flight Rules
VHF	Very High Frequency
VLF	Very Low Frequency
VTS	Vessel Traffic Services
WESTREG	Western Canada Traffic Zone

BIBLIOGRAPHY

Books

Appleton, Thomas E. *Usque ad Mare. A History of the Canadian Coast Guard and Marine Services*. Ottawa: Queen's Printer, 1969

Bernier family. *Master Mariner and Arctic Explorer. A Narrative of 60 years at Sea from the Logs and Yarns of Captain J. E. Bernier, F.R.G.S. F.R.E.S.* Privately published, 1939

Bush, Edward F. *The Canadian Lighthouses*. Occasional Papers in Archaeology and History, No.9. Ottawa: Department of Indian and Northern Affairs, 1974

Clark, Karin and Cory Hetherington, Chris O'Neill, and Jana Zavitz. *Breaking the Ice with Finesse. Oil and Gas Exploration in the Canadian Arctic*. Calgary: The Arctic Institute of North America, University of Calgary, 1997

Dorion-Robitaille, Yolande. *Captain J.E. Bernier's Contribution to Canadian Sovereignty in the Arctic*. Ottawa: Indian and Northern Affairs, 1978

Dubreuil, Stephan. *Come Quick Danger. A History of Marine Radio in Canada*. Ottawa: Canadian Government Publishing, 1998

Elliot-Miesel, Elizabeth B. *Arctic Diplomacy: Canada and the United States in the Northwest Passage*. New York: Peter Lang, 1998

Fillmore, Stanley and R.W. Sandilands. *The Chartmakers*. Vancouver: NC Press Ltd. in association with the Canadian Hydrographic Service, Department of Fisheries and Oceans, 1983

Johnstone, Kenneth. *The Aquatic Explorers. A History of the Fisheries Research Board of Canada*. Toronto: University of Toronto Press and the Ministry of Supply and Services, 1977

Keeble, John. *Out of the Channel. The* Exxon Valdez *Oil Spill in Prince William Sound*. New York: Harper Collins, 1991

Keller, Keith. *Dangerous Waters: Wrecks and Rescues off the B.C. Coast*. Madeira Park, B.C.: Harbour Publishing, 1997

Marcil, Eileen Reid. *Tall Ships and Tankers: The History of Davie Shipbuilders*. Toronto: McClelland and Stewart, 1997

Matthews, Carolyn. *Heroic Rescues at Sea: True Stories of the Canadian Coast Guard*. Halifax: Nimbus Publishing, 2002

MacInnis, Joe. *The Land that Devours Ships. The Search for the Breadalbane*. Toronto: CBC Enterprises, 1985

Oickle, Vernon. *Busted: Nova Scotia's War on Drugs*. Halifax: Nimbus Publishing, 1997

Magazine Articles

Blank, Joseph P. "Nightmare Under the Sea." *Readers' Digest*. January 1974

Douglas W.A.B. "The Nazi Weather Station in Labrador." *Canadian Geographic*, vol 101, Winter, 1981-82

Pullen, Thomas C. "Why We Need the Polar 8." *Canadian Geographic*, April-May, 1987

Reyno, Mike. "Leading the Way." *Helicopters*, Issue 3, Sept/Oct/Nov, 1998

Articles in Internal Periodicals

Anonymous. "Coast Guard Rubs Elbows with World Leaders at G-7 Summit." *Echo*, Summer, 1995

Ali, Captain F. "Operation MV *Tenyo Maru*." *CG News*, No. 213, 1992

Breig, Mary. "Air India Disaster." *Fleet News*, No.13, 1986

Breig, Mary and Captain Eric Hann. "Operation *Sea Shepherd*." *Fleet News*, No. 6, 1983

Hicks, Jennifer. "Coast Guard Meets Flood Challenge." *Echo*, July-August, 1997

McCarter, P. and P. Murdock. "Search for Answers." *Fleet News*, No.13, 1986

Toomey, Captain P. "Greenland Celebrations: 1000 Years after Eric the Red." *Fleet News*, No. 4, 1982

Official Publications

1994 U.S./Canada Arctic Ocean Section (CCGS *Louis S. St Laurent* Arctic Operation Order) Canadian Coast Guard, Ottawa, 30 May 1994, and Science Implementation Plan, 26 April 1994

Coast Guard Arctic Operation Orders (various years)

Coast Guard Operational Guideline, Winter Icebreaking Program (various years)

List of Lights and Fog Signals (various years)

Notices to Mariners, Annual edition (various years)

Radio Aids to Marine Navigation (various years)

Science Plan for Arctic 97/98 SHEBA/JOIS, 4 July 1997

TP 1318. From Marconi to Microwave. A Short History of Telecommunications and Electronics in Transport Canada, 1901-1977. Telecommunications and Electronics Directorate, March 1978

TP 10120. Polar 8 Icebreaker: Environmental Evaluation. February 1990

TP 5064. Ice Navigation in Canadian Waters. Rev. ed., 1992

Reports

Brander-Smith, David, QC. *Protecting Our Waters*. Public Review Panel on Tanker Safety and Marine Spills Response Capability. Final report. September 1990

Canadian Coast Guard, Western Region. Nestucca *Oil Spill Report*. June 1989

Canadian Coast Guard / Transport Canada. Marine Casualty Investigations. 1967-1990

Department of the Navy, Naval Ship Systems Command. *The Recovery of Bunker "C" Fuel Oil from the Sunken Tanker SS* Arrow. Washington, D.C.: NAVSHIPS 0994-008-1010.

Deschenes, Bernard M. QC. *Study on Marine Casualty Investigations in Canada*. Conducted for the Minister of Transport. Canada: Ministry of Supply and Services 1984

Evaluation of Canadian Coast Guard Helicopter Operations. ("The Higgs and Wiggs Report"). January 1980

Halley, Wayne. *Canada's Response to the Persian Gulf Oil Spill*. Canadian Coast Guard, Newfoundland Region, 26 March 1991

Hart, the Hon. Mr Justice Gordon L.S., Commissioner. *Pollution of Canadian Waters by*

Oil and Investigation into the Grounding of Steam Tanker Arrow. Report of the Royal Commission. 23 July 1970

International Oil Pollution Compensation Funds. Annual Report, 1996

MacTaggart-Cowan, Dr P.D.; Dr H. Sheffer; Capt. M.A. Martin; W.L. Ford, et al. *Report of the Task Force - Operation Oil.* Clean-up of the *Arrow* Oil Spill in Chedabucto Bay. vols I-III (1970), and vol IV (1973). Ottawa: Information Canada

Marine Incidents Summaries. Various years

Osbaldeston, Gordon F. *All the Ships that Sail: A Study of Canada's Fleets.* 15 October, 1990

Ryan, W.J. Exxon Valdez *Incident - Observations and Lessons Learned.* Canadian Coast Guard, Newfoundland Region, 1989

Ship-Source Oil Pollution Fund. Annual Reports. Various years

Special SAR Reports and SAR Operations Reports, 1968-1998

Stolee, LCdr E. *CF: Report on the Voyage in the Canadian Arctic of CCGS* John A. Macdonald, *Summer 1969 (Manhattan's* Journey). Ottawa: Queen's Printer for Canada, 1970.

Stolee, LCdr E. *CF: Report on the Voyage in the Canadian Arctic of CCGS* Louis S. St Laurent*, Spring 1970 (Manhattan's* Journey). Ottawa: Queen's Printer for Canada, 1970

Stone, Judge R.F. MV *Kurdistan.* Formal Investigation. London: HM Stationary Office, November 1981

Transportation Safety Board. Marine Occurrence Reports .(from 1990)

Transportation Safety Board. Marine Occurrences: Statistical Summaries

U.S. National Transportation Safety Board. *Capsizing and Sinking of the U.S. Mobile Offshore Drilling Unit* Ocean Ranger *on 15 February 1982.* Washington D.C.: NTSB-MAR-83-2

Periodicals

The D.O.T. (in-house magazine) 1965-1968

Transport Canada. (in-house magazine) 1969-1977

Transpo 78, 79 etc. (in-house magazine) 1978-1989

Fleet News. (in-house magazine) 1982-1992

Echo. (in-house magazine) 1994-2001

Oceans. (in-house magazine) from 2001

Safety Reflexions. Transportation Safety Board, from 1990

INDEX

INDEX OF SHIPS AND AIRCRAFT